1914   1919

A HISTORY OF THE
10ᵀᴴ (SERVICE) BATTALION THE
EAST YORKSHIRE REGIMENT
(HULL COMMERCIALS)

PRICE **7/6** NET

TO THE MEMORY OF THE OFFICERS, NON-COMMISSIONED
OFFICERS, AND MEN, OF THE I0TH (SERVICE) BATTALION
THE EAST YORKSHIRE REGIMENT WHO GAVE THEIR LIVES
IN THE GREAT WAR, 1914-1918.
"So they gave their bodies to the Commonwealth
and received, each for his own memory, praise that
will never die, . . . and their story is not only
written, . . . but lives on without visible symbol,
woven into the stuff of other men's lives".
Pericles' Funeral Oration.

Hull Commercials

A History of the 10th (Service)
Battalion the East Yorkshire Regiment

1914   1919

David Bilton

Pen & Sword
MILITARY

First published in Great Britain in 2018 by
PEN & SWORD MILITARY
An imprint of
Pen & Sword Books Ltd
47 Church Street
Barnsley
South Yorkshire
S70 2AS

ISBN 978 1 47389 556 0

A CIP catalogue record for this book is
available from the British Library.

Printed and bound in England by
TJ International Ltd, Padstow, Cornwall

Pen & Sword Books Limited incorporates the imprints of
Atlas, Archaeology, Aviation, Discovery, Family History, Fiction,
History, Maritime, Military, Military Classics, Politics, Select, Transport,
True Crime, Air World, Frontline Publishing, Leo Cooper, Remember
When, Seaforth Publishing, The Praetorian Press, Wharncliffe Local
History, Wharncliffe Transport, Wharncliffe True Crime and White Owl.

For a complete list of Pen & Sword titles please contact
PEN & SWORD BOOKS LIMITED
47 Church Street, Barnsley, South Yorkshire, S70 2AS, England
E-mail: enquiries@pen-and-sword.co.uk
Website: www.pen-and-sword.co.uk

O. H. M. S.

IT has been suggested to me that there are many men, such as Clerks and others, engaged in commercial business, who wish to serve their KING and COUNTRY, and would be willing to enlist in the New Army if they felt assured that they would be serving with their own friends, and not put into Battalions with unknown men as their companions.

EARL KITCHENER has sanctioned the raising of a Hull Battalion which would be composed of the classes mentioned, and in which a man could be certain that he would be among his own friends.

THE CONDITIONS OF SERVICE WILL BE THE SAME AS IN OTHER BATTALIONS IN THE REGULAR ARMY.

The New Battalion will be 1000 strong, and will be named the

7TH (HULL) BATTALION EAST YORKSHIRE REGIMENT.

Those who wish to serve in it will be enrolled, enlisted and clothed at the WENLOCK BARRACKS, HULL. Recruiting will commence from 10 a.m. on TUESDAY, 1st SEPTEMBER. For the present, Recruits joining will be billeted in their own homes.

I shall be glad to receive the names of ex-Officers who will help in the above work until the Officers have been appointed to the Battalion.

Major W. H. CARVER has been temporarily appointed Acting Adjutant for the Battalion at Wenlock Barracks.

GOD SAVE THE KING.

NUNBURNHOLME
LORD LIEUTENANT, E. YORKS.

A page from the original book.

The City of Hull Memorial at Oppy (France).

Contents

Original Preface

The story of the "Hull Commercials" has never been completely told. It has remained through the years in the recollections of those who served in its ranks, coming to life at reunions and then lying dormant until two or three get together to live again through those momentous days and to go once more over the old familiar ground. The 10th (Service) Battalion East Yorkshire Regiment began in the atmosphere of a happy family, and, in spite of all the changes in personnel which the vagaries of war bring to a unit on active service, a happy family it remained to the end.

This story is, therefore, in the main a family affair and not an attempt to make a contribution to the history of the War or to enlarge on tactics and strategy for the military student.

We are indebted to many members and relatives of members who have been very helpful in lending diaries, letters, cuttings, photographs, etc., and it is not possible to refer to them all by name, but among those who have given more active assistance we should like to mention and thank Captain Ivor Jackson and Mr. W. Hall for reading the manuscript and verifying facts and details; Captain C. I. Hadrill for editing and finally shaping the book; and the members of the General Committee, especially Mr. F. W. Harrison and Mr. J. B. Fay.

We should like to express our gratitude to the Historical Section, War Office, for permission to use the Battalion War Diary; to the Officer Commanding the Regimental Depot at Beverley, for access to the Battalion records in his keeping; to the Photographic Section, Imperial War Museum, for their help in finding suitable photographs; to Messrs. W. Duncan and W. H. Berry for permission to use photographs; to Messrs. The City Engraving Company for valuable advice regarding the making of the half-tone blocks for the Plates, and to the Publishers, Messrs. A. Brown & Sons, Ltd., for their willing co-operation in the production of this volume.

Finally, it will be appreciated that, owing to lapse of time, the records are incomplete, and we realise that there may be some omissions from the lists in the Appendices, although every care has been taken in compiling them from the information at our disposal.

R. B. CARVER.
J. M. FENWICK.
J. W. GRAYSTONE.
F. G. PAGE.
C. W. THIRSK

List of Illustrations

List of Maps

Foreword

By LT.-Col. A. J. RICHARDSON, D.S.O.
THE TOCSIN SOUNDED

At once many a thousand men in the prime of life left their offices, their work, their leisure, their comforts, and voluntarily bound themselves by oath to acquire skill in the use of implements they had never before handled and faithfully to stand together until the danger was hurled back to the abyss from which it had emerged.

Such is loyalty: such is Empire.[1]

This record of one thousand of those many thousands and of friends who in the long years of war joined their gallant comradeship, equals anything in the past. It will be emulated, perhaps surpassed, in the future. Human invention is cumulative, human progress ever accelerating, the implements of war ever becoming more complex, and much of the world looks with envy at this little North Sea island that controls one-quarter of the land surface, one-quarter of the population of the globe. Envy, fear and war are kith and kin, and those who make wars take no personal risks.

A. J. RICHARDSON.
North Walsham, Norfolk.

---

[1] In total 1,454 men joined the battalion before it left for Egypt.

Introduction

Editing the history of the 10th Battalion has been like visiting an old friend: the familiar stories that never grow old and with each telling reveal something new. This is a carefully sanitised story that shows the human side of the Great War, anecdotes, humour, and sadness: a story written by a group of friends for themselves as a record of their adventures and for their friends. It allows those who were not there to understand something of their war but only those parts they felt able to share openly. The true story lies between the lines.

The book is an old-fashioned, smoothly crafted understatement of the exploits of men from an educated commercial background who answered their country's call wherever it might take them; starting and ending in Hull by way of Egypt and the Western Front.

Its Battle Honours speak for them, as does the number of dead. Fortunately for the men, the battalion was one of the few Pals units that did not suffer at the start of the Somme. The 10th played its part in the battle but was not called to make an attack – that was left to its sister battalions from the Hull Brigade. Their turn came on 3 May 1917 during the Third Scarpe offensive, casualties were heavy and the name of Oppy Wood became the byword for the sacrifices made by Hull in the cause of freedom. For the remainder of the war it played its part without failing, returning home to a grateful city over four years after they had enlisted.

The final photo taken before the battalion was disbanded in 1919 shows only a handful of the men still serving with the battalion. This does not mean the missing were dead, wounded or PoWs. Their level of education meant that some were not allowed to leave with the battalion, being transferred to munitions work to be called up later; some joined other corps where their skills were needed and many were commissioned. A number were transferred to other battalions of the regiment and some ended the war fighting with other regiments.

In this edition I have changed very little but have included some footnotes to provide information not available when the book was written, extra photographs (some courtesy of Hull Museums) and an almost complete list of those served with the original battalion; it will never be complete as those who returned to industry and/or never served abroad are especially hard to track down.

David Bilton
January 2018

An Introductory Note

By MAJOR W. H. CARVER, M.P.

The Great War has been responsible for many volumes of books and historical records of the work of those who were in the leading ranks of the campaign, but I think it is fitting that some at least of the units which helped to build up that mighty army should give an account of regimental working, and how they came into being. Memories fail as we grow older, and it may not be so easy, after twenty-one years, to recall a great deal. Certain things cannot be forgotten, and the raising of the service battalions to augment the regular army deserves more than a recollection, and so it is that this Battalion Story is to be told.

I well remember Sunday evening, August 30th, 1914. Lord Nunburnholme, the Lord Lieutenant of the East Riding, was in Canada when war broke out on August 4th, and hurried home to take his part in the duties of his office. I was sitting in my room when the telephone bell rang at about 7.30 p.m., and I found myself speaking to Lord Nunburnholme, who told me he had just got back from London where he had seen Lord Kitchener at the War Office the previous day, and he had received instructions to start the First Service Battalion in Hull. This was August 29th, and was the date of my being recommissioned. The monthly Army List was suspended for a time when war broke out, and when the new issue was published my name was the first name of the Officers commissioned in the New Army, and I think this is sufficient evidence to prove that we were one of the earliest of the Service Battalions of the Regular Army, and when therefore the 31st Division was formed which contained the 92nd Brigade, composed of ourselves, the 10th Battalion, together with the 11th, 12th and 13th Battalions of the East Yorkshire Regiment, we were consequently the Senior Battalion of that Division. It was known that a great number of men were anxious to join up, and were hoping to do so with their own friends in Hull, and there were many of the commercial class who wished to do this. Lord Nunburnholme asked me if I would start the Battalion: it was a request that rather overwhelmed me at first; there were many questions to be put that could not easily be answered. I was to be Commanding Officer, Adjutant, Quartermaster – everything in fact, until a commencement was made. The great thing was to get going. (Having had seventeen years' experience in the 3rd King's Own Yorkshire Light Infantry, Militia, or

Special Reserve as it was called later on, naturally I, like many others, was anxious to offer my services, and so I said I would do my best to help him.)

The next day posters were out all over Hull, and on Tuesday morning, September 1st, I arrived at Wenlock Barracks, lent by permission of the East Riding Territorial Association, of which Lord Nunburnholme was President. In those days everyone wanted to help and we soon had Attestation Forms being filled in, for hundreds of men were waiting and more kept coming. It is difficult to mention all those who assisted. Captain E. F. Twiss came from the Depot at Beverley to act as Adjutant, Colonel H. R. Pease gave most willing help: he afterwards was given command of the 12th Battalion. Sergeant Tholander was the first Orderly-room Sergeant.

On Thursday, September 3rd, there were enough men to make a start. The four company formation, each with its four platoons, had only just come in, but I did not know it, so decided to make up eight companies, and with ready assistance we soon had men placed on parade in company quarter column on the old method. By this time we had 1,000 men, which was our complement, and recruiting for this Battalion stopped. There were many ex-officers and ex-regular N.C.O.s and they were soon fitted in to the Companies and Sections. Applicants for commissions were dealt with, recommended, and then appointed by the Lord Lieutenant. We became known as "The Commercials", or officially at first as the 7th Service Battalion, East Yorkshire Regiment. The men were first paid on Saturday, September 5th. It was not expected, though I felt it was a right thing to do, so I wired to Sir Herbert Plumer (afterwards Lord Plumer) who was then General Officer Commanding at York, for authority which he gave to me, and I called on Mr. Alwyn Smith at his Bank in Hull, and was at once given the necessary overdraft, and indeed whatever was wanted. No one minded any inconvenience; my desk was a card table in the Officer's Mess. I remember we ran out of Attestation Forms, and I hope I shall now be immune from disciplinary punishment when I say that as no time was to be lost I had more forms printed in Hull, copied from the Government form. We had no rifles and no uniforms then, and it was a case of daily squad drill and company drill on the Fair Ground, with route marches in and about Hull.

The arrival of Lieut.-Colonel A. Richardson was a real event. He had recently retired from the command of the 1st Battalion East Yorkshire Regiment, and was appointed to us on September 12th. I took him on parade, and lent him my horse, which incidentally was lent to me by the Lord Lieutenant, and his first word to his men was – "Gentlemen" – and that was perhaps typical of after events, and how he came to be beloved by those who served under him.

Lord Nunburnholme told me that he had recommended me for the command, but the War Office, I think quite rightly, decided that for the new Service Battalions an ex-Regular Officer must be appointed, and so it came about that I was made second-in-command. Colonel Richardson appointed me to this position, and it has resulted in many long years of friendship. A strict disciplinarian was what was wanted, and he found amongst his men all the material he required to fill the posts of Non-commissioned Officers.

Many of the officers were sent to me by Lord Nunburnholme for approval: some I got myself, and Colonel Richardson was very kind in consulting me about appointments, for I think most of them were known to me for some years before that, and we were all really a very happy family.

Then came the uniforms and our move to Hornsea. This move was a very hurried one: there were rumours of a German landing, and our Battalion, which had not yet done any musketry, received orders to entrain for Hornsea and Rolston Huts that afternoon. Rifles, mostly of the drill pattern, time-expired order, were collected, and we moved with celerity to a camp not yet finished off or equipped, but stores were soon forthcoming and the ever-resourceful Battalion accommodated itself to uncomfortable circumstances without a grumble. It was a welcome change, and with excitement I remember going to the cook-house next day and seeing the Battalion beef being boiled in new latrine buckets! My surprise was great, but I thought that where ignorance was bliss the meat might still be wisely cooked.

Although we had rifles, we had no ammunition to expend upon the ranges, so with the help of Lord Nunburnholme some money was collected and ammunition bought, and on Christmas Day, 1914, the men had their first experience of trying to get a bull's eye.

Some time after this, Colonel Richardson arranged to take a week's leave to settle some of his private affairs, handing over the Battalion to me. Directly after he had gone I got a message to say that Sir Archibald Murray, Chief of the Imperial General Staff, was to pay us a visit. Thinking that Colonel Richardson ought to know and that it would bring him back, I sent him a wire telling him of this very important news. His reply to me was, "Not returning, remember me to Sir Archibald". Needless to say, I did so, and found that Sir Archibald knew him very well. This visit was, I think, a success, and Sir Archibald Murray was highly complimentary on finding such a splendid body of men, and wondered why they were not out at the Front.

Everyone was keen and there was no such thing as orderly-room in the early days, for the men were only too anxious to learn and to make themselves fit. While we were at Ripon, Colonel Richardson left us. It was on October 17th, 1915, and he was told to hand over the command to me. A brilliant officer whose opinions clashed with those in superior ranks, to my own regret and I know to all under his command, he elected to go. However, later on, another Battalion had the advantage of his services, which he led over the top and was awarded the D.S.O., given to him, so he said, "for running 100 yards across 'No Man's Land'".

It is a joy to me to think that I remained with the Battalion throughout the War, although invalided home from France on two occasions, and I refused offers of what might have been promotion. The men I had helped to raise I looked upon as comrades, and friends, and as years go on our annual reunion in November, which Colonel Richardson never misses, cements a lasting bond amongst those whose patriotism was sincere, and who gave up positions of comfort to serve their country.

Those who did not return remain forever in our memory:

> "They shall grow not old as we who are left grow old:
> Age shall not weary them, nor the years condemn.
> At the going down of the sun and in the morning
> We will remember them." – Laurence Binyon.

The Croft   W. H. CARVER.
North Cave
E. YORKS.

Lieutenant Colonel A. J. Richardson, D.S.O.

Chapter 1

First Days – Wenlock Barracks – Hornsea

THE Battalion on its formation was known as the 7th Battalion East Yorkshire Regiment, the 6th Battalion, the first of the service Battalions of the Regiment being already in process of formation at the East Yorkshire Regimental Depot at Beverley.

September 5th saw the Battalion nearing its full complement, and incidentally this was the first pay-day. Few, if any, of the members of the Battalion can ever have dreamed that they would one day receive the "King's Shilling", but they not only received the 1/- per day from the day of joining, but 2/- a day additional billeting money, as they were billeted in their own homes.

During the first few days the men, as they were recruited, were formed into companies under the old eight company system; and, as each company was formed it was taken charge of by retired officers of the Regular or Territorial forces, assisted by pensioned N.C.O.s of the Regular Army, who had responded to Lord Kitchener's appeal for such to help in the training of his new army. Each company was searched for men with previous military or other training likely to make them suitable for N.C.O.s and the result of this combing out produced about 120 men who had, at least, some slight acquaintance with military or other drill and discipline. These men were put in charge of sections and squads and, from their memories, proceeded as best they could to teach their raw comrades the rudiments of "squad drill without arms".

It has been said that Napoleon's soldiers each carried a Field Marshal's baton in his knapsack. It was certainly true that within a few weeks practically every member of the "Commercials" had a copy of "Infantry Training, 1914" in his pocket.

Monday, September 7th, found the Battalion scattered in sections over the Hull Fair Ground drilling under their newly-found officers and N.C.O.s, and on the afternoon of that day the Battalion had its first route march round the city.

Training on the Hull Fair Ground continued daily and on the 11th the Battalion was re-formed on the "double company" system of four companies, each of four platoons, the companies being designated A, B, C, and D.

On the morning of Saturday, the 12th, Lieut.-Colonel A. Richardson arrived and took command. The afternoon brought rain and the expectancy of "no parade", but this hope was soon shattered, and the Battalion set off to march to Anlaby in pouring rain. It was on this historic occasion that one member, said to be in "A" Company, produced an umbrella on the march.

The following week saw the commencement of physical drill and the continuation of drilling by platoons and companies, finishing up with a route march to Anlaby and Tranby Croft – a distance of about nine miles.

It may seem superfluous in view of the future history and experiences of the Battalion to enlarge on the petty details of the early weeks, but it must be remembered that these so-called details were new and often startling experiences to most of the men of the new army, and they were an essential part of the foundation of that self-contained and self-reliant unit which was subsequently to prove itself not without distinction.

Training gradually took on a wider aspect and companies practised "Extended order drill", "Skirmishing", "Outpost Duty", and "Judging Distances", as well as company drill and physical training. The younger officers, and the men chosen to act as N.C.O.s paraded half an hour earlier, morning and afternoon, under R.S.M. George Kilpatrick, an old East Yorkshire ex-warrant officer, for physical training, which was immediately passed on to their respective platoons and sections.[2]

It was with great pride that the Battalion heard that Field-Marshal Earl Roberts had accepted the Honorary Colonelcy of the Battalion. He was only to hold it for a few weeks, however, before his untimely death in France.

On October 3rd the Battalion took part with other troops to the number of about 4,000, in a route march round the city, when General Nugent, O.C. Humber Defences, took the salute. It is of interest to mention that General Nugent subsequently commanded the 36th (Ulster) Division, which gave us our first introduction to trench warfare in March, 1916, at Engelbelmer. The beginning of October also saw the first steps in musketry training, aiming and trigger pressing, and the mysterious "triangle of error". Training of all kinds continued with unabated vigour and the Commanding Officer

---

2 During this period the battalion suffered its first death. Private Thomas Adams died on 18 September from brain fever. He is buried in Hull Western Cemetery. He was single.

commenced a series of inspections of companies in various exercises and manoeuvres, to the detriment of the nerves of officers and N.C.O.s.

On October 23rd the Battalion marched via Kirkella and Riplingham to Welton, and were entertained by Colonel Harrison-Broadley on the lawn at Welton House, marching back to Wenlock Barracks via North Ferriby. This was the longest march we had yet essayed – about twenty miles there and back – but it was successfully accomplished. Instead, however, of being complimented on the performance, we received a not unmerited rebuke from the Commanding Officer on "Litter", couched in such terms that we never again offended in that way.

The Hull Fair Ground was less frequently used now, companies going further afield to the Golf Course, the Grammar School Playing Fields, and the fields round Haltemprice Farm. Eagerness to reach these far-away grounds led one Company Commander to give his troops the command "double" up Anlaby Road, and earned for them the sobriquet of "Glossop's Greyhounds", the gallant major encouraging his troops from the steps of a tram proceeding in the same direction.

The beginning of November saw the issue of the first part of kit. Up to this time we had been training in civilian clothes with armlets, but now we were partly clothed in regulation tunics which we made to fit where possible, regulation trousers which we learnt to tuck into our regulation puttees – not too successfully in some cases – and leather equipment which we struggled to make hang correctly about us, but best of all, unlike many of the first Battalions of Kitchener's Army who were clothed for a long time in hideous blue clothing, we were issued with the regulation and serviceable khaki.

The proximity of Hull to the East Coast, and the possibility of enemy action there, caused the incorporation of about 400 men of the Battalion in a Humber Defence Force. This section was armed with what few "Drill-purpose" rifles were in the possession of the Battalion, with the addition of those taken over from the 11th Battalion, which was training at the Cricket Ground on Anlaby Road. This small force was divided into sections, each in the charge of an N.C.O., who was responsible for calling out his section at any hour on the alarm being given.

These emergency measures were rendered unnecessary by the dramatically sudden removal of the whole Battalion to the hutments at Rolston, near Hornsea, for coast defence purposes.

Before closing this period, however, one or two interesting things are perhaps worthy of note: the departure of Captain E. F. Twiss, who had acted as Adjutant of the Battalion since its formation, to be Adjutant of the 13th Battalion, just then being recruited, and the appointment in his place of Lieutenant Ivor Jackson; the last route march to Brantinghamthorpe, where the Battalion was entertained by Sir John Sherburn, whose son, Second Lieutenant Clifford Sherburn, was one of "C" Company's original officers; and the examination, held by the Commanding Officer for Junior Officers and N.C.O.s in the Paisley Street School.

This examination caused no little consternation among those called to attend.

One incident typical of many which occurred in the weeks that followed may be recorded here.

The first question on the musketry paper was: "When does a soldier charge, and when does he uncharge his magazine?"

Just as the examination was about to commence, Colonel Richardson walked into the room and said something like this:

"Look at question 1 on the musketry paper. The first 'charge' is a transitive verb. That is all I have to say".

He then walked out, leaving most of us harking back to school-days in the endeavour to remember exactly what a transitive verb was!

November 17th marks a definite period in the history of the Battalion, for it was on this day that almost immediately after falling in for afternoon parade, we were dismissed and ordered to return as soon as possible, complete with kit. The Battalion, less those men who lived out of town, paraded again at 4.15 p.m., having collected all available rifles from the 11th Battalion, marched to Paragon Station and entrained for Hornsea. The train left Paragon at 5.50 p.m., with all blinds drawn, and arrived at Hornsea Bridge Station at 7 p.m. Though we were a Hull Battalion, the homes of many of the men were at such places as Beverley, Bridlington, Hornsea, Withernsea, and there was a strong detachment belonging to Goole. Men from these places were sent home, with instructions to parade the next morning, to follow the Battalion.

These details under Lieut.-Q.M. Upton had to pack all Q.M. stores, which had been left behind in the hurried departure, and G.S. wagons were loaded and transported to Hornsea where many of us received further instruction in fatigues.

It had been the intention of the East Riding Territorial Force Association, who were responsible for the four Hull Battalions until they were taken over by the War Office, to interchange the Battalions round the hutment camps then being prepared for them at Rolston, Dalton, and Millington, near Pocklington. The sudden call on the services of the Battalion for Coast Defence appears to have altered this plan somewhat.

When the Battalion marched from Hornsea Bridge Station, in the pitch darkness of a mid-November night, it was to a half-completed camp in the middle of a field on the cliff top, ankle deep in mud. The only visible sign of life was the fitful gleam of Second-Lieutenant E. C. Williams' hurricane lamp, as he guided the platoons to their huts. The unfinished state of the camp rendered it necessary to billet sixty men per hut in place of the nominal thirty. A number of the huts had neither doors nor windows, but fortunately Second-Lieutenant Williams had been able to obtain a sufficient number of blankets to make an issue of three per man, which went some little way to mitigate the first shock of active service conditions.

The suddenness of the move was evidently too much for the Army Service Corps, as, for the first twenty-four hours there was practically no food to be had. The first issue was bread, about eight or ten men to a small loaf and about a square inch of cheese per man. This was purchased by the Battalion itself, and nearly a year elapsed before repayment could be obtained from the Army Pay authorities, so great was their faith in the efficiency of the Army Service Corps and their distrust of new Army Battalions, particularly those known as "Commercials". It is related that certain members of "B" Company set off to Mappleton about 5.30 on the first morning and managed to get some biscuits at a small shop. Returning to camp they encountered the lodge keeper at Rolston Hall, who took them home and gave them a good breakfast. When they finally reached camp they found the Battalion on parade. Fatigues occupied most of the first day, but leave into Hornsea was granted at 6.30 p.m., when a general raid on the food shops took place.

On the 19th, amid rain and snow, two platoons each of "B" and "C" Companies were moved to Atwick and Skipsea on detachment for Coast Patrol, and part of "D" Company to Hornsea. "Sunrise" to a member of "D" Company has nothing to do with the break of day, but conjures up memories of the dear old billet on the front at Hornsea, where he spent many happy days during the winter of 1914 and the spring of 1915, and many others have happy recollections of billets here with equally misleading names.

From this time onward until our departure for Divisional training at Ripon, the coast from Mappleton to Ulrome was guarded by day and patrolled by night by this Battalion. Sentry groups were posted each night at Skipsea, Atwick, Hornsea, and the camp at Rolston, and from each of these groups two men patrolled north and south in two-hour patrols, meeting the corresponding patrols from the other groups, and returning again to their own sentry group. The patrol from Skipsea northwards made contact with a patrol from the Yorkshire Hussars (later relieved by the Huntingdonshire Cyclists) and the patrol from Rolston southwards with the Norfolk Cyclists.

The troops on detachment spent much of their time digging a system of trenches on the cliff top. Those who are familiar with this coast will readily understand that these trenches were constantly falling into the sea and had to be continually renewed. The trenches were manned an hour before dawn every morning by the detachment billeted in the village behind. The troops remained in the trenches until daylight and then marched back to breakfast. Physical drill and, later, Miniature Rifle practice on the sands helped to relieve the monotony of pick and shovel work, and mild excitement was provided by occasional night excursions after unauthorised lights and the holding up of motor cars and other vehicles at improvised barriers on the coast roads.

Owing to coast defence requirements, week-end leave was very sparingly given and was liable to sudden stoppage. About the end of November, a sudden message from the Higher Command resulted in the somewhat dramatic recall of the men who had been granted week-end leave, just as they were about to enter the train at Hornsea Bridge Station.

In early December the designation of the Battalion, which had been successively 7th Battalion and 1st (Hull) Battalion, was changed to 10th (Service) Battalion, East Yorkshire Regiment, and Major W. H. Carver, who had been so actively associated with the formation of the Battalion, was officially appointed to be second-in-command.

On December 16th the whole Battalion stood to arms at 6.30 a.m. and the detachments manned the trenches along the coast in full force. This was in response to the alarm which had been circulated owing to part of the German High Seas Fleet having been missed. At 8 a.m. the now historic bombardment of Scarborough, Whitby and Hartlepool commenced. The bombardment was clearly heard by the waiting troops and caused much conjecture as to what it really meant, but a graphic description of the damage at Scarborough was soon available, and for once rumour fell short of the actual happening.

An amusing incident, which might have had serious consequences, took place at Atwick about this time, in the setting on fire one night of a hut on the cliff top.

This hut was used by the sentry group for shelter, and one youth had begged, or otherwise come into possession of, a bundle of straw for the comfort of the patrol "off duty". One of his comrades, with a thirst for knowledge, had brought a candle by which to read, and the subsequent blaze might have proved disastrous owing to the presence of six boxes of ammunition. Fortunately, these were rescued, but the blaze was visible for miles up and down the coast and caused many anxious enquiries as to the reason. The explanations which followed must have been satisfactory as nothing more was heard of the incident.

"Roll Call" parade at Wenlock Barracks.

Marching down Walton Street, September 1914.

The triangle of error, September 1914.

Not quite so happy was the sequel to the discovery by the Commanding Officer, on a tour of inspection of the Coast Patrols, of a sentry with his arm round a fair damsel and his eyes elsewhere than looking for a possible landing by the German High Seas Fleet. The young man who had visions of a commission, found that his "affair" was not a recommendation for promotion.

With the exception of the platoons on detachment, who appear to have fared sumptuously on geese and plum pudding in farms, barns and other places, "A", "B" and "D" Companies spent Christmas Day Bring on the range at Rolston.

How this came about is worth recalling as it is typical of Colonel Richardson.

The Rolston Hutment Camp was adjacent to a rifle range and the Battalion on arrival was supplied with a certain amount of S.A.A., which was "only to be used against the enemy". This combination – a supply of S.A.A., a rifle range, and a Battalion which though well versed in the theory of musketry had yet never fired a shot out of its "long" rifles – was one which Colonel Richardson was not disposed to allow to continue to exist for longer than he could help. Ever since the combination came into being at Hornsea he had written letters to all the Higher Commands of which he was aware, pointing out in his own succinct fashion this combination and the urgent necessity for the Battalion using some of the said S.A.A. on the said range so as to ensure efficiency in the use of their rifles against the enemy. Replies were unsatisfactory, but, nothing daunted, the Colonel persisted like the importunate widow, and about a week before Christmas Day, 1914, a telegram was received at Battalion Headquarters from the War Office reading as follows:

"Reference your .... Report on efficiency of rifles".

To which the Colonel replied characteristically:

"Reference your telegram....... Rifles will certainly go off, doubtful which end".

The receipt of this wire produced such extraordinary activity on the part of the War Office that on Christmas Eve authority was received from the War Office direct, to fire so many rounds of the precious S.A.A. per man – nor will those who knew Colonel Richardson be surprised that as a result such of the Battalion as were not on leave or on detachment, spent their Christmas Day in an unforgettable way on the range to such effect that by the end of the day each man had fired the allotted number of rounds out of his own rifle.

"C" Company acted as markers. This Company had, by some means best known to itself, obtained some ammunition in November and had had Grouping Practice at a target fixed at the edge of the sea at Skipsea.

At the beginning of January the camp at Rolston was visited and inspected by Brigadier-General Sir H. Dixon, K.C.B., commanding the 113th Infantry Brigade, to which Brigade the Battalion was now attached.

The four companies were settling down to serious company training of all kinds. They were commanded by the following officers: "A" Company, Major W. H. Glossop; "B" Company, Captain T. Ridsdill Smith; "C" Company, Captain W. L. Ruthven; and "D" Company, Captain Guy Lambert. The selection of specialists, such as pioneers, signallers, machine gunners, and stretcher bearers, was now commenced, and Company Commanders were called upon to recommend N.C.O.s for promotion to higher, or confirmation in their present rank. All non-commissioned ranks had up to now been "acting" only, but it was considered that sufficient time had elapsed for Company Commanders to be able to judge whether the original selection of N.C.O.s had been justified. A growing demand for men suitable for commissioned rank drew from Colonel Richardson the following statement – a position which he sternly refused to modify:

> "Commissions. Qualifications:
> "Character and determination strong enough to ensure discipline. Mental powers sufficient to assimilate the regulations and instructions that guide the army. The C.O. will recommend no one who does not give proof of possessing the above, no matter how many employers, fathers, or grandmothers try to pull the strings".

The troops on detachment were relieved from time to time, and at the end of January, Major Glossop was given command of the detachments at Atwick, Hornsea, and Skipsea. The depot company, which had been formed and of which Captain A. A. Plimpton had been given command, was well on the way to its full complement. This company was intended to provide a first reinforcement for the Battalion, and to replace casualties. A brief account of its subsequent adventures from the pen of Captain Plimpton is included later.

A series of lectures on military subjects was given on Saturday afternoons in the Royal Institution, Albion Street, Hull, and officers and N.C.O.s were encouraged to attend. Perhaps it should be stated that thirst for military knowledge was not the only reason for the excellent attendance at these lectures: an evening in Hull, with leave until the last train, may have been another.

Despite the rigours of the coast patrol, and the exposure to the inclemency of the weather during the first winter of the war, the health of the Battalion was good. By far the greater number of those reporting sick would be given the familiar "Medicine and Duty", the medicine consisting of the famous "Number 9" or a dose of the less well-known "Mist. Expectorans"; the duty meant a return to take part in whatever training or parade was the order of the day. Although such designations as "Lead-swinger", "Wangler", "Skrimshanker", and the like belonged to a later date, the types were not unknown. Route march day usually meant a larger sick parade than usual, evidently with the hope that the Battalion would have departed before the doctor's verdict was known, the result being that even if "M. and D". was awarded, the "Duty" would not be a route march of twenty-five miles. Wisdom, however, did not begin and end in the ranks, and on several occasions a senior N.C.O. was detailed to await the doctor's verdict, collect the men awarded "M. and D". and march them after the Battalion. Thus did the "Lead-swinger" learn that the way of the transgressor is hard. The following comment appears in orders about this date:

"Sick! – An excursion day – four fresh cases.

A working day – ten fresh cases".

A sharp influenza epidemic brought the figures for February up to 632.

Whilst on this subject mention must be made of Dr. Norbury, the Battalion's first M.O. He was a gentle kindly soul, a man of outstanding ability, who quickly endeared himself to all ranks. The 'flu epidemic finally laid him low, and much against his own will he was sent to hospital, by order of the C.O. This finished his connection with the Battalion, but not before he had established himself in the affections of all who knew him. He was subsequently posted to a bacteriological research section with the B.E.F. in France.

One of the "days" remembered when we of the 10th foregather, is February 23rd, 1915. It was the occasion of the march from Rolston Camp to Hull and back. Reveille was at 5.30 a.m. and we marched off at 7 a.m. by way of Mappleton, Great Hatfield, Whitedale, and Coniston, to the Victoria Square in Hull, which was reached at 11.45 a.m. Arms were piled in the square, and we were entertained to refreshments in the City Hall by Lord Nunburnholme. The return march by the same route was commenced before 1 p.m., and camp was reached at 5.50 p.m. The distance was thirty-two miles, the longest march attempted up to that time. One hundred and twenty-six men fell out on the homeward march, the numbers being fairly evenly distributed over the companies. Possibly the proximity of the Hull-Hornsea railway to the line of march throughout nearly the whole distance had something to do with the numbers falling out. The only "official" comment on the performance appeared in Orders two nights later:

> "After the Aldershot command manoeuvres in 1910 the 1st Battalion East Yorkshire Regiment, composed of younger men than most of the 10th Battalion, marched back to its station, every man carrying a complete kit, in one day. One man fell out. The distance was thirty-nine miles. In the whole Brigade six men fell out. About 100 men in each Battalion had their feet dressed after their arrival".

Training continued strenuously, inspections by O.C. companies in close order drill, musketry, and manoeuvres against a flagged enemy were carried out from time to time and produced interesting, amusing, instructive and frequently disconcerting remarks and comments. Many officers will no doubt recall the "pow wows" held in the C.O.'s room after tea on such occasions.

The recreational side was, however, not neglected and Battalion sports were held on the field behind the range, a number of excellent football teams were raised and inter-platoon and company matches played. At least one historic match was played between Officers and Sergeants, resulting in two broken ribs.

Apropos of this particular match, the Sergeants were entertained to tea in the Officers' mess at the close of the match. When tea had commenced Colonel Richardson appeared and made a place for himself among the guests at one side of the long table. Turning to the Sergeant on one side he said, "And where were you playing?" "I was referee, sir", was the reply. The same question to his neighbour on the other side elicited the reply, "I was linesman, sir!" Addressing himself to a Sergeant across the table the Colonel in his own inimitable way said, "And were you playing? Or were you just carrying something?"

A series of Battalion cross-country runs was organised and the whole of the officers and men, less the absolutely essential details, such as cooks, were ordered to take part. Colonel Richardson set a good example by himself turning out and completing the course on the first occasion. From the results of these runs a team was selected and trained to compete in a Brigade cross-country run, which was held on April 21st, 1915.

The run was from the Camp at Dalton, finishing at the Depot at Beverley, and the Battalion was given leave to go to Beverley by special train to see the finish of the run; F. Seller ("B" Co.) was first home, but the disqualification of J. Hughes ("D" Co.) cost us the team championship, which was won by the 11th Battalion.

One officer and 25 per cent of other ranks of those on detachment and 50 per cent of all pickets were left behind on coast defence to deal with any enemy invasion!

Coast defence was not without its comic relief. One bright April Sunday morning we were called out at 4 o'clock to line the cliff and deal with a reported Zeppelin. Rifles and ammunition we certainly had; the rifles, however, were for "drill purposes" only, and were deemed to be more dangerous to the user than to the enemy. It was therefore understood that the repulsion of the Zeppelin was to be by moral force only. The various company "wags" were in great evidence and a running fire of comments which would have nonplussed the enemy more than our rifle fire, was kept up.

Authority was inclined to turn a blind eye to the evidences of high spirits and might even have pleaded guilty to facetiousness itself. The cream of the joke, however, remains with the Signallers: they were by this time occupying a hut by themselves, and in the excitement of the "stand to" were somehow missed. They slept on, oblivious alike of the danger to their country and the enjoyment of their comrades, dangling their legs over the cliff top in the cool breezes of an April morning.

The formation of a band was mooted, and men with the ability to play some musical instrument were invited to declare themselves. Lieutenant Coatsworth was appointed Band President, and the first meeting of the Band was held on May 6th. A leader was found in Private F. Purcell, who had seen service with the Band of the 2nd Battalion of the Regiment in pre-war days. He was subsequently promoted to be Band-Sergeant, and did excellent work both at home and overseas in that capacity. The band instruments were provided by members of the Hull Exchange and "Pacific", many of whom were serving in the Battalion.

Baptism of fire for some of the members of the Battalion came on the occasion of the first air-raid on Hull, on the night of Sunday, June 6th, 1915, when those who were on week-end leave shared in the excitement of that midnight visit of the Zeppelin, returning to camp next morning with stories of thrilling scenes and damage done.

The time for more advanced training was drawing near and this involved the departure of the Battalion from what was really its home area to a place more suited to the concentration of larger forces.

The residents of Hornsea were genuinely sorry to part with us. Relations with the inhabitants of Hornsea and the villages along the coast had been very cordial and we had received many kindnesses at their hands.

Such little items as a mug of hot tea and a slice of buttered toast on the village cross at Atwick, left in the early hours of every morning for the village military policeman, was somebody's good deed for the day.

Distinctions are invidious, but one would like to mention the names of Mr. and Mrs. Bell at Atwick. Their home was a more or less open house for the men of the various platoons which were stationed there from time to time, who cared to avail themselves, and dozens of men must have pleasant recollections of the kindness of Mr. and Mrs. Bell and their family.

The officers – Hornsea, 1915.

Christmas Tree Hut, Atwick, 1914.

Hut interior at Hornsea, 1914–15.

Chapter 2

The Depot Company

LEAVING the Battalion en route for Ripon on June 22nd, 1915, the Depot Company proceeded to Millington Camp, Pocklington, lately occupied by the 11th Battalion and was formed with similar units of that Battalion, the 12th and 13th, into the 14th East Yorkshire Regiment, under the command of Lieut.-Colonel A. Cole, who came to us from Strensall[3] where he had been Camp Commandant. The 10th Depot Company became "A" Company of the new unit and occupied that position throughout the War. The value of the sound training earlier received was quickly in evidence, and in many directions "A" Company became the model on which the new Battalion was developed. At first, the four companies carried on independently and early memories of Millington centre chiefly round route marches, range practices, and night operations. That official schemes for night attacks are not the only ones which sometimes miscarry was forcibly brought home to the raiding party, who misguidedly chose for their objective the hut presided over by Sergeant Nicholls (who will be remembered as the burliest of the ex-Grimsby policemen). Rumour had it that there were more cold baths in a short space of time on that night than had previously been known in Millington Camp; some doubt, too, was expressed by the victims as to the source of the camp water supply.

A comparatively uneventful sojourn was suddenly broken by a move to Brockton Camp on the edge of Cannock Chase, where digging with a capital "D" was the order of the day. The camp was unfinished and the Battalion assisted in constructing the drainage system before it could be occupied. After some months the Battalion moved to Whittington Barracks, Lichfield, and life closely approached that of the Regular Army with ceremonial, barrack room inspections, inter-regimental competitions, and the like playing a prominent part. The following summer saw us brigaded at Clipstone Camp under the command of Brig.-General Claude Westmacott, and time was chiefly occupied in firing our musketry course, an event which again left "A" Company with a sense of ancestral pride.

---

3 A large army training area and home to the West Yorkshire regiment.

During this period a number of old members of the 10th found their way back to us from one cause or another, but it was not until we were suddenly moved to Newcastle in the autumn of 1916 that there were any great changes in the personnel; from that time onwards, however, movement, both of officers and men, was continuous; Battalion and Company headquarters alone remaining untouched. The Battalion now became the 90th Training Reserve Battalion brigaded with similar units from the York and Lancaster and West Riding Regiments with full Divisional establishment centred at Newcastle. The Brigade was suddenly moved on to the coast at Seaton Delaval. A line of trenches along the sand dunes was taken over and manned at night, alarms were frequent, submarines and fast naval craft made numerous sorties, Zeppelins frequently zoomed overhead at nights, mines blew up in the bay, placid-looking traders divided into two parts in broad daylight and disappeared, and as their cargo was generally timber there was much improvement in our dugouts and trench lines! We later learned that our hurried departure to the coast had coincided with the Roger Casement episode, but apart from the above excitements, we settled down to intensive training, despatch of drafts and continuous reorganisation to meet the increasing demands.

From the outset, the class started at Hornsea for the training of N.C.O.s for promotion, had been preserved in "A" Company and this, in time, became a regimental institution from which N.C.O.s for the whole of the Battalion were supplied, so much so that at one time there were few N.C.O.s in the unit who had not passed through it.

This was still more evident when calls for drafts became frequent; recruit training was curtailed, expedited and re-organised, with the result that all drafts sent out from the Battalion were passed to "A" Company for their final five weeks training in field work and Company training. With drafts leaving every week or so the responsibility that fell on those N.C.O.s may be imagined when it is stated that at times the Company Officers consisted of the Company Commander and one other.

During this time also many of the old 10th Officers and N.C.O.s were on its strength for varying periods, so many, indeed, that memory can recall only a few, but among those may be mentioned Major Glossop, who found full scope for his activities in supervising the messing and cooking arrangements, Captain Robinson, Lieutenants England, Oxtoby, Sever, Butters, C.S.M. Wheeler, and Corporal Evers, who resumed his old role of post corporal with his own particular skill.

About August, 1917, the Battalion moved from the Northern to the Eastern command into a Division stationed at Ipswich, under the command of Lieut.-General Inglefield, well known to all the Regiment and later its Colonel-in-Chief. Here Lieut.-Colonel Cole was relieved by Colonel Oliver, of the Middlesex Regiment. As the 264th Infantry Battalion of a Division at full war establishment, the Battalion was soon introduced to hectic and never-to-be-forgotten Battalion exercises, Brigade and Divisional Field Days, a summer under canvas when not in trenches, air raids almost nightly, and sandstorms which contaminated the food and resulted in much dysentery and sickness.

With a flying-boat base at Felixstowe on one side of us and an aerodrome on Martlesham Heath on the other, there was considerable activity. On the receipt of "air raid warning" we vacated camp, taking cover in small bodies in the heather and heath, where we remained until the "all clear". This soon became extremely monotonous to all officers; the partiality of other ranks for spending their nights in this unconventional manner was only explained when reports appeared in the local press of extensive depredations in large orchards a mile or two away, which were heavily stocked with ripe Cox's Orange Pippin apples for the London market.

The Company about this time was over 600 strong and with a detachment near Woodbridge, ten miles away, and another at Felixstowe, ten miles in another direction, a formidable command for a Company Commander who was O.C. troops in both places with the Company Headquarters with the Battalion at a third. There were still, however, enough of the old originals left to preserve the spirit of, and our own faith in, the 10th and ability to prevail against and overcome all that might come our way. By the time we went into billets in Ipswich at the end of the summer, having now become the 51st K.O.Y.L.I., practically all the old officers and N.C.O.s had gone, with the exception of the Company Commanders and a few of the key N.C.O.s; and when at last Captain Bilton, of the 11th and the writer, with one or two others were ordered overseas in November, 1917, it is doubtful if there were any of the original four Depot Companies left who were available for active service.

Colonel Wilson assumed command of the Battalion and in the spring of 1918 they moved to Clipstone, where they remained until the Armistice and subsequent demobilisation. It would be shortly before the Armistice that the writer was invited to revisit them and, making a search for any old faces, sought out the Q.M. and received what he then regarded as perhaps the greatest compliment of his military career from R.Q.M.S. Marriott, a charming old man who had spent his life in the Regiment and coming, I think, from the 12th, had occupied that position throughout the Battalion's existence. On my asking for the Q.M. the old man replied laconically in his slow, long-drawn musical way, "He'll be back in a minute, sir. He's outside locking up. He heard you was coming, sir!"

Possibly the R.Q.M.S. had not forgotten heavy claims for deficiencies being made on the Battalion when vacating the Northern Command, "A" Company (true to parental tradition) alone averting disaster by not only balancing its own account but providing a sufficient surplus to enable the others (there were then six companies) to do the same. A further proof, we thought, that our early training had stood us in good stead! Others may have had other thoughts.

There are no records available, but memory recalls a calculation made shortly after reaching Ipswich, which showed that more than 2,000 men had passed through the Company and gone overseas as drafts. It was ever our aim and ambition to impart to these the spirit and tradition of the old Battalion, which had ever remained in the hearts and minds of the little and ever thinning band who still "carried on". One remembers C.S.M. Dixon who, becoming Regimental Sergeant Major soon after the formation of the new Battalion, still occupied that position on demobilisation and throughout remained an invaluable ally of the Company Commander in promoting that spirit and tradition throughout the training personnel of the unit. The Battalion, under the command of Colonel Wilson, eventually went overseas as a unit of the Army of Occupation.

Chapter 3

Ripon – The Departure of Colonel Richardson

ON June 21st the Battalion left the Camp at Rolston for Beverley en route for Ripon, where the 31st New Army Division was being concentrated for Divisional Training.

The Division was made up of:

The 92nd Infantry Brigade (Commanded by Brig.-General Parker) –
10th, 11th, 12th and 13th Battalions, East Yorkshire Regiment;

The 93rd Infantry Brigade –
15th, 16th and 18th Battalions, West Yorkshire Regiment; 18th Battalion Durham Light Infantry;

The 94th Infantry Brigade –
12th, 13th and 14th Battalions, York and Lancaster Regiment; 11th Battalion, East Lancashire Regiment; with the 12th Battalion K.O.Y.L.I. as Pioneer Battalion.

Major-General E. Fanshawe, C.B., was in command for two weeks and was followed by Major-General Wanless O'Gowan, C.B.

At Beverley the troops had their first experience of billets; Captain W. Horsley was Billeting Officer. From Beverley the march was continued in the morning to Pocklington, then York, and Boroughbridge, at each of which towns billets were found. These were varied in quality; one might find a full-blown private elevated by an admiring civilian family to the best bedroom, complete with featherbed, whilst his sergeant found what soft spot he could on the tap-room settee of the local inn.

Ripon was reached on the afternoon of June 25th. By a kindly gesture of the O.C. 15th Battalion West Yorkshire Regiment (Leeds Pals), their band met the Battalion at the outskirts of Ripon, and played us up to camp. We were accommodated in the South Camp, occupying the last set of hutments on the Harrogate Road. The hutments had not previously been occupied, consequently R.Q.M.S. J. Kendall, and his advance party had been exceptionally busy fitting out the camp with camp equipment, in addition to receiving many articles of which the Battalion was still short.

Perhaps the party had been somewhat overzealous as a letter from the acting Staff Captain reads:

"To O.C. 10th Battalion East Yorkshire Regiment. –
I have instructed O.C. 12th Battalion to send a party to your lines to remove the cooking portion of a travelling kitchen which you have in excess of your establishment".

A characteristic note is appended to the above letter and reads:

"Q.M. – See that they remove nothing else, please. A.J.R".

Brigade and divisional training now occupied most of the Battalion's time, while intensive training of special sections, such as machine gunners under Lieutenant R. B. Carver, signallers under Second-Lieutenant Oxtoby, and bombers under Second-Lieutenant Carlisle, was engaged in. Much trouble was experienced in getting the necessary equipment for specialist training, which was often carried out with much difficulty. For a long period there hung near the C.O.'s desk in his room a list headed, "Things I want".

Some specialists may remember the antipathy Colonel Richardson had for certain musketry experts sent by the Northern Command. One day he overheard one of these instructors telling a squad that as the word of command "Fire" had sometimes been mistaken for "Retire", it was proposed to substitute the word "Shoot".

Colonel Richardson remarked in his most scathing manner, "But don't you think 'Shoot' might be mistaken for 'Scoot'?" Nothing further was heard of that suggestion.

Certain areas in the district round Ripon were allotted to Brigades and Battalions for field operations and training. The possibilities of using these areas were few, owing to the very stringent regulations regarding the necessity of keeping off all land occupied by hay or growing crops. The ground available in some instances was so restricted that Colonel Richardson, somewhat facetiously perhaps, suggested to the Higher Command that if the Battalion was given six weeks leave the crops might by then have been gathered in, and room to manoeuvre would be available. Whether or not this suggestion had any bearing on the subject one cannot say, but curiously enough the Battalion was granted ten days leave, one company being absent at a time.

The Battalion Band, which had been progressing under the leadership of Corporal F. Purcell, and regularly accompanied the Battalion on its parades, proceeded to Hull in the middle of September for a week for

The Band – Ripon, 1915.

recruiting purposes. C.S.M. "Sam" Cash, "D" Company, accompanied them as recruiting sergeant.

Battalion Orders of this date contained the following interesting note:

> "All N.C.O.s will be confirmed in their ranks on the 18th September, unless the officers commanding companies report to Battalion Headquarters before that date that any one of his is inefficient. In future acting N.C.O.s will not be made. Company and Platoon Commanders have had a year to study their men. If they suffer from an *embarras de richesse* they can recommend for commissions".

On September 18th the Battalion had its first taste of active service conditions; marching from camp to the moors above Pateley Bridge, we bivouacked for two nights among the heather, with nothing for protection but great coat and ground sheet. A nasty drizzling rain about 5 a.m. made things rather uncomfortable for the first night's bivouac, and it did not require "Reveille" to get the troops up next morning. In fact, many had been for several walks during the night by way of a rest. On the march back to camp we met Sir Bruce Hamilton, an old East Yorkshire Officer, then in command of the Ripon District. A further experience of three nights bivouac at Brimham Rocks and Skellgill Bridge was undergone at a later date.

The story of the Ripon days would not be complete without mention of the Rifle Ranges at Wormald Green. The construction of these ranges was supervised by the 12th Battalion K.O.Y.L.I. (Pioneers), and was largely carried out by the Battalions of the 31st Division. For a considerable period strong daily working parties marched five miles to Wormald Green, did half a day's work, and were relieved by a similar party for the other half of the day. The Battalions of the Division finally fired the first part of the General Musketry Course over these ranges. Another pleasant memory of the Ripon days is the visits paid for Battalion Drill to the Park at Studley Royal.

The formation of a Divisional Cyclist Company took twenty men from the Battalion, and along with them Lieutenant Coatsworth, who departed to take command. He subsequently became a Staff Officer with the VIII Corps. On his departure, Lieutenant R. A. Flintoff assumed charge of the band, and a very excellent Band President he made until his death in June, 1916.

Our numbers were further depleted when a deputation from the Ministry of Munitions was given a free hand with the full Battalion on parade, minus its officers, to canvass among the men for skilled workmen to return to their trades.

On October 18th the Battalion was warned of an early move to Salisbury Plain, and in Orders of the same day it was with great regret that the troops read the following notice:

> "Lieut.-Colonel Richardson has this day handed over command of the Battalion to Major W. H. Carver. On vacating the command, Lieut.-Colonel Richardson thanks all ranks of the Battalion for the very pleasant thirteen months that their hard and loyal labour has enabled him to enjoy, and it is with great regret that he recognises that there is now little probability of his seeing the result of that labour in a theatre more interesting, but not more trying, than the Ripon Rifle Ranges".

No record of the Battalion would be complete without a brief character sketch of its first Commanding Officer. Lieut.-Colonel A. Richardson was known throughout the whole of the British Army, but especially in the East Yorkshire Regiment, where he had spent practically the whole of his career. He was an acknowledged master of his profession, outspoken to the last degree, intolerant of incompetence wherever he found it, either above or below, and moreover had never learned to "suffer fools gladly".

His methods of training were his own; were sometimes severe; and, occasionally, apparently ruthless.

The private soldier, if he could march and shoot, might be forgiven much.

The officer or man who wore a stripe, or a star, or a crown, or any number of these adornments, or any combination thereof, was never allowed for many minutes to view these badges with any degree of complacency. To do so was to court disaster and humiliation. The comparative anonymity of the ranks at times seemed a desirable haven.

It is safe to say that during the first few months of his command, the Battalion bore for Colonel Richardson that "affectionate" regard which the soldier is commonly supposed to bear for the Regimental Sergeant Major of tradition!

It is equally safe to say that long before he bade the Battalion farewell, he occupied a place in the affection and esteem of officers and men which was unique and unchallenged, and which remains unaffected by the passing years.

A Battalion of men, many of whom were experts in their own professions, quickly recognised a man who knew his job, and was determined that they should know as much of it as he could teach them in the time at his disposal.

Limitations of space and the inadequacy of the written word render impossible the inclusion of the innumerable yarns about Colonel Richardson which are told by members of the Battalion or by old soldiers of the Regiment, who knew him in former days – told with a twinkle of the eye and a reminiscent chuckle, particularly in those cases when the story ends, as so many of them do, with the discomfiture of some individual, high or low in rank, who, to use a colloquialism, "asked for it".

Very few of those who were present on parade in the field behind the camp at Ripon will forget Colonel Richardson's appearance in civilian clothes, just as when he first appeared at Wenlock Barracks. Once again, borrowing Major Carver's horse, he spoke his farewell to us in these words:

"Gentlemen – Before I leave I want to take the opportunity of saying good-bye, but first I am going to start with a lecture on tactics, because I still feel a certain responsibility for the Battalion, and in future, when I watch your deeds recorded in the newspapers, I shall always feel that I myself (whoever commands you at the time) have a certain amount of responsibility.

"I want to remind you that every commander, no matter what the size of the unit, is responsible for taking all proper precautions so that his unit should not be taken at a disadvantage.

"You will find it in the regulation books, but I tell you for the last time so that it will sink into a good many heads, which otherwise might not grasp it, every commander is responsible that he should keep his senior officers and the units on either flank informed of what is taking place.

"Another thing is that when the situation is not quite clear, take a bold step. If you are not quite certain what is the right thing to do – then do the boldest and most energetic.

"That you will not find in the book, but if you indulge in reading you will discover that principle for yourself.

"Audacity may put you in the first category of casualties, pusillanimity will probably put you in the third. For four years I commanded the 1st Battalion which went to war under my successor, and having watched the casualty lists I have seen names in the first and second classes, but only eight or a dozen in the missing, and that is one that every soldier wants to keep out of.

"Now I finish my instructions on tactics and I should just like to say a few words about the reason I leave you.

"It was reported to the War Office that I was impatient of control and I am afraid that there is a certain amount of foundation for that. You see, when I came to this Battalion thirteen months ago, I rather expected we should be on active service this spring and it was somewhat upsetting to find ourselves, as one of you wrote, 'still at Ripon', and probably this might have had some effect, but there was a distinguished old friend of mine of the name of Moses, who suffered from the same impatience and if you will remember the result in his case was that he did not enter the Promised Land (laughter). Although I shall not be at the head of the Battalion when you enter Berlin, I shall have to follow you as a civilian.

"And now, Gentlemen, I want to thank you for the hard work and loyal service that you have given, and for the unfailing cheerfulness you have exhibited. There have been no complaints, and thanks to you my responsibilities have rested very lightly upon my shoulders.

"The work, the result of it you have demonstrated partly on the rifle ranges, and for that every credit is due, not to me, but to the officers, N.C.O.s and men who have learned everything that has been brought to them.

"Your behaviour has been – well, I won't say. If you remember when I first came, I told you that the command of a battalion of this nature was a great honour – well, the behaviour of this Battalion is phenomenally good.

"As a Battalion, there has been only one Court Martial in fourteen months. There has not been a deserter yet, and I have no doubt that you will give my successor the same spirit and the same trust that you have given to me, and I congratulate him on the command of a Battalion that, as I say, any man not only would be proud, but would be honoured and more than pleased to command.

"Now, gentlemen, I will say good-bye to you and I hope that you will have the very best of fighting that there may be for you. I don't wish you an easy time of it, because that is a thing no soldier expects.

"You all came in at the first flush of the War and expect to do some fighting.

"I hope that some of the officers will occasionally let me know what is going on, because I still feel a certain amount of responsibility, not only responsibility but affection, and I know that as your behaviour in England has been like angels, your fighting will be like that of the other sort.

"Well, good-bye, gentlemen, and the best of luck".

Chapter 4

Salisbury Plain and the Journey East

ON November 6th the Battalion left Ripon where it had spent several very happy months, for Fovant on Salisbury Plain. A few weeks earlier Canon Waugh, on the occasion of his leaving Ripon Cathedral, said farewell to the 31st Division in these words:

> "Your presence in Ripon has been a welcome innovation, and your conduct has been exemplary".

In this tribute, which was not the only one paid to the Division, the 10th East Yorkshires had a share.

Hurdcott Camp was reached in the early hours of the morning by a very tired Battalion. The advance party, however, had made beds for all, and as these consisted of five new, white Witney blankets, tiredness was soon forgotten. Everyone was in the best of spirits next morning.

Since the departure of Lieut.-Colonel Richardson, Major W. H. Carver had been in command of the Battalion. Lieut.-Colonel Dan Burges now assumed command. Colonel Burges came from the Gloucester Regiment and had seen active service in France. He remained in command of the Battalion until the beginning of the Battle of the Somme in July, 1916. He subsequently went to Salonika in command of the 7th Battalion South Wales Borderers, and was awarded the Victoria Cross for leading his battalion in an attack at Jumeaux (Balkans), September 18th, 1918, during which action he lost a leg.

The stay at Hurdcott was very short, for on November 16th we moved to Larkhill Camp.

A splendid march across the Plain, past the historic Stonehenge, brought us to our destination in the Canada Lines. The Lines here were very deep in mud, although the story that a Canadian soldier, in full kit and upright position, with rifle at the slope, had been dug out of the mud, was received with scepticism. It was here that we were issued with new S.M.L.E. rifles and proceeded to fire the final part of the General Musketry Course on the Durrington Rifle Ranges.

Approaching Ripon, June 1915.

Approaching Ripon, June 1915. The line indicates the owner of the original book, Private McLachlan of D Company.

Warrant officers and sergeants, Ripon, July 1915.

During the stay at Larkhill we had our first taste of trench life. A set of trenches complete with dugouts, etc., had been constructed in the vicinity, and here was practised the relief of one Battalion by another, and finally the occupation of the system of trenches for twenty-four hours.

The weeding out of the medically unfit for active service began while we were at Larkhill, and these were replaced by a large draft from the Depot Company.

On December 2nd we returned to our old camp at Hurdcott, and it was during the last stages of this march that a message was handed to the Adjutant notifying the early departure of the Battalion for Egypt. An officer and his servant per battalion of the Division had already departed for the purpose of supervising the disembarkation of the Division at Le Havre, so the change of destination was undoubtedly due to a sudden call, a possible explanation of which will be found elsewhere in these pages.

From now until we marched to Salisbury Station, en route for Devonport and Egypt, preparations were carried out with feverish energy. There were parades for inspection of embarkation kit, parades for issue of respirators, which one recalls were withdrawn inside an hour. In the orderly room nominal rolls were compiled, altered, amended and re-amended, as it became clear that a certain officer or man would be unable to accompany the Battalion, and a substitute must be found. One sergeant returning from hospital on the day before the Battalion's departure pleaded to be included, finally offering to revert to the ranks and become an officer's servant if only he was allowed to go.

Sun helmets were issued and anthropologists may be able to visualise the 10th Battalion East Yorkshire Regiment as it departed for foreign service from the following data.

Helmets required:

Size.	Number required.	Size.	Number required.
6½	14	7	289
6⅜	73	7⅛	86
6¾	142	7¼	55
6⅞	350	7½	5

After the final roll of the Battalion had been completed, the remaining officers, N.C.O.s and men, including men required for work on munitions, and men medically unfit, were left behind under the command of Captain T. Ridsdill Smith, whose great regret it was that he was not allowed to take "B" Company overseas – the company he had very largely raised and which he had commanded from the first. No embarkation leave was granted. Farewell messages were received from H.M. The King, and from the East Riding Territorial Force Association. In the late afternoon of December 7th we left the camp at Hurdcott, and marched nine miles to Salisbury Station in pouring rain, wearing great coats, full equipment, and sun helmets. The first train left Salisbury at 8.45 p.m. and arrived at Devonport at 3 a.m. on December 8th.

Little was seen of the busy naval base of Devonport, for as soon as we detrained close by the quay where the s.s. *Minnewaska* was moored, embarkation was begun. This was not completed until late on December 8th, but was rapidly carried out considering that a detachment of the K.O.Y.L.I., a brigade of R.F.A., and about 700 horses and mules had to be accommodated in addition to ourselves.

One ammunition limber slipped overboard during the process, but it was subsequently recovered by divers, the 18-pounder shells being none the worse for their immersion. The *Minnewaska* was a 14,000 ton cargo and passenger steamer of the Atlantic Transport Line, with a naval officer in command and armed with one light gun mounted in the stern. Below deck, stretching almost the full length of the ship, were the closely packed horse-lines, whilst immediately below them were the troops' quarters, the officers being berthed in cabins amidships. Nearby lay the s.s. *Persia*, the P. and O. liner which a fortnight later was torpedoed and sunk off Port Said with the loss of the 31st Division's Christmas mail. After handing in rifles and extra kit for storage in the ship's hold, we made ourselves as comfortable as conditions would permit and fell asleep, tired out with the rush and excitement of the sudden move.

We sailed at 6.45 a.m. on Thursday, December 9th, and escorted by two destroyers, the *Minnewaska* threaded her way through the naval craft in Plymouth Sound and out into the Channel. Everyone was on deck to catch a last glimpse of land, but when Eddystone Lighthouse slowly faded over the horizon rough seas were encountered, and the ship began to pitch and roll badly. There was much good-humoured fun at the first cases of sea sickness, but soon almost every man had disappeared below with the same complaint. Some tried to lie down on the hard tables or narrow forms, only to roll off among their fellow-sufferers huddled together on the floor. For two days sea sickness easily overshadowed all the other discomforts: the poor food, the overcrowded and stuffy quarters, and the effects of an inoculation against cholera, which was being carried out with much difficulty during the early days of the voyage. What a collection of dixies of untouched stew was to be seen around the ship's galley! What a boon the ship's canteen was until its supply of biscuits gave out! The plight of the horses and mules was serious: cramped in their small standings they could scarcely lie down, and in spite of the care of a small but devoted band of men, several died, including Tom, "B" Company's horse.

However, feeling a little of the exhilaration of sea-life, we soon recovered our usual bright spirits and began to take a keen interest in the voyage, and particularly in the many precautions taken against submarine attack, for the destroyer escort had turned back a few hours after sailing. The Battalion provided armed guards in the bows of the ship, and at certain boat stations and gangways, with strict instructions to keep a close watch for anything breaking the surface of the water; a look-out was stationed in the crow's nest and we steered a zig-zag course. Life-jackets were issued to each officer and man, and since they made good pillows and seats, the strict order that they must always be kept close at hand was generally obeyed. The ship's gunner indulged in occasional practice, his first shot causing considerable excitement as no warning was given. He would frequently throw an empty barrel overboard, wait until it had drifted well astern and then before our critical eyes he would blow it clean out of the water.

Sunday brought brighter weather, so that despite the big Atlantic rollers, Church parades could be held on deck; the two main services, Church of England and Nonconformist, were conducted at opposite ends of the ship, some lusty singing being ably assisted by the band under Sergeant Purcell. The Roman Catholics heard Mass in the officers' saloon. The remainder of a line warm day was spent listening to the band and concocting letters which might pass the scrutiny of platoon commanders, for active service conditions required that all letters should be strictly censored, and the day of green envelopes had not yet arrived. Submarines lurking near the entrance to the Mediterranean caused the *Minnewaska* to wait for nightfall before negotiating the Straits, so that Gibraltar was passed about midnight, and to our disappointment nothing was seen of the Rock except its searchlights constantly playing on the waters. We slowed down for a few minutes to pick up a Morse message from a destroyer ordering us to proceed to Malta.

The sea was calm and blue for a time as the ship steamed into the Mediterranean, the Atlas Mountains of Morocco and the snow-capped Sierra Nevada of Spain standing out quite plainly. Unfortunately, this respite from rough weather proved unexpectedly short, and for three days as we sailed within sight of Africa, conditions became equally as bad as they had been in the Atlantic. A cold driving wind brought violent storms with rain and hail, and once again sea sickness became the general order. The decks were often awash and the anti-submarine guards carried out their long spells of duty wet through to the skin. What a glorious change when at daybreak on Thursday Malta was sighted! We entered the magnificent

Grand Harbour, anchoring near the Empress of Britain which had on board the Leeds and Bradford Pals and the remainder of the 93rd Brigade. It was learned that their ship had won an exciting race with enemy submarines, only to collide afterwards with and sink a French troopship which was, fortunately, returning empty.

The *Minnewaska* was at once surrounded by Maltese in their tiny "bum-boats", selling oranges, Turkish delight, and an extraordinarily cheap brand of cigarettes. These latter were rapidly bought up, only to be as quickly thrown overboard when their quality was ascertained. The native boys did not trouble to dive for them as they did for the coins we threw into the clear water. There was no shore leave, so everyone had to be content with the glorious view which the bay offered; the quaint squat lighthouse, the gaily-coloured flat-roofed houses of Valetta rising in tiers from the water's edge, the strong fortifications dominating the bay; and above, a deep blue sky. That night, in a typical Mediterranean setting, we held an impromptu concert, one which few survivors of the Battalion will ever forget. A brilliant moon shone down on nearly 2,000 soldiers crowded in every conceivable position around the band which was playing on the quarter-deck; some balanced on the rails or in the ship's boats, others hung on to the rigging or perched in the crow's nest, and all were singing those old harmonised songs which later on helped us through many a rough time.

We left Valetta harbour towards dusk next day. Speculation as to the destination of the Battalion was now coming to a head, Gallipoli being the prime favourite, though as was soon afterwards known, the evacuation of that front had been decided on some time before, and was in fact being successfully accomplished about this time. Company Commanders were now happily able to tell their men that the Battalion had been ordered to Egypt as part of the Suez Canal Defence Force. It was curious how a rumour, which had been very persistent in our old Hornsea days, should now prove true.

For three days the voyage was pleasant and uneventful. The sky was blue and serene, and the weather so warm that many of us forsook our hammocks in the stuffy hold and slept on deck. The day would usually begin with a general cleaning up in preparation for a very thorough inspection of the whole ship by the Captain, followed by physical exercises and the oft-repeated submarine alarm drill, for the real danger zone had been entered. Boxing matches, band concerts and sing-songs, and learning to wrap countless yards of fine muslin round one's sun helmet to form a puggaree, provided the lighter side. One incident served to relieve the tension with regard to submarine attack. Late one afternoon a dark object suddenly appeared on the port side. Instantly the ship's gun and all available rifles were trained on it, and everyone, struggling into life-jackets, tumbled up on deck. For a minute, as the ship zig-zagged wildly, all eyes watched the water for the deadly white streak, but imagine the laughter which broke the tense silence when the object proved to be a piece of harmless wreckage floating gently along!

Breakfast time on December 20th found us entering Alexandria Harbour, where we anchored close beside the Empress of Britain to the ringing cheers of the 93rd Brigade. The busy port, with its long stretch of warehouses had a distinctly European aspect, although the high-prowed Egyptian feluccas with their carved figure-heads and curiously rigged sails, added a touch of the east. The *Minnewaska* weighed anchor at dusk and began the final and most dangerous stage of her voyage, so as to approach the Suez Canal entrance under cover of darkness. This was accomplished without incident, for the statue of De Lesseps, the designer of the canal, came into view early next morning, and the ship berthed at Aviation Quay, close to the European quarter of Port Said. Full equipment was issued during the afternoon of that day, and stores were landed with the assistance of hordes of dirty jabbering Arabs, but we did not touch terra firma until 2 p.m. next day. How fortunate we had been to arrive in safety was not realised at the time. Apparently the Germans had some foreknowledge of the movement of troops, for within two hours a Japanese steamer, the *Macceim*, which was moving out of the harbour as the *Minnewaska* arrived, and an oil-tanker which left the quay soon afterwards, were torpedoed and sunk a few miles outside the canal entrance. The long voyage, with its discomforts, dangers and pleasures, had done much to weld the Battalion together, and it was like hearing of the death of an old pal when, nearly a year later, the news came through that the *Minnewaska* had been mined and sunk off Crete.

Chapter 5

Egypt

LIEUT.-COLONEL BURGES led us on to what had been the town golf course, a long spit of sand lying between the railway and the native quarter of Port Said. After erecting tents, a speedy rush was made into the town to purchase food, for the day's ration consisted of a tin of bully-beef and three sour Army biscuits per head. Indeed, during the early part of our stay in Egypt, food was to be a problem: fresh vegetables were almost unprocurable, sandy masses of sticky dates being often issued as a substitute, while the Egyptian meat and bacon lacked freshness to an almost unbelievable degree. A native canteen soon appeared near the camp, conducted by Jim Irish, a very fat old Arab who dispensed his curious assortment of native sweetmeats whilst squatting in the midst of them, and who was reputed to have countless wives. This same wily Arab secured the catering for the officers' mess, which was a sort of Heath-Robinson hut with rush sides. At first he extorted an exorbitant figure per head for the poor food he provided, until a much-improved fare was secured by the simple expedient of refusing to pay him at all and then offering him less money, which he gladly accepted.

There was plenty of interest in the town. The native quarter consisted of narrow and dirty unpaved streets of flat-roofed houses with shady verandas. Everywhere there was the most cosmopolitan crowd conceivable: Arabs, Sudanese and Greeks in their characteristic costumes rubbed shoulders with European sailors of all nationalities. Children pestered the bewildered soldier with shrill cries of "Mangaree Tommy. Gib it", or thrust out a huge tomato for sale shouting, "Good for de belly. Good for de stomach". Heavily-veiled women glided silently by, for the most part barefooted and displaying their heavy brass anklets. The incessant babel of voices gave one the impression that trouble was brewing among the natives. The native police, though men of fine stature and mounted on superb Arab horses, seemed to add to the general disorder, as they usually tried to quell any disturbance by arguing with all and sundry. Strong armed guards and patrols supplied by ourselves in common with other units of the 31st Division which were now arriving, served to quieten the situation.

The European quarter consisted of fine spacious streets and boasted an antiquated system of tramcars drawn by donkeys, whose drivers kept up a constant drone of "Mind, Johnnie, Mi-ee-nd". The busy docks were worked by hordes of coolies, mostly dressed in cast-off army clothing; a cap comforter replacing the turban, a soldier's tunic being worn next to the skin, and over everything flowed a tattered army shirt. But how they could work! With heavy baskets of coal balanced on their heads, they would dash up a narrow plank to coal a ship in quick time, or dancing and singing around a pile of barrels, they would rapidly transfer them to a waiting barge. The native foreman would control his gang by clapping and stamping to the rhythm of the work, at the same time chanting an endless song about Allah. As one foreman expressed it, "No sing – no work. Plenty sing – plenty work".

The first Christmas Day spent abroad was naturally depressing; thoughts of home and the family dinner being hard to dispel. A new species of Army biscuit appeared in rations that day: it was almost as big as a plate and nearly as hard, so much so that one bright spirit gummed a label to his specimen and sent it home through the post as a permanent souvenir. Every officer and man received a small brass box, the Christmas present of H.R.H. Princess Mary. Thanks are due to the Rev. R. M. Kedward for arranging an English Christmas dinner at night in the European quarter, and how enjoyable it was with the band of the Leeds Pals playing carols outside!

Unfortunately, there was considerable trouble in the native quarter that night, several casualties occurring in other units of the Division, and as a result that section of the town was put out of bounds to troops, who from now on were not allowed to leave camp unarmed.

1916 at Port Said was heralded in a thoroughly Hull fashion: ships' sirens hooted and their bells clanged – all the louder as they were far from home. It found the Battalion short of "B" Company, which had been sent out on December 27th for a fortnight's detachment to relieve the 42nd Ghurkhas, who were holding a redoubt between the sea and the east side of the canal entrance and commanding the narrow coastal approach to the town. "B" Company set up outposts around the Salt Works, huge areas of flat land over which the sea was allowed to flow and to evaporate, the coarse salt which crystallised out being stacked into pyramids visible for miles. A strong guard was also supplied for the petrol and oil depot which supplied all the aeroplanes, motor vehicles and boats of the Canal Defence Force. Here the training in night patrol on the cliffs at Atwick and Skipsea helped the sentry as he plodded round the big tanks through the uneven sand with its eerie shadows, occasionally startled by strange sounds from the Armenian refugees camp in the distance.

On its relief by the 12th York and Lancaster Regiment, "B" Company returned to camp to find the Battalion well advanced with a programme of general smartening up. The usual drill operations were plentifully interspersed with short route marches, for which we wore light battle order and no tunic on account of the heat and the heavy going in the soft sand. On one march along the canal we passed a battleship, her crew returning our "Eyes right" by the "Standfast". Bathing parades in the sea or in the pools near the camp were most popular, since the water was found to be so salt and buoyant that the difficulty of learning to swim was reduced to a minimum.

It occasionally fell to the Battalion to find one company to provide the divisional guards at all points in and around Port Said, and also on neutral ships passing through the canal as a precaution against the possibility of mines being dropped. Since, at that time, the standard of a battalion was judged by the quality of the guards it turned out, guard duty was somewhat of an ordeal. The selected men, sparkling with "Soldiers' Friend", and each complete with his twenty-four hours rations, would accordingly parade in the early morning for an hour's minute inspection by the adjutant, Captain Jackson, before being allowed to proceed to their duties with bayonets fixed and marching to attention the whole way. One company will no doubt remember the famous parade when it fell in for guard duty, with here and there a man hugging a lump of beef or a sack of bread! Needless to say, this literal interpretation of the orders concerning rations never happened again.

Day by day the weather was glorious, except for one short period when a cold wet wind blew with steady intensity, driving with it the eternal sand, which stung the face and found its way into food and equipment, and clogged rifle-bolts and Lewis guns until special covers were issued for their protection. Dysentery was becoming a factor to be reckoned with, several of the more serious cases finding their way into hospital. Was it the sand which first produced those constant little bodily companions which were now becoming the bane of our lives? Soaking for hours in strong brine did not affect their ardour, exposure to the hot sun only invigorated them and no ointment seemed to do any good. Many a packet of cigarettes was used up to give them a fiery exit, but all in vain: a permanent task was now added to the soldier's daily routine. But the sand had its uses: mess-tins, dixies and harness shone up beautifully after a vigorous application of it, and the company cooks had never looked so clean as when they rolled about in the Egyptian sand. It even helped to solve the problem of washing clothes, for in imitation of the Arabs, men would lay their shirts on the wet sand near the water's edge and dance on them in their bare feet, thus driving the sand, and with it the dirt, through the cloth. The results, when dry, were fairly respectable, though somewhat stiff.

The Battalion was now becoming more acclimatised, and growing rumours of a move to a more useful sphere were strengthened when, on January 18th, General Sir Archibald Murray, then in command of the Mediterranean Expeditionary Force, made a thorough inspection of the Battalion, incidentally expressing his appreciation of "the beautiful cleanliness and smartness of the Battalion and their fine appearance – just like when I saw them at Hornsea". Orders were received later in the day for us to proceed down the canal to occupy a section of it extending from El Kab to Ballah, thus forming part of the third line of the canal defences. Most of the other units of the 31st Division had already left Port Said on similar service. An immediate result of the General's visit was a distinct improvement in our rations. It seems that G.H.Q. had seen fit to place all troops arriving in Egypt on peace-time rations, but this was now rectified and we found ourselves on full field service rations, with jam, cheese and bacon.

Camp was struck in the cool of the morning next day and at 8.30 a.m. we entrained in the open trucks of the Egyptian State Railway. The short, leisurely journey along the west bank of the canal, offered more of interest than the monotonous stretch of sand which one would have expected to see. On the immediate east, just beyond the Sweet Water Canal with its pleasant grassy banks and occasional groves of palms, lay the Suez Canal, a succession of big liners, transports, English and French warships, and heavily-laden feluccas proceeding slowly along it. To the west stretched the broad blue intensely salty Lake Menzaleh, the remains of a sea which once linked the Mediterranean with the Red Sea. It was interesting to feel that one was travelling over land hallowed for all time by incidents of Bible times.

At Ras-el-Esh, "C" Company, under Captain Ruthven, detrained for the Spit, a narrow neck of land lying between two artificially flooded areas, about twenty miles from Port Said. At the important centre of Kantara, whose key position made it an obvious object of Turkish attack, "D"Company left the train, Captain Lambert taking two platoons to hold Bridge Head and Captain Horsley the remainder of the Company to occupy outpost 50.8, about two miles away on the opposite side of the canal. The bullet-riddled and burnt-out huts of Kantara gave evidence of enemy attention, for during March, 1915, the Turks had penetrated so far as to be able to shell the canal and the ships passing through it. Battalion headquarters accompanied "B" Company under Captain Carroll to Ballah, which consisted of little more than a railway station, although the number of caravan routes converging on it showed that it was of some importance. Major Glossop, following the Battalion later in the day, established "A" Company at El Kab, a position somewhat nearer Port Said than the other companies.

All the outposts, which were taken over from the 93rd Brigade, in order to free it for forward movement into the desert, were situated on the east side of the canal except that at 50.8, which moved over later. Progress across the canal was made by flat ferry-boats hauled by Arabs, who droned their monotonous chant of "Allah Haile" to the swing of their arms as they pulled their chains. Two days later Battalion headquarters took up a more central position at Swing Bridge, the junction of the Sweet Water Canal and the Suez near Kantara. Lieutenant Harrison had quite an exciting time with his transport section during this move. He had already found, in moving the Brigade Transport a short distance of six miles on the preceding day, that progress was exceptionally slow and laborious, for there was no road, and limbers sank axle deep in the soft sand, which meant that the mules had to be rested every five minutes. Accordingly it was now arranged that all stores should be conveyed on camels provided by the Bikanir Camel Corps, so that the limbers might proceed empty alongside the railway and in the rear of the headquarters' party. In the words of the Transport Officer: "We went gaily along until one of the teams became bogged. I looked back and saw them get out all right, when the leading team with myself began to disappear. For the next hour or two we had a time! I gave orders for the drivers to unhook, leave their waggons and get their mules to the railway embankment. We tied mules to anything and everything, about ten to a telegraph post and left them, to rescue the bogged ones. I sent for help to Major Carver, who was about a mile ahead with the Signallers. We fixed drag-ropes on to the animals and hauled them out, but when we reached the last two only their heads were showing. However, we pulled them out, but why we did not pull their necks off I can't imagine".

The outposts were small redoubts, consisting of shallow trenches which were difficult to maintain in good condition for many hours together on account of the drifting sand, against which sand-bagging and revetting were of little use. Barbed wire entanglements surrounded them – apparently quite a formidable barrier – until subsequently it was noticed that an escaped camel waded through them quite casually. A further hindrance to enemy approach was the broad stretch of flat land which had been flooded by cutting the canal banks at various points. A few miles out towards Palestine the other units of the 31st Division were entrenched, either doing outpost duty or putting in excellent work in the construction of roads, light railways or water-lines so as to push further forward the front line and thereby free the canal from the danger which threatened it. Lieutenant Norfolk and his signallers kept up communication between the various detachments of the Battalion, now scattered over a ten-mile front, principally by means of field telephones, at the laying and maintenance of which the signalling section was becoming quite efficient, and occasionally with the aid of the heliograph, a strong sun making the flashes easy to observe for long distances.

Outpost duties during the ensuing month were not very arduous, except for those unlucky companies in the vicinity of Kantara, which were constantly called upon for divisional fatigues. Training in manning a post was soon reduced to a fine art, Captain Ruthven claiming that he could have every man in his Company in position within two and a half minutes of an alarm being given, whether by day or by night. Contact between posts was kept up by strong patrols by night, while by day parties were sent out to examine the canal bank for footprints on the wide smooth track, which was swept daily by camels dragging logs broadside on over the sand. Though the Turks were not likely to deliver an immediate attack in force, it was feared that small patrols might slip through the outposts by night in an endeavour to cut the railway and destroy the canal banks. In the dark hour before dawn all the personnel of an outpost would man the trenches for "Stand to", and all eyes would be strained to the east, watching for the enemy and awaiting the dawn, the beauty of which with its first delicate pink flush, rapidly changing into a crimson glow as the sun suddenly appeared, will not readily be forgotten. The usual camp fatigues and an occasional quarter-guard were all the daytime duties we were called upon to perform on account of the mid-day heat, though a flying visit by Major-General Wanless O'Gowan in his smart pinnace and attended by a line bodyguard of Mysore Lancers, would suddenly cause an outpost to spring to life. In fact, inspecting generals were so common that almost as careful a watch had to be kept for them as for the enemy. Beyond the capture of a few spies, who usually turned out to be Arab refugees, nothing of a really exciting nature occurred.

The Transport Section, operating from its lines near Kantara, was being rather heavily worked at this time, for in addition to supplying the widely-scattered companies with rations and stores, it had to provide drivers and mules for attachment to the Army Service Corps. Driving in the soft sand was difficult and slow, and mules were hard to hold in whenever camels, laden with materials for the front-line troops, passed by. Here and there the sand would all at once give way to boggy land, and the unsuspecting driver would suddenly find his mules floundering deep in it. The personnel of the Transport, though composed for the most part of men strange to the ways of horses and mules, was rapidly emerging from its amateur stage. All the mules except one had been broken in to their work. One day this refractory mule was taken in hand, harnessed and finally yoked up to a half-limber with the assistance of most of the section, from Lieutenant Harrison downwards, and sent out in charge of a very amateur driver to deliver rations at Post 50.8. By keeping to the soft sand the driver managed to carry out his orders, but returned in record time after meeting some camels, with the mules well out of hand, and heading for the lines at full gallop. Limbers were scattered in all directions, and part of the stable roof was brought down, but the services of the expectant R.A.M.C., ever ready with their stretchers, were fortunately not required.

The shortage of fresh water in the desert was a constant handicap and caused stringent economies to be practised. Looking back after twenty years of water in plenty, one wonders how a man managed to carry on in a hot climate with his daily ration of one water-bottle for drinking and washing purposes and two for cooking! The water which flowed in the Sweet Water Canal to the west of the Suez Canal, originally from the Nile, was so full of disease germs as to be undrinkable, so supplies were brought up the canal from Port Said in small water-tank boats and transferred to large tins, which were strapped to the sides of camels for conveyance to the forward troops. There was little wild animal life in the desert proper on account of this lack of fresh water. Lizards in the crannies of the rocks and a few locusts were seen, and jackals could be heard during the night. The sand was alive with ants, many of the species being fully four times as large as the English variety. Occasionally the bright colours of a flight of flamingos broke the monotonously drab aspect of the desert. Small pariah dogs managed to exist somehow in the desert scrub, and one or two animal lovers in the Battalion tried unsuccessfully to tame them and keep them as pets.

Birds of prey were fairly common, in particular hawks and vultures, and over one post there hovered for two days a great golden eagle, which on account of its markings was at first mistaken for an enemy aeroplane. It had, no doubt, been attracted by the dead body of a camel which had been dragged out of the compound nearby. At the posts nearer the marsh lands, wild bird life was very abundant; herons, pelicans and kingfishers were to be seen, and white ducks and snipe were present literally in thousands. One longed to exchange the service rifle or revolver for an English sporting gun; in fact, Captain Harrison-Broadley did manage to secure one from an Italian engineer, and with it he undertook the pleasant task of replenishing the larder with wild fowl. Lieutenant England is credited with having brought down an eagle whose wings had a spread of seven feet, and Lieutenant Addy shot a heron which was not much smaller. The shallow water in which the water-fowl fed was well stocked with small fish which swam about in shoals, so much leisure time was very profitably spent in mastering the art of casting the native nets.

Some leave was now being granted for Port Said, and the immediate outcome of it was the establishment by the officers of small canteens, to give variety to the food and to supplement the supply of cigarettes, for since the introduction of an army tobacco ration nearly everyone had become a confirmed smoker. The post-corporal's visit was always eagerly awaited: he had brought, on January 11th, the first precious letters from home, the previous ones having been lost with the s.s. *Persia*; he was now appearing with mail-bags of most welcome parcels, which enabled us to celebrate a belated Christmas in our tents. Our main interest was the canal, watching the ships pass by: a great liner from which cigarettes and newspapers were thrown, a splendidly-fitted hospital ship with its broad green band painted from stem to stern and its great cross amidships, some monitors, which except for their big 12-inch guns, looked for all the world like New Holland packet steamers, or a transport laden with troops for Mesopotamia and India. At these times rousing cheers were given and returned. By night the ships carried powerful searchlights which lit up the canal for miles ahead, leaving intense darkness as they passed. Out of such darkness one night a sleepy sentry was startled to hear a cheerful cry, "Good old Hull! Anyone there from Beverley?" One evening two young officers from Battalion headquarters boarded a Clan Line steamer tied up to the canal bank in the hope of being offered a drink, only to be greeted by an elderly bosun with the remark, " 'Ere,' op it. The likes of you ought to be abed". The brighter side of canal life was somewhat clouded for "A" Company and Battalion

Ration parade, Egypt 1915–16.

HMT Minnewaska *en route for Egypt, December 1915.*

headquarters; they passed many days and nights to the accompaniment of the horrible noise of mud-dredgers, which flung their slimy product and its consequent smell well over the canal banks.

The "Sweet Water Canal" near Kantara.

Deck shuffle-board. Captain Ivor Jackson – HMT Tunisian.

Swimming sports, in which all the neighbouring battalions took part, became increasingly popular as the weather grew hotter. One such meeting, held as usual in the "ditch", deserves special mention, in that it was quite the equal of many a peace-time effort. Organised primarily for "A" Company by Lieutenant England, it attracted over 200 entrants and included: 60 yards Breast-stroke, 60 yards Side-stroke, 60 yards

Pontoon bridge – Kantara, January 1916.

Port Said – embarkation on HMT Tunisian, *February 1916.*

Any Stroke, 30 yards Beginners, Cigarette Race, Blindfold Race, Pillow Fight, Neat Dive, High Dive, Plunge Dive. Twenty-two prizes, ranging from 2/6 to 10/6 were subscribed by the officers, who showed themselves untiring in their efforts to provide something to interest their men. It was easy to lure the Arabs into swimming contests, in spite of their aversion to cleanliness. For the reward of a piastre (2½d or 1p) or a cast-off army shirt, Mohamed, Ahmed or Hassan could be bribed to dive into the canal and swim the 150 yards across and back with their fast overarm stroke, somewhat resembling the Australian crawl.

The hundreds of Arab camel drivers and labourers attached to each of the posts were a constant source of worry, and the only safe place for them was inside the barbed wire of their compounds, under the armed guards which we rather unwillingly provided. In this connection, Captain Williams recorded at the time: "Thieves – I've never met the like of them. We get packages of food down here from Port Said by train. You've got to meet the train, count your boxes as they come off, and if you turn your back to sign the invoice the chances are that one of your packages has gone. Only today the Rev. R. M. Kedward, who is our chaplain, brought three sacks of bread by train; he went from the platform for ten seconds, and was back in time to see two Indians running away with one sack and some Arabs with another at the opposite end of the platform. Others had taken the lids off packing cases and were helping themselves to tins of jam". Lieutenant Pierson mentioned the side-tracking of about

£100 worth of foodstuffs which he had bought for the men's canteen, and the difficulty he had in securing its delivery. On one occasion the Camel Transport Corps turned up with the rations minus the precious sack of sugar. Colonel Burges at once informed their officer, who immediately told his gang of Arab drivers that they would be stopped two days' pay unless the sugar was forthcoming. It was amusing to see how each Arab stripped and carefully searched his neighbour's person and camel gear, so distrustful were they of each other. The sack, needless to say, was found and handed back intact.

January closed with heavy rain and hail accompanied by a gale, which blew our tents down and smothered everything in sand. Under cover of the bad weather the Turks, whose outposts had been located by our native cavalry on some small hills about twenty-four miles in front, advanced their main forces a little, but expectations of an immediate attack did not materialise. However, there were signs of increasing activity on our front: a captive balloon was observed to rise over Kantara, Lewis guns were set up at Battalion headquarters as a protection against hostile aircraft, and the R.E. flung pontoon bridges over the canal to replace the slow-moving ferries. Fresh troops began to arrive. Among these were the 6th East Yorkshires, who although a battalion of pioneers, had acquitted themselves with much distinction as infantrymen at Suvla Bay. The East Riding Yeomanry were not far away at Cairo, while the 2nd East Yorkshires, in co-operation with French forces, were helping to hold the Bulgarians at Salonika: a total, with the four battalions of the 92nd Brigade, of seven local units engaged in the eastern theatre of the war.

It was now becoming clear why we, in common with so many other battalions, had been concentrated in Egypt. During the winter of 1915-16 there had been considerable doubt as to the enemy's next big move. There was the fear that the Turks might attack Mesopotamia and even Egypt, and that the Bulgarians might attempt a move against Salonika; there was the probability of a German offensive in France, and lastly it was thought that reinforcements might be needed for India. The upshot was that for a few months a strong force had to be maintained in Egypt, from which central position it could rapidly be moved East or West as soon as the enemy's intentions became apparent. This Imperial Strategic Reserve consisted of the 31st Division from England, the 46th Division from France, ordered out by Lord Kitchener after he had been out East to review the situation himself, the divisions liberated from Gallipoli, and one or two Indian divisions. This concentration was broken up when it was found that the main struggle of 1916 would be in France, so that nearly all these troops found themselves there before the summer of that year.

Persistent rumours of a pending move to Mesopotamia were now current, for the night patrol on February 10th had brought the news of General Townshend's enforced surrender at Kut with his large force. In fact, later in the month, the 31st Division actually did receive orders to proceed to that area, but for some reason the orders were withdrawn, and the 13th Division was sent instead. News began to filter through that the French were being hard pressed at Verdun, so it was not surprising when it became known, towards the end of February, that the Battalion was destined for France. On February 28th the 4th Royal Scots of the 52nd Division from Gallipoli took over all the outposts. Earlier in the day the Battalion Transport had handed over all its animals and waggons, with the exception of a few officers' chargers, to that unit, and after concentrating with the transport sections of the rest of the Division at Kantara, had proceeded by train to Port Said for embarkation on H.M.T. *Northlands*. The Battalion here said good-bye to one of its most notable personalities in Major Glossop, who left by the same ship for leave to England, prior to taking up a command with the 14th East Yorkshire (Reserve) Battalion. His genial and kindly disposition, which lurked beneath an explosive exterior, had made him much liked, not only by his own Company, but by that "gang of thieves and vagabonds" forming the rest of the Battalion. Everyone will remember his strenuous efforts to place his Company, familiarly known as Glossop's Greyhounds, first in everything, and the good-humoured rivalry which ensued. Fortunately, Captain Harrison-Broadley was at hand to take over the command of "A" Company.

By mid-day the relief was complete, but it was not until noon next day (Leap Year Day) that the Battalion, now concentrated on Kantara, renewed acquaintance with the open cotton trucks which quickly transferred us to Port Said. When we embarked on the Allan Liner *Tunisian*, which we did the same day, our sun helmets, the last link with Egypt, were still in our possession. At 5.30 p.m. the ship sailed for France, carrying with it thirty officers and 926 other ranks of the 10th East Yorkshires, eight men having been left behind in hospital and a few remaining temporarily attached in various capacities to the Mediterranean Expeditionary Force. The short service in Egypt had done much to make the Battalion thoroughly self-supporting; its various sections, such as the Signallers and Transport, had gained much valuable experience; contact with Brigade and Division had been strengthened; while we had learnt to rely more fully on our superiors and to pull with one another in that unselfish way which was to be a marked characteristic of the Battalion during the more strenuous times ahead. It is comforting now to feel that the 10th East Yorkshires had done some, at any rate, of the spade work which made possible the victorious advance from

Egypt into Palestine during the closing stages of the War. The G.O.C. XV Corps sent us the following message:

"The Corps Commander, in wishing the 31st Division farewell and good luck, expresses his gratitude to all ranks for the good work they have done for him. It has been a great pleasure to him to be associated with such a capable body of officers and men. They have borne the brunt of the work in the XV Army Corps sector and have done wonders, and there exists a very fine spirit in the Division. He wishes all ranks the best of luck and hopes soon to have the pleasure of being associated with them again. He is confident that they will fight as well as they have worked".

Conditions on board the *Tunisian* were far better than they had been on the *Minnewaska*: food was good and accommodation plentiful, the big ship being shared by the 10th Battalion, part of the 11th, and Brigade Headquarters. Many of us were able to enjoy the luxury of a real bed in a cabin, and the atmosphere below deck was much improved by the absence of horses. For the earlier part of the voyage scarcely a ripple broke the surface of the blue sea. The usual thorough precautions were taken against submarine attack: we continuously steered a zig-zag course, Lewis guns were mounted in the bows, life-boat drill was frequent, and lastly, many of us slept on deck until the danger zone was left behind. One day we passed a lifeboat and wreckage from the torpedoed French transport *Provence*, but the number of British merchant vessels which were steaming by in safety was a constant tribute to the power of the navy.

Soon Malta was sighted and passed, when the weather became cold and a heavy sea was encountered, but sea sickness was not very general as the big liner did not pitch or roll excessively. Sicily was soon passed, and Sunday Church parades were held on deck as the *Tunisian* ploughed through heavy seas within sight of the rugged coast of Sardinia. Next day conditions improved considerably, for we had now entered the Gulf of Lyons and were heading for the French coast. Many of the Battalion will remember the farewell concert on the last night at sea. Artistes from both the 10th and 11th Battalions helped to make the occasion a great success. A glorious panorama unfolded itself early the following morning as the *Tunisian*, passing the famous Château d'If, entered Marseilles harbour. Ahead lay the port, in a gap between the gleaming white cliffs and backed by hills, surmounted here and there by the ruins of some old castle. In the distance the snow-capped Alpes Maritimes sparkled with a bluish tint in the glorious morning sun.

Chapter 6

France – First Tour in the Line – "The Four Wet Days"

AFTER disembarking about noon on Tuesday, March 7th, some time was spent on the docks, watching gangs of German prisoners at work, or experimenting with schoolboy French on the dockers, until a move was made to the harbour station of the Paris-Lyons-Mediterranean Railway. Instead of the expected collection of cattle trucks bearing the inscription "Chevaux 8, Hommes 40", a train composed of third-class carriages was waiting. Eight men scrambled into each compartment, piling their equipment knee-deep on the floor and stretching themselves over the top of it in whatever positions of comfort they could. At 11 p.m. the train began its three days' journey towards the Western Battle Front. Frequent halts were made for exercise or for the brewing of tea, the obliging engine-driver supplying hot water. Progress was for the most part slow, so that if after a halt an occasional man was left behind, no one worried for he was usually able to overtake the train. Whenever we drew up in a station crowds of cheering civilians thronged the platforms eager to see the British reinforcements, for the word "Verdun" was on all lips.

For a whole day the track lay along the valley of the blue Rhône, where smiling vineyards climbed the hillsides and orchards were numerous. The ancient city of Arles and its Roman arena, Avignon with its centuries of fascinating history, were passed as the train steamed into a land of viaducts, narrow gorges and tunnels. At Valois, a glance through the carriage window showed the countryside to be inches deep in snow: a beautiful sight, but what a shock after the warmth of Egypt! A dose of hot rum and coffee, served by French soldiers and nurses, was here very welcome. We were now moving through the busy manufacturing district around Lyons, where the Rhône was crossed by a fine suspension bridge and the valley of the Saône entered, with the snow-covered Cevennes to the West. Hospital trains, full of wounded from Verdun, and others packed with steel-helmeted French troops for the Front, were passed as Dijon was approached. Much to our regret, the Ceinture Railway, a loop-line round Paris, was taken, although a glimpse was caught of Versailles and its famous palace.

Signs of war were much in evidence as the train passed through St. Germain and Amiens, finally stopping close on midnight at Pont Remy, where we detrained and set off on the march, shivering with cold and cramped by the long journey. Small wonder that the night march, along rough unfamiliar roads and through a snow blizzard, seemed the most strenuous we had yet done. At 4 a.m. we found ourselves in the streets of Longpré-les-Corps-Saints, a small town which was evidently on the army's practical joke list, for we remembered passing through it in the train some hours before. Unfortunately, billets were not immediately forthcoming, as the local "Maire" could not be induced to leave his bed at that hour, so we had to sit about in the snow until 7 a.m. Finally, "B" and "C" Companies were given a stone-paved railway goods shed, while "A" and "D" secured smaller and more comfortable billets. Later in the day the Transport re-joined for duty, having been completely refitted with mules, limbers and harness at Abbeville.

The succeeding fortnight was one of intensive training, calculated to harden and acclimatise the Battalion; route marches, bayonet fighting and musketry on an improvised range, alternated with instruction in trench warfare and particularly with regard to gas attacks. Goggles were issued to combat tear-gas, and incessant practice with stuffy and elementary P.H. gas-helmets was necessary before they could be put on rapidly yet effectively. Parties were attached to the Army Schools at Hocquincourt and Hallencourt for instruction in mining and bombing, Lieutenants R. Addy and Carlisle specialising respectively in these branches. On March 22nd, ten officers and forty N.C.O.s under Captain Ruthven left by bus for the trenches in front of Engelbelmer, about four miles north of Albert, and were attached to the 36th (Ulster) Division, the officers and men of which treated them with great hospitality. They received valuable first-hand instruction in trench warfare from the 9th Royal Irish Fusiliers, and watched the relief of that battalion by the 12th Royal Irish Rifles. The experience of this party, which withdrew from the line on March 26th, proved a steadying influence on the Battalion when a few days later it was called on to receive its baptism in the same trenches.

In leisure hours attempts were made to master the French money system and to differentiate between the various types of tattered notes, which replaced coins to a very great extent. The higher valued notes bearing the stamp of the Banque de France were current anywhere, but notes of smaller value, even as low as 2½ d. (1p), were issued by each "commune" and could only be used in the immediate locality. "Pas bon ici" was the reply which the soldier received to his cost when he tendered one of these notes in the wrong district. Visits were made, chiefly out of curiosity, to the estaminets, which were plentiful in Longpré. Here we could gaze on countless varieties of sugared drinks with unpronounceable names, or listen to the unconsciously humorous entertainment provided by the proprietor with the snatches of English which previous troops had taught him, whilst we sipped a very weak bière or handed back an undrinkable dark liquid labelled "English Stout". The general apprehension felt by French civilians with regard to enemy spies was evident from the notices posted on the estaminet walls calling for caution in speech: "Taisez-vous. Méfiez-vous. Les oreilles ennemies vous écoutent". The civilians generally were very obliging to us, and though tremendously overworked owing to the absence of all their men of military age, they preserved a bright appearance, any disappointment or mishap being dismissed with a cheerful "Ça ne fait rien! C'est la guerre!"

Whilst at Longpré, leave to England was granted to a few officers and men, precedence usually being given to those whose relatives had suffered during the Zeppelin raids on Hull, news of which was just reaching us. Final preparations were now being made for a move up to the line; new service caps were issued to replace our sun helmets which, owing to the frequent snowfalls, now appeared to be constructed of corrugated iron, and equipment was overhauled; only the bare minimum of kit being retained. The luxury of a bath was even provided: on one occasion 250 men were tubbed in half a dozen barrels at the disused brewery of Bettencourt-Reviére in the remarkable time of one and a quarter hours. The mystery surrounding the term "iron rations" was now solved: company quarter-master-sergeants issued to each officer and man a bag containing a tin of bully-beef, some small hard biscuits and a tin of tea and sugar, to be carried in their haversacks and to be used in case no rations were forthcoming for twenty-four hours, and then only on the order of the officer commanding. Their issue happily coincided with the gift to all ranks of chocolate from British Colonists in Trinidad, St. Lucia and Grenada.

On March 25th we began a strenuous three days' march to the line. The route lay in the Somme area, along poor roads which blistered the feet rendered soft by the stay in Egypt, and all the lively tunes the Band could play were needed to keep us going. An occasional plane overhead, a beautiful wayside shrine or a striking crucifix at a cross-roads would now and then take a man's attention from the pull of his pack, but it was a great relief when after marching twenty-three kilometres via Hangest and Vignacourt, Flesselles was reached and billets were secured for the night. Lieutenant Fletcher, R.A.M.C., our medical officer, held a record sick parade as a result of the march, there being more than a hundred cases of blistered feet which had to be repaired before the next day's move. Before "lights out" our first rum ration was issued, with due solemnity by platoon commanders. One keen officer lectured his platoon very thoroughly beforehand on the reason for the issue, emphasising the care that he had to take to see that every man received his exact ration, and concluding by remarking that any rum left over would have to be poured down the sink by him immediately. It is to be hoped that he never knew how certain of his men, anxious to prevent this waste, paraded before him three times, first in tunics, then without, and finally in greatcoats.

After an early start next day, we marched fifteen kilometres in rain and snow through Talmas and Maison-le-Val to comfortable billets in straw-filled barns at Beauquesne, which was later to be Sir Douglas Haig's advance headquarters during the Somme battles. The civilians, fresh from church, for it was Sunday, gave of their best in the way of "Deux oeufs et pommes de terre frites". The layout of the farms struck one as curious: the buildings formed almost a closed rectangle around a big manure pit, into which not a few men stumbled to their dismay, and the only water supply was a pump or well, usually alongside this manure pit. The rush of men to fill their water-bottles was stopped by the farmers, who managed to explain that the water was "Pas bonne à boire" and very kindly offered weak beer and coffee as a substitute. Later on, this contaminated water, liberally treated with chloride of lime, was to be our sole supply for weeks together. In the afternoon the party from the trenches re-joined us, and each member of it quickly became the centre of an eager audience, for officers and men alike were keen to acquit themselves well when the time came.

The last stage of the march lay along roads which the enemy occasionally shelled. Consequently, steel helmets were issued, and what a nuisance they were at first! The unaccustomed weight made it impossible to wear them long without a headache and on no part of one's equipment would they ride comfortably. A start was made late in the afternoon, so that the approach to the line might be made under cover of darkness. Once again rain fell heavily as we plodded through Acheux and Hedauville, where Ulster troops out on rest shared their hot tea with the rain-soaked Battalion. At nightfall the long line of Verey lights and occasional gun flashes showed for many miles the direction of the British Front. Billets were found that night with the 11th Battalion in the battered village of Engelbelmer, close to the line. Late on March 28th, "A", "C" and "D" Companies marched up to Auchonvillers and filed into the trenches to hold the sector in front of Beaumont Hamel, which was to be the scene of much bitter fighting a few months later. On the right and left flanks were the 11th East Yorkshires and the 15th West

Yorkshires, while immediately in front lay Y-ravine, a strongly entrenched position which is preserved to this day in its war-time condition as part of Newfoundland Park, the memorial to the Newfoundland troops. We were now in the VIII Corps of the Fourth Army.

The trenches were surprisingly dry and well kept, and some of their names such as First Avenue, Essex, Felthard, and Pompadour still rise readily to the mind. Beyond occasional machine-gun fire, a little intermittent shelling, and a little sniping, the sector was quiet, which was just as well, for we found that we had many lessons to learn in the conduct of trench warfare. On wiring parties or on patrol in "No Man's Land" at night the temptation to lie flat when German Verey Lights went up had to be resisted, and we learned to remain motionless in whatever position we were caught, until the flare died away. We learned, too, not to lose our heads when a harmless group of tree stumps gradually assumed the appearance of an enemy patrol or a big rat creeping up to the trench would seem to be a man's head, and all the time a watch was kept for the mysterious "three green lights", there being a persistent rumour at the time that these were to be the signal for peace, which was supposed to be imminent.

Here, too, we made acquaintance with the Minenwerfer, the first of which was greeted with derisive laughter as a "dud" because of the delay in going off; but we soon learned to treat them with respect, as our first casualty was due to one of these "Minnies", Private S. Horsfield,[4] of "C" Company, being killed at dusk on our second day in. It was fitting that at this stage Captain Horsley should leave the trenches for a course on trench mortars, later returning in command of the newly-formed Brigade Stokes' Gun Battery, which was to form such an effective answer to the Minenwerfer. During subsequent tours in the line, whenever the enemy made himself particularly troublesome, the Stokes' gun proved very useful, for it could be fired so rapidly that several shells from the same gun could be seen in the air at the same time.

It was in this sector that we were introduced also to the nightly harassing fire of the German artillery. This came on regularly at dusk and soon came to be known as the "Evening hate", but most of the shells seemed to be directed towards the roads behind us, evidently in an endeavour to catch the Transport with our rations and supplies. "B" Company, which had been left behind in close support at Engelbelmer, came up nightly to supply digging and wiring parties, and also to assist a Tunnelling Company, which was driving a sap under "No Man's Land" and preparing the big mine

---

4 Private Stanley Horsfield was aged 24 when he was killed. He is buried in Auchonvillers Military Cemetery.

which was blown ten minutes before zero on July 1st. Towards the end
of our stay in the line we suffered two further casualties, one man being
killed by a sniper's bullet and another wounded by shrapnel. On April 3rd,
Brig.-General Parker, commanding the 92nd Brigade, brought up a party
of officers of the famous 29th Division, a unit of which – the 1st Border
Regiment – relieved us the same day, the trenches being handed over by
midnight. One officer and four other ranks per company were left in the
line to assist the relieving battalion in acquiring the necessary knowledge
of the sector. We then withdrew to Engelbelmer in close support, and after
a long refreshing sleep and a clean-up, we were relieved by the 1st Royal
Fusiliers, so that we were able to proceed to huts at Bertrancourt, five miles
away.

For a week we became one gigantic working party, usually all available
officers and about 600 other ranks assembling early each day under Major
Carver for work under the direction of the R.E.s, opening out old trenches
or digging new ones near Colincamps, carrying heavy materials for the
construction of dugouts or gun emplacements, and re surfacing the narrow
roads which were pitted with shell-holes. One night we had just turned in,
tired out after one of these parties, when a violent bombardment broke out
at Auchonvillers on the 29th Division's front, which was suddenly raided
by the enemy, and we "stood to" in full battle order, ready to move forward
at a moment's notice, until the "all clear" signal was given. Little training
was possible at this time, although Lieutenants Dugdale and C. Addy took
special Lewis gun courses, and Lieutenant Pierson went to the Divisional
School for a bombing course. Lieutenant Carver organised the Battalion
Scouts as an Intelligence Section, which was shortly afterwards taken over
by Lieutenant R. Addy and was to prove of some importance later.

On April 11th we were ordered to move forward to Courcelles-au-Bois
for four days in close support prior to occupying the sector immediately north
of the one we had just left. We were now to have our first big experience
of supplying working parties to the trenches by night. Strong parties spent
their time nightly under the R.E.s, either in pushing trolleys laden with coils
of barbed wire, "corkscrews", "concertinas", "gooseberries", and sump
boards down the light railway from Euston Dump to the support lines, or
else they filled in the dark hours with the eternal digging, stumbling back
with picks and shovels to their cosy barns miles away in Courcelles at
dawn. Almost did it seem better to be holding the line.

Leave to England was very meagre at the period and turns were very
slow in coming. The lucky few to secure the precious seven days, which
really amounted to five when allowance was made for travelling, used to
set off to the railhead at Acheux, piled up with commissions from their

less fortunate comrades, and proceed by rail to Le Havre. The Channel crossing from that port to Southampton was made by night, since German submarines were very active there. At one time all leave was suddenly stopped, officers and men at home being recalled to the Battalion, and R.S.M. Thirsk had the unpleasant task of awakening several men during the night and interrupting their pleasant dreams of "Blighty" by taking their leave warrants from them.

On April 15th Lieut.-Colonel Burges and Major Carver made a tour of inspection of the trenches in front of Colincamps, prior to the Battalion occupying them the next day, which was Palm Sunday. During the late afternoon of that day the Battalion moved off by small sections at intervals of 200 yards along the open roads and finally arrived at Euston Dump. Here we entered the long communication trenches of Eczema, Flag Street, and Patrick Street, passing the support trenches, Palestine, Hittite and Rob Roy, and finally reaching the front line, which ran through four small copses, curiously named Matthew, Mark, Luke and John. Here the 12th East Yorkshires were holding a front extending from Luke Copse on the north to Board Street, a position east of the Sugar Factory and directly facing Serre. The relief of that battalion was not completed until midnight, owing to a sharp enemy bombardment, in which we lost one man killed[5] and three wounded, and the 12th two men wounded.

Soon after the relief, "Boots, gum, thigh" were issued, for most of the trenches, in particular Warley Avenue, Dunmow and Monk, where battalion headquarters were situated, were deep in water. Rain began to fall and continued without a break for three days, so that the long waterproof capes, the gift of Lady Nunburnholme to each man, proved very useful. The condition of officers and men moving about in trenches which were little better than ditches, for dugouts were few, became rapidly serious; in fact, the only warm time was when the rum ration was issued, immediately after "stand to". We conscientiously rubbed our feet with whale oil, but this did not stop the occurrence of "trench feet", a number of the more serious cases being sent out of the line to hospital. "A" Company at No. 7 post were having a particularly bad time, and had to be relieved by "B" Company, then in support. Communication was being constantly interrupted by the trench sides caving in and snapping the telephone wires, Lieutenant Norfolk with his Signallers having a rough time locating faults and repairing them. The Transport had great difficulty in getting the rations up at night, since part of the route lay across country, and the drivers had to urge their mules

---

5 Private Edgar Hyde was born in Hull but lived in Hornsea. He was 25 and is
   buried in Sucrerie Military Cemetery.

forward with limbers axle deep in mud as far as Observation Wood. This point was well forward in the trenches and was approached by a narrow bridge across a busy communication trench. On one occasion a mule fell from the bridge into the trench and lodged there upside down, completely blocking the way. It defied all the efforts of a party of fifty men with ropes to haul it out of the glue-like mud, and had finally to be shot and removed in sections by the Battalion butcher.

The bad weather had the welcome effect of settling the activities of both sides, so that wiring parties and listening posts went unmolested, and patrols met little opposition. There was some enfilade machine-gun fire from the direction of Beaumont Hamel, where the line turned, but it was not until the last day, when the weather brightened, that any activity occurred, and even then it was confined to a little hostile shelling mostly with "whizz-bangs", two other ranks being wounded. On the same day, Thursday, this short spell in the line was brought to an end and the 16th West Yorkshires relieved the Battalion at midnight.

Bus-les-Artois, 1916.

Longpré-les-Corps-Saints, March 1916.

The Sucrerie near Colincamps.

The journey out was a veritable nightmare. Weighted down with mud and weary with lack of sleep, we stumbled down the seemingly endless communication trenches, several men collapsing when open roads were reached. Of this march one man writes: "Dimly I saw the first houses of Colincamps, and fearing myself about to fall I sank on to what seemed to be a grassy bank by the roadside and slept. I remember my head being raised by an R.E. and a kindly voice saying, 'Drink this, chum.' How delicious the tea tasted and how soft and cosy the bank felt, until on trying to rise I found myself embedded in a heap of mud".

At Courcelles the Rev. R. M. Kedward had set out buns and hot drinks in a barn, to help us on our way to Bus-les-Artois, where we entered camp as Good Friday was dawning. The spirit of camaraderie showed itself on that march: many a man, though dead-beat himself, took a rifle to ease the load of his worse-off pal, and those few men who had been left out of the line worked hard that night, repeatedly coming down the road from Bus to meet the men, and help them in by relieving them of their equipment. The Battalion Runners, who arrived last of all at daybreak, had followed in the rear in charge of R.S.M. Thirsk, to help along any stragglers. Commencing with twelve Runners, this party had grown to about thirty-five men. The fitter amongst them were carrying anything from three to six rifles apiece, together with box-periscopes, tin-helmets, and other appurtenances of war.

It was full daylight when they arrived at the entrance of the field where the huts were situated.

A bright, cheerful youth, who had just returned from leave, accosted the leading section of fours, notebook in hand, and demanded names and companies.

One of the Runners, Clifford Street, said, "What for?"

"Oh", said the youth, "I've been told to get the names of all stragglers".

"Stragglers be damned!" was the reply. "We're a highly organised party under the R.S.M".

Chapter 7

"Somme" Preparations

AT Bus we found ourselves in canvas-covered huts, and as it rained the whole of Good Friday we could not dry our clothing, and the mud from the quagmire outside flowed in through the open ends of the huts. The C.O. very sensibly gave us a full day's rest, and this was much appreciated. Daytime working parties began once again next day for all those who were not doing bombing or other courses. How often in those days were the R.E.s, into whose tender hands the working parties delivered themselves, condemned to perdition in polite, humorous and sulphurous language. But it soon became clear, even to the most disgruntled soldier, that the work had to be done: evidence was now forthcoming that a big move was being contemplated, so the Battalion threw itself into the work of preparation with the same spirit that had brought it into being in those far-off days of September, 1914. New assembly trenches were dug, forward gun emplacements were constructed, and much heavy material was carried on our backs into the line.

The Battalion quickly trained itself into a more efficient fighting unit. The Lewis gun section first received attention: the number of its guns was increased to eight, and 150 men were trained as reserve gunners, for it was in this direction that the Germans had until now enjoyed such a distinct superiority. The training of snipers was also taken in hand, our best shots having their rifles fitted with telescopic sights. Men were even trained in the ways of pigeons, so as to provide a means of message carrying in case the Battalion should be cut off Gas drill was strenuous: the chemically-soaked P.H. helmets were tested on Easter Sunday by the very direct method of sending officers and all ranks through a hut full of gas, while the gas-instructor stood by watching for casualties. As a final test the men, after donning gas-helmets in the regulation time – a few seconds – were ordered to attack in full battle order a mythical enemy 100 yards distant at the double. After fifty yards uphill the ranks were seen to thin rapidly, while very few reached their objective, breathing being so difficult. About this time Captain Ivor Jackson began his long career of temporary attachments to various staffs, which subsequently ended in his appointment as Staff Captain 137th Infantry Brigade, 46th Division. His position was temporarily filled by Lieutenant R. A. Flintoff, and finally by Lieutenant A. V. Rhodes.

More attention was being paid just now to the comforts of the men. The good food and healthy appearance of both officers and men was a tribute to cooks, the Quartermaster and the A.S.C. The Divisional Baths were visited periodically, although water was scarce on the Somme, and a clean change of clothing was issued at them. The services of a Foden disinfector were requisitioned, so that the verminous state of blankets and clothing was to some extent remedied. Opportunity was given for us to visit the Army dentists at Etaples, but the stories brought back by the live heroes who went made the trenches seem preferable even with toothache. Our Battalion water-man rather overdid his duty at this time. Since all the water he could obtain in the district was surface water, and therefore according to Army regulations unsafe, he added that full measure of chloride of lime which the said regulations prescribed and made the water almost undrinkable. The petrol-flavoured water which he sent up to the trenches in Pratt's tins was certainly much better, although the flavour lingered somewhat.

On May 6th we moved up into close support at Colincamps and relieved the 14th York and Lancasters. "C" Company and part of "A" Company moved further forward to occupy the support trenches of Hittite, Ellis Square and Fort Hoysted, the transport and quartermaster's stores remaining at Courcelles. The wrecked village will best be remembered by its church, whose tall spire was neatly pierced by a shell-hole in the exact position where one would expect to see a clock. Quite a number of French peasants clung tenaciously to their ruined farms in the surrounding district, working their land in spite of the constant danger, and there was some difficulty in getting them to evacuate when the sector livened up a few weeks later. The straw-thatched barns, whose walls were of brushwood and mud, looked like making cosy billets, especially as they had been fitted with tiers of beds made of wire netting, so that some of them could accommodate fully 100 men.

These beds, however, proved of little use, for neither officers nor men were allowed to undress while the Battalion was in close support. Instead, the trenches claimed them by night for working parties, a few hours' sleep being snatched by day. One big task which the Battalion undertook, and indeed completed in a single night, was the digging of a new trench, in many parts through solid chalk, not many yards behind the front line. The rapid and efficient way in which each man tackled his six-foot section, though hampered by German flares and the consequent bursts of machine-gun fire, was commended by the R.E.s. During the July 1st offensive the forward platoons were glad of the presence of this assembly trench when the front line had been completely blown in.

On May 10th we relieved the 12th East Yorkshires, who were then holding the line, taking over the left sector of the divisional front extending from John Copse in the Hébuterne direction to the much-raided No. 7 post on the right, where contact was made with the 11th East Yorkshires. The relief was carried out by daylight and went off much more smoothly and comfortably as a result, and there were no casualties. The four days' tour in the line was reasonably quiet, the enemy confining his attention to sending over salvos of "whizz-bangs", of which Battalion headquarters received more than its fair share, and the strafing of parts of the front line with "Minnies" and rifle grenades. Our few casualties were minor ones, three men being wounded by shrapnel and two suffering from shellshock. One rather heavy bombardment, which the enemy laid down on the front line, was smartly stopped by retaliation from Captain Horsley's Stokes' Gun Battery.

Listening posts by now had acquired a glamour all their own. No one who has ever lain out in "No Man's Land" with nerves tingling and every sense alert, grasping his bomb which seemed to grow enormously large as the moments passed by, will ever forget the sensation. One volunteer party, after a suitably serious lecture by their platoon officer, was posted by him at nightfall in one such post. The men crawled forward on their stomachs through a hole in the parapet and then lay down in the sticky mud. They heard nothing and saw nothing as the time passed by, and the silence was so intense and the night so dark that all four of them remained on duty. Dawn came and revealed to them that they were lying in a disused dugout! Needless to say, they volunteered for the same post the next night, but a cute sergeant discovered the reason for this excessive zeal, and the post was abandoned.

We put in a lot of hard work in this sector, improving the front line, countless sandbags being filled in the process, and putting out more wire. Working parties from all units in the Division not then holding the line appeared each night. Dugouts soon became more plentiful, the deep shell-proof German kind, and the comfortable but more vulnerable "elephant" type being constructed. The trenches were made more habitable by the digging of deep sump-holes to drain them and by the laying of duck-boards. Latrines were at last dug in spots where the German snipers could not give one an unpleasant five minutes. The Company cooks under Sergeant Regan established themselves in Basin Wood, a dell sheltered by a few splintered tree stumps, and although frequently they were cursed for the smoke they sent up and the attention they caused the trenches in the vicinity to receive

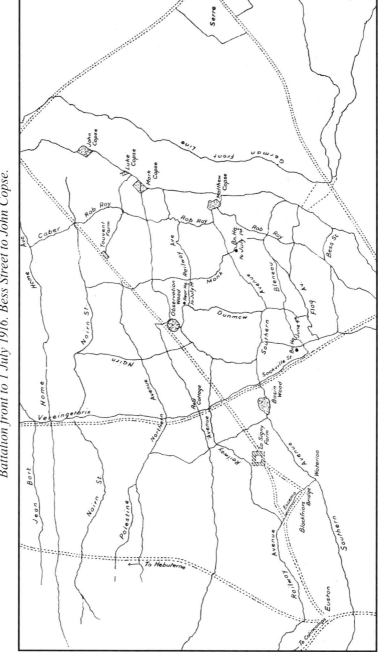

Battalion front to 1 July 1916. Bess Street to John Copse.

from the enemy, the tea and stew they managed to make, despite the rain, was very welcome. This tea and stew was sent up to the various platoons in tall containers resembling huge thermos flasks, which were carried slung on long poles by pairs of men, who floundered about in the muddy trenches as the containers swung from side to side.

The Germans opposite seemed to be well informed as to the Division's movements. One day there appeared to the right of No. 7 post a notice board on which the enemy displayed the colours of the 92nd Brigade. On Sunday, May 14th, these colours were replaced by those of the 93rd Brigade, a unit of which – the 16th West Yorkshires – actually did appear that day to relieve us. We were able to move out in broad daylight with comparative ease, and progress was made without a single casualty via Bertrancourt to huts in Bus-les-Artois, where a good night's sleep was very refreshing. The next day we moved further back into Warnimont Wood, which lay in the valley between Bus and Authie and here we occupied huts and tents pitched out of sight under the tall trees. The distance of this camp, about seven miles, from the line agitated men's minds not a little, since it was expected that trench working parties would have to be provided as usual, and the long tramp back to camp in the hours before dawn would be an ordeal.

Fortunately, there was no need for this uneasiness, as the nine days' stay in this delightful spot proved a complete rest after the weeks of strenuous trench life, and conditions were very much like they had been in the good old days at Ripon. The whole gamut of platoon, company and battalion drill was revived and varied with instruction on all matters connected with trench warfare, with an occasional visit to Bus for a much-needed bath. Major Carver, who was in command of the Battalion at this time, did his best to make life pleasant for us, after the discomforts of the last tour in the line. The band brought out its instruments once again and made the woods ring with all the brightest tunes of the day, whilst we lay around in the thick undergrowth. When it became too cold to remain in the open any longer we retired into our huts and our vocal efforts replaced the more tuneful music of the band. How great it was at night to hear the boom of the guns and yet to feel that for a short time at least one was out of it all and free to sleep! Concerts arose in the evening without much arrangement- almost spontaneously. Those men who were later on to form the "Tonics", as good a concert party as any brigade possessed, used to make the woods re-echo with songs like "Nirvana". Their voices have been heard many a time since, to the delight of their pals fresh from the trenches, and in fact at frequent intervals during these long years after the War, but never so sweetly as in those happy days in Warnimont Wood.

Battalion orders one night warned us for a 6.30 a.m. parade next day, but very strange to say the orderly sergeant overslept himself, and at 7.30 we were still peacefully sleeping. When we finally assembled, one and a half hours late for parade, the solemn-faced rank and file chuckled inwardly at the efforts of perspiring C.S.M.s struggling to make up for the time which the Army had lost. An extract from one man's diary will serve to show the contented state of the Battalion: "For once I was excused parade, so I spent the time wandering for miles under the beautiful trees, through which a glorious sun was streaming. I returned to camp feeling happier than I had ever been since leaving home, and I was just in time to catch a glimpse of the whole Battalion drilling under Major Carver. It was quite a surprise to see how smartly the movements were done, just as well as in our palmy days at Ripon. The Major was delighted with us and so were we. It was laughable to see those officers and N.C.O.s who had been quite reckless in the trenches, apparently nervous and scared on this parade".

A draft of N.C.O.s and men, forty in strength, joined us about this time, the steady drain of casualties, the transfer of men to Brigade and Divisional headquarters, and the departure of men for commissions, since the Battalion had proved a good training ground for future officers, having reduced the strength of other ranks to 925. Captain E. M. Carroll, of "B" Company, was invalided home to England, and the command of his Company fell to Captain E. C. Williams, a keen soldier. There was one big working party for the trenches towards the end of our stay in Warnimont Wood, but the long tramp to and from the line was done quite cheerfully, for we were now in the pink of condition and we sang on the march. A heavy bombardment was put down by the enemy during the few hours in which we did our digging, but the "Lucky Tenth", as we were then called, did not have a single casualty. The Bradford Pals, however, who were holding the line, suffered rather heavily.

It was with great regret that we handed over our quarters in Warnimont Wood to the 16th West Yorkshires on May 24th, and moved into divisional reserve at Bus, where our camp was found to be in an orchard amongst trees laden with apple and pear blossom. From here it was evident that the sector had become distinctly lively, for heavy bombardments by both sides were breaking out frequently both by day and by night. Working parties operating in the neighbourhood of the Sucrerie brought back the news that the divisional cemetery there had considerably increased in size. The 12th East Yorkshires, who were then holding the line, were having a particularly bad time, so it was not surprising that Division should issue a series of instructions as to how to quieten the enemy. A diary records the instructions thus: "If any German sniper is particularly troublesome at any time, the whole of the battalion snipers are to concentrate their fire on him and to root him out". When the Germans send rifle-grenades or "coal-boxes" over we are to return twice the number and at once. If they send out a bombing party at night we are to send out two and give them a warm time. And so for the artillery, which is to return twofold any bombardments the line may be subjected to". The order concludes: "Only in this way may the Germans be taught not to be impertinent, and only in this way may the sector once more resume its wonted quiet". The newspapers which occasionally filtered up to the front from now on frequently recorded that "considerable artillery activity occurred last night in the Hébuterne district".

We were all very chummy together these days, for the tales of what was happening to the 12th East Yorkshires in the line made us wonder very much about what the future had in store. Luckily there was plenty of work to occupy our time. Bus proved itself to be a regular hot-bed for working parties. Some were attached to the R.E.s in the district, meeting convoys of lorries laden with trench materials and forming dumps at convenient points. Others, detailed for the trenches, carried water mains to the Sugar Factory, and were happy in the thought that a water supply would soon be available within reasonably easy reach of the front line. A few had the comparatively pleasant task of repairing the roads in which the shell-holes appeared with monotonous regularity. At the same time parties were constantly leaving us for training in all the special branches of trench warfare. It was now quite obvious that preparations for an attack on a big scale were well under way. The one bright spot was that leave had continued steadily throughout the three weeks' spell out of the line, so that quite a fair proportion of officers and men had re-joined the Battalion refreshed with the sight of home.

On May 29th, having been reinforced by a draft of twenty-one men, we left Bus to take over the right sector of the divisional front. We were very lucky not to be trapped in Colincamps during the march, for here a bombardment of H.E. shells had caused havoc to billets and transport just before we passed through. The 12th East Yorkshires were pleased to see the Battalion, which once again arrived by daylight and quickly took over the line through Matthew Copse, just opposite to the mysterious Quadrilateral, where the enemy was so touchy. Things were found to be distinctly lively, since the enemy observation was very good, our trenches being dominated by the higher land around Serre. Much repair work was necessary as both wire and trenches had been badly smashed, and the work was not easily done with an enemy constantly on the alert. His snipers and trench mortars took a steady toll of casualties, one man being killed[6] and

---

6 Private Herbert Gale was aged 21. He is buried in Sucrerie Military Cemetery, Colincamps.

Lieutenant Vickers with ten other ranks being wounded during the first few days.[7] In addition, one sergeant of a party of Hampshire N.C.O.s attached to the Battalion was killed. The communication trenches and support lines received much attention from enemy 5.9s, and at intervals long-range shells destined for the back areas went screeching overhead. They came chiefly at nightfall, so that the transport which was bringing up the quartermaster sergeants with their companies' rations had some hectic moments near to Euston Dump, the Sucrerie, and La Signy Farm.

Our retaliation, in which machine guns, trench mortars, and artillery co-operated, was usually heavy and generally carefully planned beforehand so as to secure the maximum effect. A section of the Heavy Trench Mortar Battery moved up into emplacements in the support lines, from which they fired those big spherical shells, which we had previously carried up to the trenches for them and had very appropriately christened "footballs". These shells pounded at the deep German dugouts with good effect, although the long iron bars blown from them as they exploded usually returned to our lines screeching merrily. The R.F.C. were very active at this time over the enemy lines, doing photography and artillery observation work. Their stunts added some variation to a life which was becoming dreary, and we watched them with much interest. One plane, reputed to be that of the much-talked-of "Mad Major", gave us considerable entertainment, and was generally greeted with a cheer whenever it crossed our front line.

Saturday, June 3rd, after a quiet night in which the only noise was the rattle of our Lewis guns firing at certain gaps in the enemy's wire, opened fairly quietly. As the day wore on the Germans became distinctly jumpy, for it was the King's birthday, and judging by their frantic efforts to locate our Stokes' gun and "football" emplacements, they were in expectation of something. In fact, a raid was to be carried out that night: the East Lancashires were to send a raiding party over with the object of bringing back prisoners, and generally wreaking as much destruction as possible on the enemy in a short time. It was anticipated by certain officers that enemy retaliation would certainly cause heavy casualties, owing to the poor state of the trenches, to "A" and "C" Companies in that sector, and a desire was expressed that half the men should be withdrawn for a few hours to the new assembly trenches just behind the front line. However, higher authority decided against this procedure, so the affair proved a real tragedy for those unlucky companies.

---

7 Private John Thornton Galt died of wounds on 31 May. He is buried in
   Gezaincourt Communal Cemetery Extension.

At dusk a strong party of the East Lancashires appeared, camouflaged with sandbags and faces begrimed, and armed with revolvers and Mills' bombs. Punctually at midnight our barrage opened on the enemy front line, the raiding party lying out in "No Man's Land" until the barrage moved forward at 12.30, which was to be the signal to advance. Hostile retaliation was prompt and heavy, and continued until 1.40, some twenty minutes after our guns had ceased, and every available German gun seemed to be firing on the short sector held by "A" and "C" Companies. The front line trenches were blown in almost beyond recognition, scarcely a fire-bay remaining intact. As expected, casualties came rapidly, but the men stood up heroically to a rain of shells to which they could not reply. The following, recorded by a survivor, then a private in "A" Company, is typical of what happened:

"It is difficult after twenty years to remember all the names, but I know that I was in a bay with six men. Within a few minutes of the opening of the bombardment, a shell fell immediately behind the trench and two men were hit. One, Tich West, who was next to me, was struck high up in the back. Lifting him, I placed him across my knee and was endeavouring to rip his tunic to fix his field dressing when another shell blew in the parados, burying us all. Fortunately, the trench had been banked up with a lot of new sandbags, so that for a few minutes at any rate, some air came through the crevices, which would not have been the case had the parados been of earth alone. I was buried in a kneeling position, grasping a man I then knew to be dead. One forgets time in such circumstances, and how long I was so fixed I do not know. However, Sam Conyers came from the next bay to pull away the bags and was killed in the act. The platoon sergeant then made an attempt, but was badly wounded, and finally I believe my rescue was completed by Joe Allen, who got my head free, which was all that could then be done. I believe the rest of the men in the bay were killed. By this time the front of the trench had gone altogether, and I was in the open, pinioned from the shoulders downwards and unable to move until the shelling ceased, when someone freed my arms and gave me an entrenching tool to dig the rest of myself out. I suppose I must have been somewhat light-headed, for I remember singing and telling my leg I could not possibly go without it, until a young newly-joined officer, who was doing heroic work digging others out, bid me shut up for fear the Germans heard me and came across".

It is a coincidence that the narrator of the above, when an officer in another unit, should be decorated for rescue work in a similar incident two years later.

When the shelling had ceased, there was an instant rush from the support companies to get out the wounded, many of whom were still buried, and for hours frantic digging was carried on. Lieutenant Palmer, a very popular officer, and Second-Lieutenant Spink, who had just joined the Battalion, were killed, in addition to twenty men.[8] Lieutenants Rice and Norfolk were wounded, and forty-seven N.C.O.s and men, many of them severely. Lieutenant Rice subsequently re-joined the Battalion in January, 1917, but the heavy going and the strain of the fighting in Slug Street at the end of February, 1917, caused his wounds to reopen, and he died in June of that year. Owing to the impassable state of the trenches, the rescue work was so difficult that the day was well advanced before all the casualties had been removed, and the Battalion M.O., Lieutenant Hart, with his assistant, Sergeant Crookes, worked feverishly for many hours in their forward dressing station. The enemy was very quiet during the whole of Sunday, no doubt busy with his own casualties, which the raiding party had reported to be heavy. The East Lancashire raiders, according to one of them, had gone over the parapet in a flash at the pre-arranged signal, and had done their work of destruction rapidly, throwing bombs into trenches and dugouts. They had as quickly withdrawn when the agreed word "Kantara" was passed down, unfortunately arriving back without the required prisoner. As both sides were exhausted and busy with their casualties and repair work, our relief by the 15th West Yorkshires at 6 p.m. that day passed off without incident. It was a very silent Battalion which filed out of the trenches past its twenty-two dead, who were lying at Sackville Street Dump on the light railway and awaiting stretcher parties at nightfall, when the bodies were to be conveyed to the ever-growing cemetery near the Sucrerie.[9]

We marched quietly back to Bus, to be met by men of the other Hull battalions, who, in spite of the lateness of the hour, were out on the

---

8 L/Cpl. Lewis Edward Peek, Privates John Henry Monday, George Henry Johnson, Albert Blakemore, George William Bray, Frank Johnson, George Archer, Walter Richard Raney, Harry Storr, William Bernard Ascough, Percy Brown, George Kilby Deighton, John Richard Farnill, Harold Herbert Pawson, William Vincent Miller, Charles Samson Joys, Arthur Ernest West, Oscar Rounding Leighton, Samuel Conyers and Leonard Webster.

9 Over the next few days a further six men died of wounds received that night: Sgt. Thomas Huntington, L/Cpl. William Arthur MacPherson and Privates Benjamin Ireland, Frank Kellett Woodcock, John Bell Atkinson, Cyril Winterton Riley and Samuel Conrad Neill.

roads, anxious about the safety of their pals. Billets were comfortable, a liberal supply of blankets and straw and a long sleep serving to steady the shattered nerves somewhat. But it was hard next day looking for missing faces or hearing that some close friend had succumbed to his wounds. The news of the death of Lord Kitchener reached us at this time, and as we were amongst the first of the service battalions he had raised, his loss was deeply felt. Some days were now spent in re-organisation, particularly so as to strengthen the weakened companies commanded by Captains Harrison-Broadley and Ruthven, the latter of whom had just attained the rank of Major. Lieutenant Norfolk's duties as Signalling Officer were taken over by Second-Lieutenant Richardson, son of the Battalion's first Commanding Officer. Working parties became numerous once more, but the weather was reasonably fine, the countryside was putting on its summer clothing, and best of all, leave was continuing steadily. In the afternoon and early evening the band used to beguile the time of those of us who were warned to set off to the line for the night. On such occasions, as we lay in the long grass or strolled about listening to the music, the war seemed to fade far away, and we felt ourselves transported back to Hull to imagine that the scene was one of the parks, until the crash of a long-range shell or the cry of "Working party! Fall in!" destroyed the illusion.

Soon after dawn on Whit Monday, June 12th, we left Bus for a short spell to take over the sector south of John Copse. The relief of the 16th West Yorkshires, who had had a good time with the enemy but a bad one with the weather, was completed soon after noon – the earliest yet. The trenches were found to be in a bad state, full of mud or flooded with water, the front line especially so. The portable pumps, with which the line had now been equipped, were very useful so long as the mud did not clog them or the streams of water they squirted over the parapet did not draw hostile fire. On the whole the Germans were quiet, especially during the second day. The number of crosses bearing the names of French soldiers killed at this spot on this same day a year ago made one expect a strafe, which, fortunately, was not forthcoming. During the early morning of the next day the enemy became active, three other ranks being wounded, but our guns and trench mortars replied with interest and quelled the shelling.

In the early afternoon of June 14th the 12th York and Lancaster Regiment appeared to relieve us. On the journey out we were surprised to see how far the preparations for the rumoured big attack had been made. One man's diary described it as follows:

"It was lovely weather at 5 p.m. as our platoon left Matthew Copse and stepped out down the communication trenches; so bright and

Lewis gun section, near Doullens, July 1916.

Transport on the march, near Doullens, July 1916.

clear that the Germans, looking out of their observation balloons, would not let us get out at our usual exit at Euston Dump. Instead we had to keep under cover all the way to Colincamps. Here we fairly opened our eyes with surprise: every preparation for an immediate advance seemed to have been made. There were stacks of big heavy shells everywhere, new batteries of heavy guns had been brought up and camouflaged by grass screens, dugouts and safety trenches had been made and big bomb stores erected. The village had been cleared of its last inhabitant, who had clung so long to his home. We passed him on the road, pushing his few household effects on a rickety old cart. On the road to Bus, as dusk set in, we passed one long string of artillery wagons carrying tons of ammunition up to the guns. At Bus, too, there were great ammunition parks, and the whole civilian population was talking about the coming advance. We didn't discuss it much, for we were glad to get into our billets and turn in".

Our billets at Bus were very cosy – just barns, but well filled with soft warm straw. Like most farm buildings on the Somme, they consisted of a rough wooden framework filled in with mud and thatched with straw. A shell landing anywhere near would usually cause the walls to collapse outwards and the thatched roof to drop downwards on masse, so that some cover was always left. During the ensuing week heavy guns drawn by caterpillar tractors shook the village as they tumbled through, and batteries of light French guns, the famous quick-firing "75s", cantered through its main street. Huge reserve ammunition dumps, representing fortunes soon to be flung at the enemy, were being formed. Soldiers' talk was mainly about the coming offensive and how soon the war would be over – there was no thought but that the Germans would be driven far back as soon as the word was given. The optimistic spirit of the British soldier had now definitely taken the upper hand.

Most of the other units of the Division were now well advanced in their training for the coming attack, and it became known that we would not necessarily take an offensive part in the scheme of operations. Accordingly, having been reinforced by a draft of six officers and seventy-one men, we threw ourselves with keenness into the arduous work of final preparation. Tasks of all types were undertaken, such as the quarrying and breaking of stone for road construction, the boring of deep wells under R.E. supervision, the digging of assembly positions for the attackers, the carrying up of all types of ammunition and the moving of heavy bridges into positions from which they could readily be flung over trenches to allow our artillery to follow the expected advance. The construction of those ingenious barbed-wire contraptions, which could be thrown out of the front line to fill gaps in the wire entanglements, occupied much time, but the difficulty of making them was as nothing compared with their transportation to the front line. Many a man, his clothes torn by the barbs, finding himself repeatedly entangled with the telephone wires hanging from the trench sides, took a hasty and risky cut over the top to deliver his prickly burden.

The job of one working party, which few of the Battalion will forget, since nearly all available officers and men took part in it, was the carrying up of gas-cylinders to the front line. The party unloaded a convoy of lorries at Euston Dump, and with gas masks at the alert, set off at dusk in a long file, each pair of men carrying a heavy cylinder slung on a long pole, another pair of relief carriers walking behind. Progress was slow and exhausting up to the emplacements which had been dug for the cylinders under the front line fire-steps. The rear men of the party did not get rid of their burden until dawn was breaking. On June 23rd we said goodbye to this period of heavy labouring, which, considering that most of us had been recruited from non-manual trades, had been surprisingly well done. At 1p.m. that day, after a heavy thunderstorm, we marched out of Bus, each in full battle order and wearing two extra bandoliers of ammunition, some carrying a bag of bombs or parts of a Lewis gun, and headed for the trenches to take over the divisional front for the coming attack.

Chapter 8

Final Preparations – July 1st

ALTHOUGH the Battalion played no spectacular part in the First Battle of the Somme, the period immediately prior to the July 1st attack formed such an important landmark in its history that some consideration of the general situation would not be out of place. As far back as December, 1915, Joffre and Haig had agreed on a joint offensive in the Somme area on a big scale the following summer. However, the terrific onslaught commenced by the Germans at Verdun in February, 1916, with such appalling loss to the French, soon made it obvious that the British would have to bear the brunt of the offensive. The British forces found themselves suddenly compelled to take over another twenty miles of front, and this, together with the fact that the proposed offensive might have to be launched much earlier to ease the pressure on the French, had caused the hurried departure of the 31st and other Divisions from Egypt to France.

The VIII Army Corps, consisting of the 4th, 29th, 48th, and 31st Divisions was under the command of Lieut.-General Sir A. Hunter-Weston, and formed part of the Fourth Army, whose attacking frontage of twelve miles extended from Maricourt in the south to John Copse, close to Hébuterne, in the north. Two divisions of the Third Army further north were to make a subsidiary attack on the Gommecourt Salient, from which no great result was expected, its principal purpose being to divert the enemy's attention from the main attack. Between Gommecourt and John Copse no attack was to be launched, but the 48th Division, holding the line, were to make a demonstration in the way of artillery bombardment and the release of smoke and gas in order to occupy fully the attention of the Germans opposite them. Amongst the fourteen divisions taking part in the operations, were no less than six battalions of the East Yorkshires, for in addition to the four battalions of the 92nd Brigade, the 1st and 7th were at Fricourt. Of course, the impending attack could not be concealed from the Germans, whose observation balloons lined the front and whose planes were thick in the air, but they did misjudge the actual frontage of the attack, anticipating that the main thrust would be to the north. Consequently, that part of the enemy's line was more heavily defended than the southern part, and this was largely the cause of the failure of the VIII Corps attack.

The 31st Division found itself on the left flank of the main attack, with the 48th and 4th Divisions to the north and south respectively. Its front extended from Flag Avenue, about 500 yards south of Matthew Copse, to John Copse, and its particular task was to take Serre and form a defensive flank facing north. Serre was admitted to be one of the strongest of the German positions, sharing with Gommecourt the honour of being one of the two villages to resist all attacks until evacuated by the Germans on their general retirement to the Hindenburg Line early in 1917. Its powerful defences were the product of two years' consolidation: thick barbed-wire entanglements, elaborate systems of deep dugouts and solidly protected gun emplacements. It is now known that G.H.Q. did not expect any great advance on this northern frontage, but considered that the enemy reserves would be so confined that the divisions attacking further south would be able to make good headway. This proved to be the case, but it was not expected that the nine divisions operating from La Boisselle to John Copse would be brought to such a complete stand-still as, in fact, they were.

The 93rd and 94th Brigades were selected some weeks before July 1st to lead the attack of the 31st Division, and as this involved them in special training, the task of holding the divisional front devolved on the 92nd Brigade. It fell to the 10th East Yorkshires to hold the whole of this front during the preliminary bombardment, which was to begin at dawn on June 24th and to last five days, "Z" day originally being June 29th. In the afternoon of June 23rd[10] the Battalion took over from the 11th East Yorkshires that part of the divisional front extending from Bess Street to Warley Avenue. Its front was extended still further north early next morning as far as Nairne Street, just north of John Copse, the 11th East Lancashires being relieved so that they might complete their training in Warnimont Wood. All available Lewis guns were placed in the front line, which was held at intervals by small posts, each company providing one platoon which it relieved every twenty-four hours.

The preliminary bombardment began rather mildly in dull stormy weather on June 24th, our 18-pounders concentrating their fire on the German wire, the gaps blown in it being as eagerly watched by our front line sentries through their periscopes as they were by the Artillery F.O.O.

---

10 On 25 June Private Samuel Caley was killed in action and Private Arthur Harold North died of his wounds. The next day Private Alfred Barrett North was killed in action. They were not related. Also killed on 26 June was Private George Blenkin. In the following days before the attack, the battalion suffered a further four deaths, Privates George Walter Buck, John Brunyee, Joseph Cheney and James Stanley Watson.

Except for a short period, the enemy's retaliation was not very severe on the 24th, but next day, when our guns began some destructive shelling of gun-emplacements and dugouts, hostile fire was heavy and our trenches soon began to assume a battered appearance. Serre was receiving much attention from our heavy guns, including a 15-inch howitzer, the village rapidly disappearing. On the 25th, our aeroplanes, acting in conjunction with the Artillery, made a concerted attack on the German observation balloons, shooting down three of them in succession, to our great delight. However, this had little effect in checking enemy retaliation on our lines, and from now on we had to stand up to heavy bombardments with periods of particular intensity, but the careful selection of the positions of the posts was having the effect of keeping down casualties.

The next two days were noteworthy for the number of violent artillery duels, in which the front line and the communication trenches immediately near it suffered so badly that by the end of this period they were almost flattened out. Moving about in the line by daylight was something of an adventure, and it was found impossible to occupy it except by night. By day, small parties would rush forward to it from the support line, Rob Roy, and gas was released on two or three occasions, but this operation was difficult and risky, as many of the gas cylinders were completely buried and others were leaking owing to the heavy shelling. "D" Company suffered several casualties on this account, Lieutenant R. A. Flintoff, who had always been so careful about his men with regard to gas training, being killed.

On the night of June 26th a raiding party of the 11th East Yorkshires left the line to secure prisoners for identification. They were, however, held up by insufficiently-cut wire, and forced to return unsuccessful. Further attempts made by the 12th East Yorkshires on the nights of the 27th and 28th met with no better luck, the parties being received with bombs and determined machine gun fire, the thick wire still proving an obstacle. It was later known that the failure of these and similar raids taking place on the rest of the VIII Corps front, was causing an uneasy feeling at G.H.Q Evidently our bombardments, though very heavy when judged by previous standards, were not sufficiently powerful to subdue the keen and active Germans of the 169th Regiment in the trenches opposite to us.

Orders came through on the 28th that owing to the spell of bad weather, Zero day had been postponed at the request of the French from June 29th to July 1st, and the Battalion was given the option of holding on for a further forty-eight hours or of being relieved by another of the Hull Battalions then in divisional reserve. It was decided to stay in the line as the heavy strain of the previous five days had rendered the men unfit to take any immediate offensive part if called on to do so. This postponement proved very unfortunate for the VIII Corps, since the Germans at the last moment were able to bring up strong Artillery reinforcements into the Serre-Puisieux area. One incident will serve to show the curious state to which the prolonged bombardment had reduced us. A lance-corporal was walking up and down his little charge, a small fire-bay which had so far remained nearly intact, although shells were dropping all round it. He was entirely oblivious of this, however, and stopped from time to time alongside his two sentries who were peering out into the darkness, to quote to them for their edification long speeches from Shakespeare and Dickens. Realisation that there was a war on was suddenly brought to him when a shell blew in his bay, pinned his sentries, and cut short one of Hamlet's soliloquies.

On looking back from the support line, which one did not do very often just then, one was surprised to see how close up the Artillery had approached. 18-pounders peeped out wherever there was the slightest sign of cover, in positions so obviously untenable that one wondered what actually did happen to them on the day of the attack. Fortunately for the gunners, the R.F.C. had by now gained a certain measure of control in the air, and many thrilling air duels were witnessed. The advanced headquarters of the attacking brigades had been established in the line, their positions being well chosen from the point of view of control, though with little consideration for safety. Their "elephant" dugouts formed excellent protection against shrapnel, but were of no use whatever against direct hits, and one feels curious as to the feelings of a certain headquarters staff when a shell pierced the dugout top and poked its way half in, most fortunately failing to explode.

On June 30th, ten per cent of our officers and men were sent back to an entrenched position immediately in front of Colincamps. They were to form a nucleus around which the Battalion could be rebuilt in case of heavy casualties. That same day Lieut.-Colonel D. Burges left the Battalion, and Lieut.-Colonel W. B. Pearson, of the 1st Lancashire Fusiliers, took over command. At night, after first providing parties to cut "lanes" through our own wire to give our attacking troops a quick means of egress into "No Man's Land", we were relieved by the 93rd and 94th Brigades, which were to attack on the right and left sectors respectively of the divisional front. Three companies withdrew to Palestine trench in support, leaving "D" Company, under Captain Lambert, to carry on. That company spread itself along the whole of the divisional front, to remain there during the attack and to serve as a "net" to collect stragglers.

Progress through the trenches, now packed with men, back to the supports, was not difficult, for the night was comparatively quiet after the days of intense bombardment. The enemy had evidently transferred his attention just now from the trenches to the back areas, for there was much long-range shelling, and Colincamps was observed to be in flames. The Transport had as usual managed to get through with our rations. It had endured some particularly rough times on the roads near the line, especially in the neighbourhood of La Signy farm, and deserved, together with the band, which had formed itself into a stretcher-bearing party, a word of praise.

The three companies in "Palestine" passed a quiet time during the night, but there was no thought of sleep and the time dragged slowly by. Our final bombardment began at dawn in real earnest and reached its crescendo an hour before Zero. For an hour it kept up an intensity which no words can describe until 7.30, when ten minutes after the great mine in the direction of Beaumont Hamel had been exploded, the attack was launched. Actually this was an absurdly late hour for an attack and was against the desire of G.H.Q., but had been agreed upon in deference to the wishes of the French. Little news concerning the attack filtered back to us for some time, and what did come was very contradictory. A succession of orders and counter-orders with little exact information kept us on tenterhooks during the whole day, for the possibility of a German counter-attack was very real and had to be provided against. One company was ordered forward to reinforce the 93rd Brigade at 10 a.m., but it finally found that it was not required, and it was not until then that it was realised that the attack along the 31st Division's front had failed with heavy casualties.

It seems that the Germans had very carefully conserved their manpower during our bombardment by packing their deep dugouts with men, who were waiting in comparative safety, ready to rush out the very moment the alarm came from their sentries posted at the dugout entrances. The instant our barrage lifted and the attacking battalions were climbing out of their assembly trenches, masses of Germans poured out into the open, setting up their machine guns in advance of their own line, and these, together with the terrific barrage put down by their artillery, took a very heavy toll. It became known later that parties of the 93rd and 94th Brigades did actually get into the German lines, some even reaching Serre itself, where their unburied bodies were found in February, 1917, when the enemy retired. But these isolated parties were too weak either to establish themselves or to link up with one another, and in the course of the day they were either killed or taken prisoner. During the general slaughter of this attack, our losses passed almost unnoticed. Actually, when the Battalion withdrew, its ranks were considerably thinned, more than 100 of its officers and other ranks being either killed or wounded.

During the afternoon of July 1st[11] the Battalion was once more warned that it might be required, so Lieutenant R. Addy went forward to the 93rd Brigade headquarters for information, but found that we were again not wanted. A call for more bombs at Matthew Copse caused a carrying party to leave Palestine trench loaded with boxes, and it was the men of this party who brought back the first definite news as to how completely the attack had been broken up. They had experienced great difficulty in getting forward through the communication trenches, which were packed with wounded and small parties of survivors. About 9 p.m. it was heard that the 92nd Brigade was to renew the attack for the 31st Division, but this order was countermanded two hours later by instructions to move out of the line into Corps Reserve at Bus. We were soon on our way back, remembering little of our midnight march except the burning buildings of Colincamps and the shattered appearance of Courcelles.

And so the "Eight-days Bombardment" ended and also – with the relief of the Battalion and its withdrawal in the early hours of July 2nd, after nine days in the line, to huts in Bus Orchard – our close acquaintance with this particular sector for the next four months. The tension of the last spell in the line had had a marked effect on all ranks, but the persistent rumour that our next move was to take us out of this area to one of comparative peace, did much to dispel within the next day or two the atmosphere of tired expectancy which was so apparent on the day of our relief

Two events during these three days are worthy of recording. July 2nd, mid-afternoon, found the N.C.O.s and officers assembled for a talk by Colonel Pearson. After giving – as far as his information allowed – a brief survey of the Battle of the Somme in its first stages, the C.O. stirred his audience, perhaps with varying emotions, by concluding: "We shall be in it again before long, never fear, and we shall suffer casualties. But the Battalion will still go on. You may not be there, but there will be, at the end of it all, a 10th East Yorkshire Battalion to march proudly down King Edward Street".

The second incident provided that mixture of pathos and comedy which was so often to be found in those days of excursions and alarms. On the morning of July 3rd the whole Battalion, in all conceivable form of undress, was enjoying to the full the colossal mail which had accumulated during the last ten days. Parcels littered the floor of every hut, the chances of a royal high tea for each and every one were definitely rosy. Rudely into this

---

11   Sgt. Reginald Percival Jones and Private William Henry Dalton were killed in action during the day. The next day Privates William Edwin Adamson and Stanley Coop died of wounds.

veritable "Nirvana" of the trench-weary soldier came the order "Battle order in ten minutes". And so, half an hour later, saw the Battalion staggering out of Bus Orchard – parcels with their untouched delicacies consigned to the incinerator – each man carrying his full load of specialist impedimenta – bomb waistcoats filled to capacity, Lewis gun parts and loaded pans, signalling tripods and box lamps. The route taken was away from the line, but gradually, as the afternoon wore on and the men's tempers wore out, working round to Vauchelles only three kilometres from Bus. Here we turned left towards Bus, and the C.O. asked that all should have a cheery smile as the photographer was just along the road. Sure enough, there he was, with his movie camera by the roadside, merrily turning his handle as the Battalion marched past. What a pity it was before the time of sound pictures! The remarks would have given the true Somme atmosphere. The amusing sequel came in the following October. A party of N.C.O.s, when going up the line in a "General" bus found, decorating the interior, a page of a popular weekly, the article being "The Somme Smile!" To give point to the title was included a section of the film (part of "D" Company) taken with the caption, "Gallant East Yorkshires smiling as they go into action!"

The march which commenced on July 5th, however, though perhaps not as strategic as the foregoing, was much more to the liking of the whole of the Battalion. By easy stages, each one of which took us further from the evacuated areas, further into the heart of apparently peace-time Picardy, we came at last to Auxi-le-Château. An interesting and stimulating interlude had been introduced at Thièvres. Here the Corps Commander, Sir Aylmer Hunter Weston, addressed the Battalion and, though his written message had been previously handed to every man under his command, he here spoke in the highest terms of the part played by the whole of the 31st Division during the first day of the Battle of the Somme. Such an address given when the spirits were considerably higher than they had been a week previously, did much to dispel from the minds of the men concerned any feeling of defeat or inferiority that may have possessed them immediately after July 1st, and sent the Battalion marching into the unknown with a definite "tail-up" feeling.

From Auxi-le-Château, the much maligned but nevertheless definitely acceptable cattle-trucks conveyed the entire unit to Thiennes, by way of Frevent, St. Pol and Bethune. The detraining was completed at 1.45 a.m., July 9th, and immediately the road was taken for Robecq. The only members of the Battalion who look back with any pleasure on this journey are the Billeting Party under Captain R. Addy, who on July 8th made it on bicycles, for all the world like a pre-war cycling party, even to the periodic halts at various estaminets by the way. As for the Battalion, the *route pavée* in the darkness of this Sunday morning was a veritable *via dolorosa* after the soft

Somme roads, and it was a pathetically footsore crowd which staggered into Robecq as dawn was breaking. But, as was always the case, the cares and worries of a day died with that day, and the calm and quiet of Robecq that Sunday in mid-summer proved perhaps the most potent tonic the Battalion ever experienced. This ideal day too, proved but a prelude to the most restful and enjoyable week spent during the whole of the sojourn in France. The hospitality of the villagers, the lazy days spent amongst surroundings in which all the peace time avocations were still being pursued, all left an imprint in the memory which has never been erased. The thoughts of many went out in sincere sympathy to this kindly area in the spring of 1918, when the tide of war swept forward to its very doors.

For the next week training and refitting occupied our time. We were now in XI Corps (Lieut.-General Sir R. Haking).

During this period the influence of Colonel Pearson began to show itself, and a certain amount of "gingering up" was felt throughout the Battalion. He also revived the band, which had suffered a good many casualties during the previous few months. This wise and welcome move was much appreciated in the months to come, as not many Service Battalions could lay claim to such a cheering influence.

The week's rest ended, the Battalion moved on July 15th to huts at Riez Bailleul, where it was in support with a view to relieving the battalions of the 61st Division. When the Battalion at length, on the 20th, took over a sector of the line at Fauquissart to the north of Neuve Chapelle, from the 12th East Yorkshires, the novelty of the area was almost in the nature of a nine days' wonder. The breastwork defences, whilst inspiring for a time a sense of insecurity in the rear, eventually appealed to the majority because of the feeling of liberty of movement. Actually, only "A" and "B" were in the front line at Fauquissart, "C" and "D" being in billets at Pont du Hem. Major Carver was in command of the two front-line companies; Battalion headquarters at Lonely Post.

The sector was definitely "quiet", so that the initial experience of this type of defence system was distinctly favourable. We were relieved on the 23rd,[12] and on the 24th moved to Richebourg St. Vaast – a vast heap of rubble and broken machinery (the result of the Neuve Chapelle battle) which was the Battalion's next "resting place". Although by this time all had fully realised the utter devastation that a modern war must cause, the

---

12 Relatively quiet. On 22 July Private Charles Herbert Kingdom was killed in action and the next day Private Mark Wilson was also killed in action and Private David Douglas of the 4th East Yorkshires who was serving with the battalion died of wounds.

"D" Company near Louvencourt, July 1916, are seen leaving the front-line and heading back to rest. This photo, used in numerous books, wrongly claims they are "Gallant East Yorkshires smiling as they go into action".

fact that we were on the spot where one of the early vital battles of the war had been fought stirred the imagination and curiosity of the whole Battalion. Groups of sightseers wandered about the village, noting – with many and varied conjectures – the sand-bagged windows, the few mud walls left standing, still pock-marked by shell or bullet, or both, and the great heap of debris which had once been the church. The huge bell, lying amongst the gaping vaults, was of special interest, the date of its casting (1370) being clearly decipherable.

It was at Richebourg that the Battalion canteen came into definite being, Sergeant S. O. Watson being appointed Sergeant-in-Charge, a post which he filled until the very end. It would be fitting here to pay tribute to "Tommy's" conscientious discharge of his duties in this sphere, and the efforts he made to keep his "shop" well stocked for the boys on their return from the line. No journey was ever too long, no weather too vile, so long as he found the goods.

It was here, too, that the embryo Battalion Concert Party was produced. "A" Company utilised the shell-stricken village school to produce their first concert, and though the standard fell short, perhaps, of that set by the then

Richebourg – Boar's Head (aerial photo).
Scene of the raid, 18/19 September 1916.
X = Point of exit from British Line.
A, B, C, D are the points of entry into the German trenches.

super-concert party "The Curios", who had enlivened the evenings at Bus a few weeks previously, nevertheless the initial attempt was uproariously received, especially the famous "Shell-Hole" sketch as the final item.

Outstanding, too, in this direction, but in a much more serious vein, was the classical concert given on July 27th in the courtyard of Battalion headquarters, for the entertainment of the Brigadier (Brig.-General O. de L. Williams, C.M.G., D.S.O., who had recently taken over command of the 92nd Brigade) at dinner, as the guest of the Battalion. The importance of the occasion was very obviously felt by one of the soloists, for he was at no small pains to ensure that the tenor should stand on one particular cobblestone in the yard, from which position his voice, in all its strength, would carry through the window to those inside. To the uninvited guests – headquarters' other ranks – lying in the shadows, this careful attention to the acoustics of the "stage" seemed a trifle unnecessary, as they remembered how a month or two before the same singer had filled Warnimont Wood with the music of "I hear you calling me" and "Nirvana". It is worthy of record before leaving this dinner-party that the Brigadier's visit was rudely cut short by a sudden intense bombardment on our front. So unusual was this at that time in those areas that the guest, desirous of being informed of what this might portend, hurried back to Brigade headquarters, not on his charger, with orderly in attendance, but on a push bicycle. This bombardment proved to be a German raid on the 93rd Brigade, and the Battalion had to "stand to" for an hour or so until things quietened down.

And so the summer of 1916 passed, there being long but quiet spells in the line – with, however, a steady toll of casualties because of the inadequate protection of the breastwork defences – followed by quieter spells behind, spoiled only by the constant demand of that arch-enemy of all infantry battalions, the R.E., for his nightly working party. On July 30th we relieved the 12th East Yorkshires in front of Richebourg l'Avouée. The breastworks did not afford much protection and communication trenches were very shallow, but casualties were few.[13] On August 5th we handed over to the 12th East Yorkshires and returned to Richebourg St. Vaast until the 11th, when we again relieved the 12th East Yorkshires. This proved to be rather a long spell, as it was not until the 20th that we were relieved once more by the 12th East Yorkshires and returned to King's Road. From August 23rd to 28th, September 4th to 10th, September 16th to 22nd, September 28th to October 4th,[14] we were again in the line. There will be many to whom the names of that area bring still a vivid memory, perhaps comic, perhaps tragic. The ruins of the Factory, always reminiscent of Bairnsfather's pump;[15] the Rue du Bois, a long straight stretch of utter desolation; King's Road, with its comfortable billets and its fields of ripening corn; Lacouture, a village deserted but almost intact; Seneschal Farm, that housed the whole Battalion; and lastly, Merville and Bethune, to which one used to lorry-jump to make contact, at long intervals, with a world that seemed almost unreal – a world of shops and tablecloths, of little children and house-proud women.

Colonel Pearson contracted trench fever and left us on August 10th to go into hospital, and Major Carver followed him on the 13th, leaving Major Ruthven in command until Colonel Stapledon, of the Manchester Regiment, arrived and took over command on the 24th.

If any period of trench warfare could be called pleasant, it was surely this, and it was appreciable in the spirits of the Battalion as a whole,

---

13 Three men were killed and one died of wounds.
14 During this period the battalion suffered eight men killed in action and nine men died of wounds.
15 A reference to a piece of artwork from the Bystander magazine drawn by a serving officer. In the picture a soldier, The Fatalist, is drawing water from a noisy pump in front of a ruin.

culminating in the successful raid of September 18th-19th on trenches near the Boar's Head.[16] For a week previous to this date, the 31st Division had practised a "non-offensive" policy, mainly with intent to lead the enemy to believe that he had a peace-loving unit billeted opposite. Added to this was the determination of Colonel Stapledon, in face of much criticism from the Higher Commands, that this first raid should dispense with artillery and depend for its success on surprise. Accordingly, Bangalore torpedoes were decided upon to do the cutting of the enemy wire. Never was confidence and optimism more apparent. The raiders themselves – one officer and twenty-five other ranks from each company, the whole under the command of Captain Lambert – were convinced of the soundness of the Colonel's judgment, and so went over never doubting of success. Some of the Transport Section willingly carried the torpedoes to the front line and Headquarter Signallers went up shortly before zero hour to connect the charges. The result was a great success. Unfortunately, "A" and "D" Companies' torpedoes failed to explode and by the time these parties, under Lieutenants McILroy and Pierson had succeeded in cutting the wire, they found the trench deserted. "B" and "C" Companies, under Lieutenants Clark and Stewart, had better fortune, and they went forward with such dash that they took the Germans completely by surprise and were able to do a good deal of damage. Eight were taken prisoners, together with a machine gun in perfect condition. The captured corporal looked very woe-begone at Battalion headquarters, as over a dixie of tea and a cigarette, he told how another two minutes would have changed the whole story. He had nearly completed the assembling of his gun – a new one just arrived – when our raiders appeared over the parapet.

Our casualties were very slight, being mostly scratches, and the only touch of sadness was given by the failure of Sergeant Tindall to return. Although strong search parties scoured "No Man's Land" until nearly dawn, nothing was heard or seen of him. This loss of one of our most respected N.C.O.s was felt keenly by all.

Congratulations poured into the Battalion headquarters from Brigade, Division and beyond, where the value of the raid was appreciated when our prisoners proved to be of the 104th Regiment, 40th (Saxon) Division – a unit whose presence on that front was news to the Intelligence Department.

It was in his congratulatory speech to the raiders that the Divisional General (Major-General Wanless O'Gowan) hinted that a return to the Somme area was a strong possibility. This materialised on October 8th when, after spending a night or two in billets outside Merville, the Battalion took the waggons "Hommes 40 Chevaux 8" to Candas.

---

16 Privates Edmund Keene, Alfred Webster and Sgt. Arthur Tindale were killed in action during this raid.

Chapter 9

Hébuterne – German Withdrawal to the Hindenburg Line

THE march through the night from Candas to Vauchelles ranks with the approach to Engelbelmer and that to Robecq. With all our possessions on our backs, together with the varied and ever-growing collection of specialist paraphernalia, the five and half hours march taxed the strength of every man in the Battalion.

During the week spent in Vauchelles, however, autumn came to us pleasantly. Mornings spent in Brigade exercises, attacking our old home, Warnimont Wood, afternoons playing the other Hull battalions at rugger and soccer – it was here that the 11th piled up 46-0 against us, but at soccer we came out with considerable credit – soon restored the men to their accustomed fitness and spirits.

An advance party sent up to John Copse to look over our old sector was made aware that the Somme offensive had not yet fizzled out. An imposing assembly of tanks at Louvencourt and the considerable increase of artillery on the Colincamps Plain gave promise of further activity to come. On October 16th we moved forward to bivouacs near Sailly-au-Bois and on the 17th back to Rossignol Farm. This promised to be very comfortable, but we had to turn out again next day and moved up once more to Sailly.

On October 20th we made our first acquaintance with Hébuterne, a village which for the next two and a half months was to accommodate the Battalion for its spells in the line. Who cannot still picture, scarcely dimmed by the passing years, those avenues of rubble along which we hurried at 100 yards distance, our steps quickening when a shell shattered one of the few bits of wall still remaining erect? Who does not remember those nights when, for what seemed hours, gas shells poured into the village with their sickening hiss and dull thud as they struck? Who cannot recall those holes of mud and water called trenches – Whisky, Woman, and Welcome – down which fatigue parties and reliefs plunged and slipped to reach their objective? And who does not still feel that twinge of envy that possessed him when he discovered that in one or two places in that desolate and devastated village during that wet and dreary autumn there were dry and roomy cellars, rendered shell-proof by the wreck above, where men might sit and even lie in warmth and comfort?

And behind the line, how did the Battalion fare? Bivouacs or ruins at Sailly-au-Bois, with the framework of barns providing fuel (much to the dismay of the Town Major's staff), the barns of Rossignol Farm and Authie, and hutments at Couin, Coigneux and Warnimont Wood, these served their turns as the authorities decided.

On October 21st we were relieved and moved into huts in Warnimont Wood. Throughout the second part of the month and early November the rumours of an attack gained in strength, especially when, on October 30th, a patrol was sent out to reconnoitre, previous to a raid being attempted. The raid itself was afterwards cancelled, but the preliminary patrol cost us dear in that Lieutenant Pierson and one other rank were missing, subsequently known to be killed, and one other rank was wounded.

But the expected attack on a big scale was not much longer delayed, for in the wet and gloom of the evening of November 12th the Battalion moved up from Bayencourt to Vercingetorix, the deep wide support line to the south of Hébuterne.[17]

Throughout the late summer and autumn of 1916 the Battle of the Somme, commenced, in the case of the 31st Division on July 1st with such unavailing heroism on the part of the 93rd and 94th Brigades, and to the south with such unqualified success, had continued with varying intensity, and was now moving to its final stage.

This was to be an attack by seven Divisions on a considerable front stretching from Hébuterne southwards to St. Pierre Divion. The role of the 92nd Brigade was on this occasion no enviable one. Being on the extreme left flank of the whole attack, the Battalion had to form a defensive flank for the 3rd Division which was to undertake the assault on our objective of four and a half months before – Serre. The right of our Divisional front was on this occasion John Copse – that shell-scarred hollow whose blasted and stricken stumps had marked the left flank on July 1st – the left was at Jean Bart.

The attacking units of the 92nd Brigade were the 12th and 13th Battalions, the former (on the left) being ordered to take and consolidate the first and second lines of enemy trenches, while the penetration of the 13th was to be to the German third line. Tanks were to have been employed, but the mud was so bad that they could not be used.

---

17 During the build-up and during the attack the battalion suffered eight men killed in action and two dying of wounds.

Zero hour was 5.45 a.m. on Monday, November 13th, and was signalled by the opening of a very intense barrage. The 10th Battalion in support in Vercingetorix anxiously awaited news, not only of the battle in general, but of those members of the Battalion who were actively taking part. These were two distinct parties, the task assigned to each being both vital and hazardous in the extreme. Four sections each comprising one N.C.O. and twenty men, the whole under the command of Second Lieutenant Anderson, provided the carrying party, their job being to deliver further supplies of bombs to the 12th and 13th Battalions when they should have gained their objective. Although the main body of the Battalion back in Vercingetorix were not worried with a single shell all day, the area from Caber – the assembly trench-forward across the whole width of "No Man's Land" – was pounded by an enemy barrage, the passage of which might well have been deemed impossible. To the lasting credit of the Battalion as a whole, and of each man in particular, the impossible was achieved, three of the parties successfully delivering their bombs to their comrades in the advanced position. The individual achievements and acts of heroism and determination performed by the members of these parties are still, after nearly twenty years, spoken of with enthusiasm and admiration, Sergeant Edgar Herman's superlative courage being, perhaps, the high-light.

The other members of the 10th Battalion directly taking part in this memorable engagement were the two Lewis gun sections who, under Corporal S. Edlington,[18] were attached to the 12th East Yorkshires. It is, perhaps, presumption to describe any one task of this tragic day as "the most hazardous", but few, if any, will grudge this term to the position assigned to these gunners. Theirs was the responsibility of occupying the German front line on the extreme left flank of the attack, and for almost twelve hours they withstood countless enemy attempts to annihilate them -attempts made not only from the front, but also from the left flank, and still again from their rear, for bombing parties of the enemy, creeping out into "No Man's Land", assailed them with bomb and bullet. As may be expected, the toll taken of the two teams was heavy, their casualties at the end of the day being three killed, three wounded, and one wounded and missing. Privates Hanby and Fisher did especially splendid work.

And what of the battle as a whole? By 6.45 a.m. – an hour after zero – the walking wounded were filing through Vercingetorix, each giving – usually in the cryptic phrases so easily comprehended by all ranks – his

---

18 Awarded the D.C.M. for the attack on 13 November when in charge of two machine-guns he repelled several German bombing attacks, and accounted for many of the enemy.

own version of the position. Prisoners, too, appeared, the majority of them showing considerable jubilation at being on this side of "No Man's Land". One indeed, a sergeant-major, possessing the Iron Cross, actually danced his way along the whole length of Vercingetorix, so elated was he to have escaped the shambles a bare quarter-mile away.

It is only fair, at this point, to pay tribute to the courage and kindliness of several of these Germans. Our carrying parties afterwards reported that on their way to our lines they stopped, even where the shelling was very heavy, to bandage or help along a wounded Englishman.

From these, the walking wounded, and later from more authoritative sources, the true state of affairs was learned as the morning advanced. The Battalion's Lewis gunners had reached and were holding the pivotal point on the extreme left, the 12th East Yorkshires had gained the German second line, while the 13th, with orders to advance to the enemy third line, had reached the second, from which, because of the mud preventing their keeping up with the protecting barrage, they were unable to advance. Back in our lines, the 11th East Yorkshires, who were assembled in Caber waiting (and as events turned out, uselessly) for the order to reinforce, were subjected the whole day to a murderous enemy barrage which inflicted considerable casualties in that unit. To the immediate right, Serre – that stumbling block of July 1st – perched as it was on the summit of one of those slight rises so characteristic of the Ancre Valley, and thus commanding an almost bird's-eye view of our lines, had completely held up any advance by the 3rd Division.

And so the units of the 92nd Brigade found themselves isolated in the enemy lines, their right flank completely "in the air", their left flank being saved from a similar fate only so long as the fast-dwindling remnants of the two 10th Battalion Lewis gun teams could continue to beat off the determined attacks of the enemy. The only course was evacuation.

At 3.45 p.m. this was commenced and the remnants of our carrying parties and the six surviving gunners, with one gun intact, the other having been put completely out of action, re-joined the Battalion in Vercingetorix. At 7.30 p.m. the 13th York and Lancaster Regiment relieved us and we marched back to Bayencourt. On the 14th we moved back to Warnimont Wood.

It should be mentioned, however, that the Battalion bombers and the stretcher bearers, the whole under the M.O., spent the whole night searching the battlefield for the wounded. Their numbers were later augmented by a party of Brigade details, and such was their success that they were officially mentioned for their "excellent work".

Thus ended the second major operation in which the 10th had been directly concerned since its arrival in France eight months previously, and though for the second time no permanent success was achieved on the Divisional front, the Hull battalions have every right to remember with pride this glorious failure of November 13th, 1916. We may be confident that when, a few days later, Major-General Wanless O'Gowan, in complimenting the Battalion, said, "Our attack attracted the enemy fire and enabled the battalions on the right to take Beaumont Hamel and Beaucourt", he was not merely giving utterance to empty words, but was assessing the day's work at its true value. In fact, the Battle of the Ancre was largely the cause of the German retirement in February, 1917, and the sacrifices made by the 12th and 13th East Yorkshires were not in vain.

For the next two months life was wearisome in the extreme. Trench periods alternated with support and reserve spells at varying distances behind and with varying degrees of comfort. It was, and still is, a debatable question as to which was preferable – the quagmire-like trenches in and around Hébuterne with their complete lack of comfort, but still with a fairly definite assurance of periods on and periods off, or the so-called "rest" billets at Sailly, Courcelles, Couin, Coigneux, or Warnimont Wood, from which places the ever-necessary working parties trudged night after night up to the line, to return in the dawn of those December days with scarcely sufficient energy to make camp.

And yet, somehow, many pleasing memories of those "turns out of the line" persist in breaking through. Company and Battalion football matches will be readily recalled. Perhaps the match which has left the most lasting memory is the "A" Company v. "C" Company (3-2), for it was whilst the game was in progress that a touch of home was brought to us by the visit of the then Lord Nunburnholme and Colonel Easton. One can also, without much effort, live again those excursions to Authie, where Suzanne and her helpers could always be relied upon to serve a satisfying meal at any hour of the day. It was at Authie, too, that the Battalion, on January 4th, 1917, celebrated their second Christmas on active service.

Mention must here be made of the Battalion Band. Revived by Colonel Pearson after July 1st, 1916, and strongly encouraged by Colonel Stapledon, they had by the autumn become welded into a definite "unit", so that they were able to give performances which not only enlivened many an evening, but were both excellent and memorable. "The Tonics", too, were in constant service, but of them we will write more fully later.

A further point, worthy of recording whilst dealing with this period, is the promotion of several of our N.C.O.s to commissioned rank. Some took up their new responsibilities without even leaving the Battalion, whilst others managed a short spell across the Channel to return as Second Lieutenants, or, as the phraseology of the time would have it, as "temporary gentlemen". Of these, one and all, it may truly be said that never in the subsequent months did they belie the confidence placed in them. The ready acceptance of these few as officers by the men who but yesterday were their equals – and sometimes superiors – in rank, is testimony that the Battalion as a whole endorsed the opinion of those recommending the promotions.

Despite the diversions first alluded to, however, few members of the 10th felt any strong pang of regret when, on January 11th, 1917, our backs were turned on Authie, a lengthy rest in the back areas being in prospect. By route march we proceeded to Amplier, at which village the first part of the rest period was spent. Eleven days later, however, the Battalion moved once more, this time to Gezaincourt, where a further nine days were passed. This in turn was followed by yet another move, this time to Berneuil, a village only a few kilometres from Bernaville. At Berneuil our rest period was completed, the eighteen days there bringing the time in the back areas to five and a half weeks, by far the longest spell out of the battle area since the Battalion's arrival in France nearly twelve months previously.

A draft of seventy-four other ranks arriving on February 4th found us engaged in very light manoeuvres, Battalion and later Brigade attacks being the usual morning's routine. These operations, carried out in most peaceful surroundings and over country frozen to granite by a six weeks' unbroken frost, left us considerable freedom to renew acquaintance with civilisation at such places as Doullens, Bernaville, and even Amiens. It was at Bernaville that many of the Battalion saw the "Somme Film", in which the "gallant East Yorkshires" (our Battalion) were shown "going into action". Need we say that this part was the film mentioned earlier in the narrative?

The frost, the keenest and longest ever experienced by the majority of us, remained unbroken by a thaw for the whole of our stay in these back areas. In fact, a nightly rum ration was issued during this period – a thing unheard of previously. It was then that the art of "scrounging", so ably acquired by all during the last twelve months, was exploited to the full. Firewood, never a ration to the rank and file, became a necessity, for billets were cold and estaminets few. The neighbouring woods were raided surreptitiously, but even they could not produce sufficient small fuel, and many and varied were the means used to make supply and demand approximate. It is on record that one specialist section sacrificed to the flames the wash bench with which their billet yard was furnished. Perhaps, because of their long absence from such barrack-life equipment, it was only when the inventory was checked at the end of their stay that they realised what it really had been! The Battalion was fined one franc per man for barrack damages and the total, about 700 francs, was paid from canteen profits.

A further incident during this period of cold, and one worthy of recording, was the gallant attempt of the band during the route march to do their bit. One of Sousa's swinging marches was commenced, the jaded steps of the Battalion becoming appreciably lighter. Gradually, however, the tune wilted and finally faded into utter silence. The instruments, each in its turn, had frozen!

And so the weeks passed, rumour as ever, playing a changing theme throughout, but, as in most rumours there is the germ of truth, so eventually a story gained currency which materialised into a definite order, so that February 18th saw the Battalion changing quarters, once more to the line. These five and a half weeks, however, had undoubtedly served their purpose, for dispelled, and dispelled effectively, was that trench weariness that had become so apparent in each single man of the Battalion during the wet and weary welter of the weeks spent in and around Hébuterne.

For some considerable time, in fact ever since the attack of November 13th, the Fifth Army had been engaged in a series of nibbling activities to the south of Serre, with such results that by February the enemy had decided to evacuate a considerable frontage and withdraw to the Hindenburg Line. It was this move which brought the Battalion from the seclusion of Berneuil. From his point of view, the enemy had timed his evacuation to a minute, but from our side the same can scarcely be said. The frost which had gripped the earth with ever-increasing strength for six long weeks broke in a night, and that the night before the 92nd Brigade left the Bernaville area for the line. It was, therefore, along roads, at one time stretches of loose flints, at others long reaches of liquid mud, that we plodded through Beauval to Terramesnil, and the next day through Authie and Coigneux to Bayencourt, which was left the next day for rude shacks on the scarred slopes of Sailly Dell. Here the much-postponed final of the 92nd Brigade Inter-Company Football Competition was played, goal-posts being improvised from G.S. waggon poles lashed together. The field had a 9.2 howitzer mounted on each touch line and the gunners ceased fire to watch the match, which was won by "C" Company of the 10th, who beat "C" Company of the 13th East Yorkshires by 3-0. For four days this was our home, and a more depressing environment and conditions were never encountered. The sides of the dell, stripped of almost every vestige of timber and covered with huts, shacks and bivouacs, built for utility, not beauty, rose steeply on both sides of what was once the road, but was now a mile-long ribbon of mud, crowded at all times of the day and night with parties representing almost every branch of the British Army – troops and artillery moving forward, limbers squelching through with supplies for men and ammunition for guns, lorries lumbering along (and occasionally being ditched), and among it all the inevitable working party, often provided by the 10th, endeavouring to remake the road even as the legions passed over it.

But what really mattered was happening meanwhile three miles east, in and around Serre.

There, the 11th East Yorkshires had penetrated without opposition to the German third line, which position they were holding when at 1 a.m. on February 25th we were ordered to be in Papin Trench (Pylon Avenue) by 6 a.m. It is to the credit of each man that this was achieved. To the darkness of a February night was added the further handicap of fog, whilst the road from Sailly to Hébuterne had simply disappeared – swallowed up in the sea of mud which had been Hébuterne Plain.

After spending the day in Papin, "A" and "C" Companies at 5.30 p.m. crossed over, without opposition, to the German third line, but patrols which were immediately pushed forward by these Companies had, by 8 p.m., established touch with the enemy.

Early on the following morning, February 26th, Battalion headquarters and "B" and "D" Companies moved across the old "No Man's Land", having spent the night at the junction of Pasteur and the old front line. These parties, strangely enough, were subjected to considerable sniping and machine gun fire. Despite this interference, the majority of those making the crossing were strongly affected by the almost eerie silence and desolation which stretched away to the distant skyline. The effect of our many heavy bombardments was obvious, shell-hole overlapping shell-hole, the stagnant water in which filled the still February air with a stench nauseating in the extreme. Here and there, rising in straight pillars, columns of smoke identified German dugouts, fired by their late occupants before being evacuated.

Headquarters were established in Nameless Trench and contact with the 19th Division on the right and the 93rd Brigade on the left was made.

As was to be expected, information regarding the disposition and strength of the enemy was of the scantiest. It came as no surprise, therefore, when at 1 p.m. the Battalion was ordered to advance towards Slug Street and, if possible, to occupy this trench from Point 76 to La Louviere Farm. This advance was entrusted to "A" and "C" Companies.

"C" Company successfully occupied the farm and a portion of Slug Street, but on the left "A" Company met with such considerable resistance, especially at Point 76 that, handicapped as they were by the clinging mud and the totally unknown trench system, they were obliged to retire to Dugout Lane.

Whilst these two Companies were thus engaged, however, further orders were received instructing the Battalion to change direction left and occupy the sunken road (from A to B on the map) and if possible before dark to take the trench Berg Graben. This attempt, too, was unsuccessful,

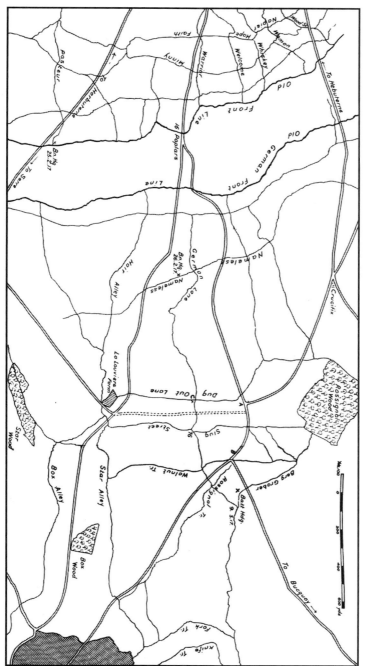

German withdrawal from the Somme Front, February–March 1917.

The Old Front Line, Serre, May 1919. (Looking north from Matthew Copse)

but in the darkness of the next morning, February 27th, the same Company made a further determined attack, unfortunately with little or no artillery support, which the enemy repulsed, chiefly by machine guns, from the south-east corner of Rossignol Wood and Berg Graben. It was in this skirmish that Captain S. E. Jones was reported killed, a report we were all delighted to hear negatived a few months later, when news came through that he was a prisoner, severely wounded. Second-Lieutenant Fricker was reported missing, and we learnt subsequently that he had been killed, as his body was recovered and buried.

These two encounters had shown that the enemy had either reached the limit of his retirement or was determined to fight as stubborn a rear-guard action as possible. Although future developments showed that the latter was the enemy's real intention, the need of the moment was the consolidating of the newly-acquired area. Strong points were established and when, sometime later, news was received that the units on both flanks had each been slightly driven back, "A", "B" and "C" Companies were withdrawn down Dugout Lane and constructed defensive positions along that trench (at point C on map) and German Lane, and the trench joining Nameless to Dugout Lane. Meanwhile, an Officer's Patrol had re-established contact

Hébuterne as the war left it.

Robecq, 1916–17.

Authie – Suzanne's.

with the 93rd Brigade on our left and 19th Division on our right. These measures were scarcely completed when, at 4 o'clock in the afternoon, the 12th East Yorkshires took over, and the Battalion squelched back to Sailly, and thence marched to hutments at Couin, where the following day, February 27th, the Divisional Commander expressed to the C.O. his pleasure at the work accomplished by the Battalion.

The cost of these last forty hours was officially computed as killed one officer, six other ranks; wounded one officer, thirty-three other ranks; missing one officer, two other ranks.[19]

A later tour in the sector on March 3rd[20] took us over the ground so recently assailed unavailingly by "A" and "B" Companies, Battalion headquarters actually being in Berg Graben near Rossignol Wood, amongst the stumps of which by this time our 18-pounders were firmly established. We were relieved on March 5th by the 11th East Yorkshires and moved

---

19 A German account states that the British suffered heavy losses, losing eighty prisoners and 200 killed in a rear-guard encounter near a little wood on the Gommecourt-Puisieux road. British official records give the losses as 8 men killed and three men dying of wound, one of whom, Sgt. Saunderson had won the DCM.

20 During this period the battalion lost three men.

back to Vercingetorix. On the 9th we again moved forward and relieved the 13th Battalion in the line. It was during this tour that rumour was most active. Gommecourt, Serre and Puisieux had already fallen – and it is interesting to recall what a comprehensive panorama we obtained from the ruins of Serre, of our old haunts – Monk Trench, Observation Wood, the Copses, Euston Dump, and Colincamps! The fate of Bucquoy was the chief topic of conjecture, and rumour assigned the taking of it to each battalion of the 92nd Brigade in turn. Our artillery, on March 9th, were concentrating on wire-cutting in front of that town, and on March 10th "D" Company were in position to launch an attack which was eventually called off, the mud rendering the carrying forward of the requisite ammunition impossible. But March 12th[21] saw the end of the tour without the Battalion having been called upon to make any further attempt to move forward. The continued retirement of the enemy to the Hindenburg Line completely erased the salient on this front so that when the 7th and 46th Divisions closed in on March 12th and took over our defences, the 31st Division was squeezed out, and the 10th again – and for the last time – made the long trek to the huts at Couin.

When, on March 19th, rumour having been effectively silenced by the cold truth of Battalion Orders of the previous night, we turned our backs on Couin in column of route for Terramesnil, few, if any, but gave vent to a sigh of relief – some even became definitely articulate – that the Ancre Valley was being left behind.

"The ills we wot not of"[22] were over the horizon, nebulous, the mud and squalor of our last sector were definitely material, even if not solid, and with each step westward spirits rose and memories faded. Our route from Terramesnil took us through back areas hitherto untouched by the Battalion, and in many places, apparently, by the war. Bonnieres was reached in a snowstorm on March 20th, but the next day's march to Croisette and Wignacourt via Frevent and Ecoivres was made in spring weather through delightful country. The 7th Battalion were at Oeuf; the next village, when we stayed at Croisette and old friends were visited. A further day's march via St. Pol and Valhuon brought the Battalion, on the 22nd, to Pernes, where a picture show – crude but acceptable – was available. A day's rest here enabled the band to show once more that its repertoire did not consist solely of Sousa's compositions, for they gave an exceptionally good concert, enjoyed by the villagers and troops alike.

---

21 One private was killed and one died of wounds on the last day of the tour.
22 Hull dialect - things to forget.

It was at the end of the next day's march that, at Estrée Blanche, a village with a dual personality – part old world and part colliery with typical rows of cottages – we made our first acquaintance with our Portuguese allies.

March 25th proved our last day on the road, our halting place this time being Robecq, which village we had left so grudgingly eight months previously. Although the weather was definitely wintry, the next fortnight spent here was keenly enjoyed, many old friendships being revived and new ones made, so that as a result of good billets, light training exercises, plenty of football, and long nights of unbroken sleep, it was a thoroughly reinvigorated Battalion which set off on the morning of April 8th for a cold and snowy march to Marles-les-Mines.

Chapter 10

The Third of May

THE news of the wonderful success at Vimy Ridge reached the Battalion the next morning, and the most elementary knowledge of map-reading was sufficient to permit the rank and file to deduce our next reappearance in the line. Such deductions, however, did not prevent the Battalion enjoying such touches of the outside world as came its way. At Marles-les-Mines, during a three days' halt, many had a night at the pictures, the main attraction being the "Bomb.Wells[23] – Colin Bell" fight. A further three days followed at Bruay, a substantial mining centre where, in addition to experiencing the comparative luxury of being billeted in private houses, the Battalion to a man enjoyed the best bath taken since leaving Ripon, the up-to-date pit-head showers being placed at the disposal of the troops.

It was at Bruay that any delusion that the past month's wanderings might have engendered that the 31st Division was on a Cook's Tour was finally dispelled when Lieut.- Colonel Stapledon left us to take an advance view of the trenches, and on April 14th the Battalion took a further step towards them by a nine-kilometre march to Diéval, a village sufficiently far from the line to be safe, but not so far as to suggest total severance from their old homes for a considerable number of refugees from Lens now settled there. It was interesting, but also strange, to learn that these refugees were looked upon by the villagers as foreigners and that little or no attempt to establish friendly relations had been made. Here, too, we met for the first time the 63rd (Naval) Division and we were not a little amused to find men wearing beards who spoke of their N.C.O.s as "Petty Officers" and whose cookhouse was the "Galley".

Nine days were spent here on training and practice attacks on the one hand, and sports and games in the afternoons. "A" Company's sports meeting was a most laudable effort, successfully organised under heavy handicaps.

The bombardment in the distance came as an unbroken rumble throughout the nights, but on April 23rd a thirteen and a half kilometre

---

23 Bombadier Wells – a heavyweight boxing champion.

march to Mingoval and Villers Chatel effectively altered its volume, and all realised that the long trail was almost ended. The outward and visible signs of war were again becoming apparent, our billets, two huge concrete-floored huts, being typical of the devastated areas. A bright spot, however, was provided by a visit to the near-by small town of Aubigny, at this time packed with troops of all types.

Three days later, April 28th, found the Battalion being added, as so many drops, to augment the seemingly endless stream pouring eastwards towards the Ridge. The roads, ankle deep in dust, which accompanied the column as a stifling cloud, were a revelation as to what state congestion may reach and yet allow progress to be made, and eventually the Battalion reached its destination for the night – Maroeuil.

We had billeted in villages far more battered than this, but there was about it a something difficult to define, a sense of desertion, of eeriness, which affected one and all. As one diarist puts it: "Went to bed early, nothing else to do", an entry worthy of Pepys in its expressiveness.

Our next three resting places brought us into closer contact with a greater desolation than we had hitherto known. Who does not remember the short march from Maroeuil to Ecurie – or rather "Ecurie, village, site of " – the extensive plain, until lately our support and reserve trenches, dominated by the imposing ruins of Mont St. Eloi,[24] the broad tracks now crossing it, beaten hard by the feet of those thousands who had been or were still to be hurled into the mad world, just over the far skyline? And finally our home (for that night), the Old Front Line, just south of the famous Labyrinth, on the Arras-Thélus Road?

And can one forget the next step forward? Map references in plenty we knew during our months in France, but none was so ineradicably seared into our minds as H.1.c. In peace time a pleasantly wooded dell leading off the Arras-Bailleul Road, now a shell-torn depression, its trees splintered to within a few feet of the ground, its sides honeycombed with old German galleries and dugouts, and, on the farther bank – grim reminder of that magnificent effort a fortnight before – the derelict tank.

It is interesting to record that here, during a later stay, was staged, despite the unorthodox contours and restricted dimensions of the ground, an inter-section football match, the winning team each receiving a five-franc note from their enthusiastic subaltern.

---

24 In 1915 heavy shelling reducing the height of the Mont St. Eloi towers from fifty-three to forty-four metres. In 1921 they were listed on France's register of ancient monuments.

It was on the way to H.1.c. in a road inches deep in the red brick dust from the shattered village of Roclincourt, that we again met, and exchanged greetings with, the gallant Naval Division, on their way out after acquitting themselves so well in attack and counterattack round Gavrelle Windmill.

And it was at H.1.c. that each man, in the dusk of April 30th, learned his part in the coming attack, and for each man this part seemed definitely unreal. The ignorance of the sector as a whole, the mystery of the land beyond that skyline only a short half-mile ahead, obscured the preparations with a haziness which was most undesirable. Certain officers and N.C.O.s from each company went on the night of May 1st to see the assembly position in front of Oppy, reporting to Brigade headquarters in the railway embankment on the way up. Returning on the morning of May 2nd, they spent the rest of the day issuing wire cutters, bombs, etc., to their respective companies. The same night they were back again leading their respective parties to the jumping-off position, and many officers and N.C.O.s were in poor physical state to meet the strenuous conditions which were to begin in a few hours' time.

The rest of the Battalion moved forward on May 1st, under cover of the dusk, to disused trenches and gun pits near Maison de la Coté, on the very crest of the Ridge, which fell away rapidly to the east, with the ruins of Bailleul immediately below us and the trees of Oppy Wood showing over the far skyline. From this vantage point, throughout Wednesday, May 2nd, we watched counter-battery duels, Oppy Wood and Bailleul being the respective targets. The shell-bursts in the village, of which we had almost a bird's-eye view, with the resultant clouds of brick-dust, the colour intensified by the setting sun, provided a picture gripping in its awfulness. And so came the night, and at 9.30 p.m. we moved forward to the great adventure.

Although Thursday, May 3rd, 1917, is looked upon by the survivors, and indeed by the City of Hull, as a whole, as the most fateful day in the history of the Brigade recruited from the city, it has to be admitted that when viewed in its proper relation to the French and British projects on the Western Front in general, the attack takes its place as an operation of no historical importance in spite of the number of troops engaged.

It will be recalled that by this time the French attack of April 16th on the Chemin des Dames had definitely failed, leaving the French Army temporarily demoralised. This meant that the Arras operations themselves no longer had any real objective, but it was obvious that the British would have to exert constant pressure on the Germans to give the French time to recover. A big attack at Messines and Ypres was being prepared, but until this could be launched the French had to be relieved of the enemy pressure as much as possible. With this in view and also in order to mask their true intentions to the north, the Higher Command had ordered a series of minor operations, with shallow objectives only.

Such a minor operation was that of May 3rd, although twelve divisions were engaged, these divisions being drawn from the First, Third, and Fifth Armies, and the total length of front attacked was nearly twelve miles.

From the 31st Division, the 92nd and 93rd Brigades supplied the assault troops, the Hull Brigade being on the left with the West Riding Battalions on their right. The disposition of the three attacking battalions of the 92nd Brigade, from left to right, was 12th, 11th and 10th East Yorkshires, so that we found ourselves between the 11th East Yorkshires and the 93rd Brigade.

The objectives, as stated previously, were shallow, the Support Trench of the enemy's system being fixed as the limit of penetration, this depth, on our front, embracing the whole of Oppy Wood. It is admitted in the Divisional records that no great results were expected from this attack – its main object being to keep the enemy occupied – which only adds poignancy to the tragedy of May 3rd.

It must here be recorded that the same front had been attacked by British troops only a few days previously, April 28th-29th, and the chaos resultant upon that vain endeavour was still in marked evidence when the Battalion, leaving the crest above Bailleul at 9.25 p.m. on May 2nd, moved forward to take up assembly positions by 11 p.m. The assembly trench itself was a map reference rather than an actuality, for the taping party of May 1st had found it to be merely an isolated untraversed length of trench barely four feet deep, with no communication to the rear, nor any means of contact to left or right. So exposed was the position that the 13th East Yorkshires, who had been holding the line for the previous two or three days, had already suffered some 100 casualties.

It was into such forbidding surroundings, with no familiar landmark either to cheer or direct them, that our men felt their way. The first wave was to be in two separate lines, twenty yards and ten yards, in front of the assembly trench, the second wave in the trench itself; the third 100 yards in the rear, while the fourth, "D" Company, was to establish a strong point in the trench, which they were to hold under orders from the G.O.C. 92nd Brigade.

Such were the operation orders, and officers and men, individually and collectively, valiantly endeavoured to put them into effect. A combination of circumstances and incidents, however, proved too strong, so that none of those present when the attack was launched wondered that it proved abortive.

At least three of the incidents must be mentioned. Firstly, during the assembly of the attacking troops in their battle positions, the moon, within a few days of being full, rode low in the sky, so that the lines of men,

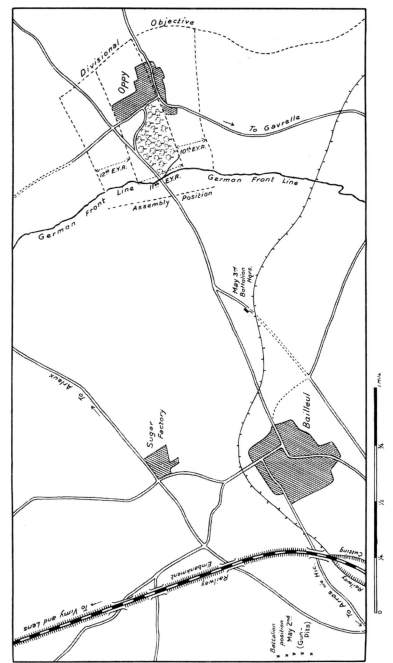

Oppy Wood Operation, 3 May 1917.

moving forward over the series of ridges to the low ground in front of Oppy Wood, formed perfect silhouettes as seen from the German lines.

A second disturbing factor was provided by an enemy aeroplane which, flying low through the night, passed over the assembling troops. That the observer was able to realise what was afoot there can be no doubt.

Finally, about midnight, an enemy patrol of four or six men was sighted. The hurried retirement of this enemy group was taken as a definite sign that they had seen or heard quite sufficient to make an immediate report to their headquarters imperative.

It is certain that one or other, or all, of these incidents must be held responsible for the intense barrage which fell on the assembly trench at 12.30 a.m. The companies, tired though they were by the carrying of stores the previous afternoon followed by the short but unnerving march to the forward positions, had perforce to set about making their shell-holes still deeper. After twenty minutes a lull in the bombardment gave the various commanders an opportunity of re-organising their units.

This respite, however, was all too short, for at 1.30 a.m. a second barrage, more fierce than the last, fell on our lines. This, excepting a few short periods, continued right up to zero hour. So prolonged was this bombardment, indeed, that though casualties were few, confusion was caused by the men moving away from it, for a move of even a few yards from one's original position made it impossible to recognise that position again under the conditions which then obtained.

Such then was the disposition of the Battalion at zero, 3.45 a.m. – theoretically in four distinct waves, actually occupying a maze of shell-holes measuring 100 yards from front to rear, the whole area being mercilessly pounded by the enemy. Then, on the stroke of zero, the British barrage opened in all its intensity, and, as though he were now convinced that an attack was being launched, the enemy augmented his own bombardment, the combined result being a chaos indescribable.

The word to go forward, however, was given and, by all who were able, acted upon. In the darkness which had succeeded the setting of the moon, murderous machine gun fire swept the whole front, and rockets and Verey lights of every colour shot up from the German lines, but the attacking waves moved steadily forward, although the enveloping blanket of mist and fumes made the keeping of direction an impossibility. Is it to be wondered that by 5 a.m., as dawn crept over the sky, the forward movement was checked? In that brief hour the impossible had been attempted and much heroism had been achieved by almost every man in the forward positions, but, granting that these pages were the place, the tale is too long to be told.

Each of the survivors must cherish the individual and personal memories of that morning which he himself carries.

That some pierced the enemy defences is certain. One man – Private Green,[25] of "A" Company – actually brought in eight prisoners, whilst after-the-war tales reveal that most of the prisoners taken by the enemy were captured in Oppy village.

Private Green's account when reporting to Battalion headquarters after taking the prisoners to the Brigade Prisoners' Cage may be quoted from memory as follows:

"I went forward with the first wave of 'A' Company. I found myself alone and approaching a trench in which there was a German machine gun with a crew of twelve. They had stopped firing for a moment and I threw a Mills bomb which wrecked the gun, killed four men and wounded one, and the others then threw up their hands. Just then, Captain J. C. Addy jumped into the trench and when he saw the prisoners he said, 'You'd better take them back, Green, you seem to have done your bit for to-day.' I brought the prisoners back, left the wounded man at the Advanced Aid Post and was told where the Prisoners' Cage was at Brigade so I took them there".

Here is a short account of the day as submitted by one who was taken prisoner:

"When our barrage opened, we moved forward. Although there was considerable enemy machine gun fire, little was directed at us, so that, walking across 'No Man's Land,' I almost had the feelings of a spectator. Two of us crossed the German front line – levelled by our bombardment – without seeing anything of the enemy. At a huge shell-hole, we parted to pass on opposite sides, and I saw him no more (he was afterwards reported missing and believed killed).

"Still walking forward in the growing light, I became aware of a small party from 'A' Company, under Lieutenant Akester. Under his orders, we took up a position in an old trench, with Oppy village sixty or seventy yards away on our left front. We appeared to be isolated, and the sound of firing and bombing from a considerable distance to the rear seemed to indicate that the enemy's front line had not been taken.

---

25 Private Green was awarded the D.C.M. for destroying a machine gun post and taking some of its crew captive.

"The officer left us to endeavour to make contact with some other party which might also have broken through, and, as our position had now been discovered, we engaged in a machine gun duel with an enemy party about 150 yards ahead. I was with a gun on the extreme right of and somewhat detached from our party, and so was not aware of all that took place. When a group of the enemy left their cover and advanced towards us, I prepared to open fire on what appeared to be the best target yet presented. A yell, 'Cease fire,' however, caused me to pause, and I learned that some sign of surrender had been made further to the left. And so an action which would have been dubbed 'base treachery' was narrowly averted. It should be added that the officer named was no party to the surrender – he had not returned from his reconnaissance".

And for those laying out in front of Oppy Wood commenced as harrowing a day as any had either experienced or imagined. Day, a brilliant spring morning, had broken. Movement with safety was impossible. Even the shell-holes and the wrecked assembly trench were insufficient cover, for the enemy snipers in the trees overlooked these, and inflicted heavy casualties.

Back at Battalion headquarters considerable anxiety prevailed as to what the coming night might bring, and runners gallantly made the crossing to the advance positions, dodging from shell-hole to shell-hole, to carry messages and to ascertain the true position, and so enable some order to be restored. Telephonic communication was impossible – lines had long ago disappeared, attempts to re-establish them being discontinued after over an hour's work by the Signalling Officer, Lieutenant J. St. C. Richardson, and two men, who got no more than fifty yards from headquarters, but Lieutenant Richardson, with one orderly, subsequently made his way down to the front line in his own inimitable manner as if out for an afternoon's stroll.

And the enemy artillery kept up a barrage of varying intensity the whole day and our shells poured unceasingly into the wreck of village and wood.

But the day, apparently interminable, ended at last, and with the dark arrived the 11th East Lancashires to take over. The remnants of the Battalion dragged themselves first from their shell-holes, then over the top to Bailleul village, and lastly along the long road to the divisional huts near Ecurie, the last named being reached by dawn of May 4th.

It was then that the result – and the cost – of the last twenty-four hours could be definitely assessed. The Battalion went into the line for the attack about 550 strong. The total casualties were 231 including the four Company Commanders and all officers other than those at Battalion headquarters;

Oppy and Vimy Front, back areas, 1917.

Captains J. C. Addy and R. Carlisle, who had been with us since the very first days being amongst the killed.

The first casualty returns showed: officers – one killed, seven wounded, six missing; other ranks – seven killed, 103 wounded, 107 missing; but most of the missing were subsequently reported killed and many of the wounded succumbed to their injuries.[26]

In addition to the incidents already described which undoubtedly contributed to this grand failure, one must mention the fact that consequent upon the attack launched on the same sector on April 28th-29th, and the frequent bombardments, Divisional headquarters had surmised that the attack of May 3rd would be met by shaken and demoralised troops, whereas events showed that our attempt followed immediately upon the strong reinforcement of the enemy lines by fresh troops.[27] In fact, it is now thought that the Germans were themselves preparing an attack on this front, but, however that may be, "May 3rd" remains a day the memories of which the survivors and, in fact, Hull as a whole, will always hold dear.

---

26 Soldiers Died in the Great War gives the total as 4 officers and 68 men killed and one died of wounds the next day.

27 The German troops in Oppy were the 1st and 2nd Guards Reserve Divisions, described by the regimental history as 'some of the bravest of the enemy's troops'.

Chapter 11

Vimy Ridge – "The Tonics"

For the first few days which followed, the remnants of the Battalion were formed into a composite Company, and when the strength had been made up again by fresh drafts, there followed a series of short tours in the line, followed by equally short periods in support and reserve.

During one of these tours,[28] a 5.9 fell on a Battalion ration party, killing five of them and leaving the rest dazed and apparently not capable of making any attempt to go on. The arrival of the R.S.M. and an N.C.O. however, galvanised them into activity and such of the rations as had escaped the effects of the shell-burst were taken on their allotted journeys, but it seems to be generally agreed that rations were short that day.

Ecurie, Roclincourt, St. Catherine, and St. Eloi each knew us in turn, and for nearly a month almost every night brought intense bombardment along the whole front, with the consequent "Stand to" for the Battalion, although, except for the repulse of an enemy bombing raid during the night of May 6th-7th, no further engagement fell to our lot during this time.

It was on June 6th and 8th at St. Eloi that, as an antidote to the nerve-racking effects of the past few weeks, our first Battalion Sports were organised, officers and men entering with extreme keenness. The events provided some exciting contests, and the final pull in the Tug-of-War between "A" and "D" Companies was a really great effort.

The Higher Command however, was still desirous of deluding the enemy that the Arras Battle continued to be a major operation. To achieve this, two raids on the enemy position were launched on June 22nd and June 28th respectively. In the latter stunt the Battalion was not called upon, being held as Brigade Reserve, "A" and "B" Companies being in East Bailleul Post, with headquarters and "C" and "D" Companies in the Red Line.

For the raid on June 22nd, however, each Battalion of the 92nd Brigade provided two officers and fifty other ranks, the whole being under the command of Lieut.-Colonel Ferrand of the 11th. The objective was the enemy trench known as Cadorna, to the south of Oppy.

---

28 This was 7 May when four men were killed and one died of wounds.

The raid was a complete success; our barrage commenced at 10.20 p.m. and under its protection, Cadorna was rushed. Enemy garrisons were encountered in front of the trench, and these were dispersed or captured. Cadorna itself proved to be obliterated and untenable, but beyond, the wire was found to be in excellent condition. The chief enemy counter-activity came from Oppy Wood, whence a machine gun swept the line of attackers. The purpose of the raid having been effected, the withdrawal was ordered, the Battalion's contingent bringing with them seven prisoners.[29]

From then on, throughout the summer and autumn of 1917, the life of the Battalion was made up of a long series of tours in and out of the trenches. Our rest billets for this period were at Ecoivres, Bray and St. Eloi, our reserve position at Roclincourt, Ecurie and Neuville St. Vaast, whilst our sectors stretched from Vimy on the north to Gavrelle in the south. An unfortunate bombing accident occurred during training at St. Eloi, resulting in the death of Captain Clark and the wounding of Lieutenant Willis and several other ranks. On July 11th the Battalion, along with other troops, was to be "inspected" by H.M. King George V, and we marched to Madagascar Road near La Targette corner, where we fell out on the roadside. We were informed that the King would drive in an open car down the road where we were supposed to have just fallen out for the usual ten minutes halt while on the march. His appearance was to be the signal for us all to be very surprised at seeing him and to get up and give a hearty cheer as he went by. The day, however, was dull and chilly, and as we had waited in expectancy much longer than we anticipated, by the time His Majesty appeared, we found it difficult to carry out the Higher Command's orders to look surprised and pleased, and it must be recorded that the cheering lacked something of spontaneity and enthusiasm. The King looked worn and pre-occupied and we marched back to camp feeling that with better timing of the whole thing it might not have fallen quite so flat.

It was in July, too, that we relieved the Canadian forces for the first time, their optimism and happy-go-lucky attitude to the war and life generally, appealing strongly to us all. An example of this casualness is afforded by the following conversation which took place as one of our Company Commanders entered a dugout to relieve the Canadian occupants:

Canadian officer: "Hello, boys! Are you the Imperial troops? "
10th officer: "We are".

---

29 Privates Percy Martindale and Walter Raymond Homan were killed during the raid.

Canadian: "Well, son, we'll be off, then. Here's a jar of rum, and there's the map. So long!"

The periods in the line were almost devoid of interest, the only other incident worthy of mention being the raid of September 12th, carried out by three officers and forty other ranks. The raid was entirely successful, valuable information being brought in, but this success was marred by the death of Second-Lieutenant Southern.

Throughout the whole of this period, however, the anxiety in the minds of the Higher Command was apparent even to the rank and file of the Battalion. Every occupation to which the troops were put was given a sinister interpretation, and rumour, far from being the inconstant and lying jade we had so often proved her, stuck to the same tale throughout the whole of the autumn and winter of 1917 – the enemy was going to attack.

Needless to say, few idle days were spent, especially out of the line. There, our tasks were varied, but all had the same purpose – the achievement of fitness and efficiency.

Near the line, in reserve, the Battalion provided innumerable working parties, who, leaving quarters (perhaps bivouacs on Roclincourt Plain, perhaps huts at Ecurie cross-roads) in the soft light of a perfect August evening, or (later on in the year) in the mud and mist of a November afternoon, would spend the night digging, either consolidating existing systems, building a strong post here, a machine gun emplacement there, or scarifying hitherto untouched areas in the making of new and complicated defence systems. It is good to realise now that this dreary round was not time wasted. The works then constructed contributed materially to the smashing of the German offensive of March 28th, 1918, against Vimy Ridge.

Further back, when at Ecoivres, St. Eloi, or Bray, fitness and efficiency in another direction were achieved. Football matches were arranged at the shortest of notices, and were played at the most unorthodox times and places. Do many remember the match at Ecurie, the field ringed round by horse lines, when the enemy decided to shell the balloon with 8-inch shrapnel?

But the main business was training, and training as intensive as it could be made. The rifle and bayonet range at Bray saw much of the Battalion, and memories of Hornsea and Wormald Green came back. Field days were frequent, almost every contingency being anticipated and practised.

An outstanding event in this connection is worthy of inclusion. On November 15th, 1917, a platoon of "B" Company, who some time previously had qualified for the signal honour by an inter-brigade contest, competed in the final of the XIII Corps Platoon Competition. The officers of the two finalist platoons were given (on the map) the position and limits of a hypothetical strong point. The contest was to decide who made the better attempt at its capture. The occasion whilst partly in the nature of a diversion for the actual participants, was of immense importance to the Corps Staff, and the contest was watched by numerous staff officers, from the Corps Commander to our own Brigadier and their following. A sector of the Old Front Line near Ecurie was chosen, the ploughed-up nature of which provided sufficient obstacles to give realism. Our platoon attacked first, followed by their rivals. The result was a flattering reflection on the efficiency of the 10th, both officers and men alike, for the final marks allotted read: 10th East Yorkshire Regiment, 88.6 per cent; rival Platoon, 54.0 per cent.

At Christmas everything was in favour of the proper festivities. To begin with, the Battalion was out of the line for a full month's rest, the 93rd Brigade taking over the line for this period as promised by G.O.C. Division. Secondly, and equally important, was the unexpected dispersal to the Battalion of all back pay since the "dependants" allowance was paid in full by the War Office from the previous September, and the Battalion was not slow in taking full advantage of this fortuitous combination of circumstances.

Towards the end of the year, the possibility of an enemy offensive had become noticeably stronger. This was apparent in our later tours in the line, for the S.O.S. signal was frequently sent up, and the assigning of S.O.S. positions to the trench garrison was a regular feature of trench manning; but it was not to fall to the lot of the Battalion to be in the line when the enemy struck, for on March 4th, a month after the Brigade had been reorganised into three battalions – the 10th and 11th East Yorkshires and the 11th East Lancashires, the other two Hull battalions being broken up – we moved from Mont St. Eloi by train and march route to Monchy Breton, near St. Pol.

The re-organisation, in February, 1918, of Brigades on a three-battalion basis was carried out by order of the Army Council, the original idea, according to one historian, being to allow of the eventual brigading of American troops in British Divisions.[30] A large party from the 12th Battalion had joined us, and the friendly feeling which had always existed between the two Battalions ensured that the newcomers were soon at home with the "10th".

---

30 The reorganisation was due to insufficient troops being released for overseas service although tens of thousands were available.

Oppy Wood, 1917 (aerial photo).

Mont St Eloy from La Targette Road.

The ground behind Oppy Wood, 1917.

March 4th proved to be the last day we should spend in the Vimy area. From now on we were to see other parts of the Western Front and to find other adventures. From now on our journeys took us to sketchy outpost lines and semi-open warfare, and never again were we to see the seven-foot deep front and support lines trenches and the three and four-mile long communication trenches with which we had grown so familiar during the last nine months.

For us, though we did not know it, the stalemate of trench warfare was over.

Before leaving this sector, however, it will be both opportune and fitting to pay tribute to that small but gifted group who, in fair and foul, did so much to lift us above the squalor of war and show us glimpses of a world where music and laughter still had their places.

> "We're the Tonics gay, and we sing and play,
>   In a pierrot way every night.
>   And with song and jest, we all do our best
>   To cheer up your lives when you're out on rest.
>   When you've done your time, six days in the line
>   And you want to be merry and bright,
>   Come and see the Tonics, yes the good old Tonics
>   In their pierrot show at night.

How often and in what varied settings has this opening chorus served as a prelude to an evening's entertainment full of variety, yet having each and every item bearing the hallmark of talent.

It would have been strange had not the 10th Bn. East Yorkshire Regiment, recruited as it was in September, 1914, possessed many who, though very imperfect soldiers at that time, were already firmly-established favourites with the music lovers of Hull and district. The fact that there were many such was apparent during the Hornsea days, for it became a usual thing for a visiting concert party to augment its numbers from the ranks of the Battalion, the items of these volunteers being by no means the least appreciated.

Later, at Ripon, where amusements were not of the intimate nature of the Hornsea canteen concerts, the two-fold desire of this group – a desire for self-expression in the midst of routine military life, together with the perhaps greater desire to share their gifts with, and relieve the monotony of, their fellows – found its outlet in those memorable occasions when they hired the local Assembly Rooms and gave good value to soldiers and civilians alike.

On these occasions the performance of the Town Horn Blower, heard in the distance during an interval, served rather as a foil than as a rival.

From June 1915, however, to June 1916, few opportunities came along for further combined efforts. Nevertheless, there was that memorable evening of December 16th, 1915, in Valletta Harbour, when, in the slanting rays of the setting sun, with the ship's hatches for platform and the whole ship's company ringing them about, the artistes sang the familiar songs, and cracked jokes which, though old, succeeded in bringing back the smiles which the previous week's buffeting had banished.

Nor must we forget those delightful efforts in the dusk and shadows of Warnimont Wood in the spring of 1916, the novelty of the setting and the quality of the renderings making a bright spot in an otherwise colourless period.

But it was September 1916 which saw the inauguration of "The Tonics" proper. By this time the members of the party had, along with the rest, realised that the war was likely to last some considerable time and had decided to do their bit on more orthodox lines. To this end white pierrot costumes with black poms and skull caps had been obtained, the appearances in service uniform becoming with this innovation a thing of the past.

It was September 23rd, 1916, when "The Tonics" were honoured for the first time by a visit of the Brigadier-General and his Staff. The General was undoubtedly impressed by the quality and tone of the performance, and showed a kindly trait when he suggested a "repeat" for the benefit of those who had been unable to gain admittance. Needless to say, the "repeat" was immediately given, and there must be many who remember that huge barn at Vieille Chapelle, with its platform only slightly raised, the hangings and curtains of that flimsy canvas-like material which one usually associates with the farthest corner of a camp, and the canteen candles, stuck in biscuit tins, to serve as footlights.

Whether this visit of the General marked the end or the beginning of a train of thought on the subject of a Brigade Concert Party we do not know, but it was shortly after this that "The Tonics" were informed that they were to be transferred to the 92nd Brigade headquarters, and were to be relieved of front-line duties so that rehearsals and preparations might be uninterrupted.

Captain Douglas Oake, 92nd T.M.B., was appointed officer-in-charge, a piano was purchased, and Corporal Bartindale, having been given the post of producer, was despatched on leave to purchase costumes and draperies.

At Brigade the "patron saint" of "The Tonics" was undoubtedly Captain L. Thorns. It was due to his tremendous enthusiasm and kindly help that the early troubles of the party were so effectively overcome, and it was he who, whenever possible, obtained for the party billeting accommodation suitable for their requirements.

It must not be supposed, however, that from then on "The Tonics" ceased to be soldiers. Far from it, for their duties were many and varied, especially when operations demanded an advanced Brigade headquarters. There, the members of the party provided gas guards, acted as guides and runners and as sentries in charge of ammunition dumps. During the March and April retirements of 1918 they all did excellent service.

A tragic note was struck on August 8th, 1918, when the party was robbed of their deservedly popular officer, Captain D. Oake, who on that day was killed by a premature Stokes shell. As a sign of the esteem in which he was held, the evening performance was cancelled.

And so "The Tonics" went on to the very end. Their "theatres" were those places which happened to be available and convenient – or that could be made convenient by the efforts of the Pioneers. The open-air, old barns, hangars, Y.M.C.A. and C.A. Huts, churches, officers' messes, civil theatres (Audricq and Halluin), a cotton mill at Maroeuil – all these in turn resounded to the applause and chorus singing of men temporarily lifted above the stagnating influence of war.

The programmes throughout were of a very high order. The generally-accepted theory that the *risqué* song and joke was an essential in such shows was entirely disproved and throughout their existence "The Tonics" both of their own accord and also by the wish of the Brigadier, served up a show at the cleanness of which none could cavil.

Occasionally unrehearsed incidents occurred, but "The Tonics" were sufficiently alert and experienced to profit from them. In this connection might be mentioned the occasion at Couin, when during the performance in the Church Army Hut, three long-range shells fell uncomfortably near. The comedian, who was just preparing to "do his turn" seized the opportunity and brought the house down by making his entrance in his tin-hat!

It will be realised by all that in a brief survey such as this of the Battalion as a whole, it is impossible to refer at length to the many items given by "The Tonics" during their two very full years as Brigade entertainers. It must suffice to mention but a few, trusting that these few will be immediately augmented by the memory of the reader.

Perhaps the most outstanding sketch presented was the burlesque, "The Orderly Room". The trials and tribulations of a C.O. were perfectly caricatured, whilst the entry of the "German prisoner" never failed to convulse completely every man in the packed house. "George, V.C". and "The Revue" both enjoyed deservedly long runs, whilst Harry Tate's

"Motoring" with the famous moustache working as effectively as its creator intended it should, invariably "got across".

The appeal of the high-class items, whether solo baritone or tenor, or duets, was never questioned, the truth of this being apparent when, as at the Annual Dinner, our friends of "The Tonics" are pressed to give some of the old numbers.

As a last mention, we must include the duet "If you were the only girl", in which the histrionic powers of the female impersonator, though taxed, proved equal to the occasion, so much so, that "she" went on from success to success.

The high quality of "The Tonics" soon took their name beyond the confines of the Brigade, so that they were frequently "loaned". A very successful tour of Canadian Y.M.C.A.s was made, several C.C.S.s were given "free shows", whilst adjacent R.F.C. squadrons successfully solicited their services.

Here fit mention may be made of the great assistance rendered by the band of the 11th East Lancashires, under Bandmaster Perry, who provided the musical accompaniment for "The Revue".

The full personnel of "The Tonics" might be of interest: (The late) Captain D. Oake, Officer I./C. and Light Comedian; Sergeant M. Wikner, Character Comedian; Corporal W. S. Bartindale, Comedian and Producer; Lance-Corporal A. A. Lamb, Light Comedian; Private E. E. Draper, Baritone; Private A. Tinn, Tenor; Private R. C. Hall, Female Impersonator; Private Farnill-Clayton, Pianist.

Guest artistes who frequently augmented the programme included Captain Cyril Oake, Lieutenant T. Brandon, and Private Betting de Boer.

Chapter 12

The German Advance of March 21st, 1918

NEVER was a large-scale enemy attack more certain than in early 1918.

The Russian front had disappeared during February, releasing enormous numbers of men and guns for use against our Western Front. France was so exhausted that the British Army had taken over another twenty-eight miles of her line around St. Quentin in January, though our army was very weary after Passchendaele and Cambrai.

But Germany knew now that her submarine campaign had failed, and that the Americans were surely coming. So it was clearly 1918 – or never – for her; our turn might come in 1919.

Knowing that the Germans had as many men in the West as the allies, with probably 500,000 in reserve, the British Army had spent the winter months in organising its front, for defence, into three zones – a forward outpost area, a main battle area, and a final defensive area.

Thus, as has already been described, the Battalion in company with the rest of the 31st Division, had been working steadily at the wiring of the defences on the Arleux-Gavrelle front-defences which were destined to help to break the big German attack on March 28th. But spring, 1918, found us resting twenty miles behind the Arleux sector, and carrying out training about four miles east-north-east of St. Pol, at Monchy Breton.

The first hint that the long-expected German offensive might have begun came on March 21st. Throughout that day, at regular five-minute intervals, the important railway junction of St. Pol was shelled by a long-range enemy gun. The actual discharge could be heard; seconds after came the slowly-increasing hum of the approaching shell until the air overhead was filled with the horrid din, which as gradually died away to complete silence; perhaps two seconds more would pass before the dull "boom" of the shell's explosion was heard – and this from dawn till dusk all that memorable day. So little, however, did this long-range bombardment, or the heavy strafing from the direction of the line concern us at the time that "D" Company beat the Transport Section by 5-3 at football when the day's work was over.

But we saw matters in a different light at midnight, when Battalion Runners awakened everyone with orders for a 4.30 a.m. "Reveille", because of the enemy attack on the Third Army front.

So we paraded at 7.30 next morning, and marched through La Thieuloye, where the 11th Battalion had been billeted, on to the main Arras-St. Pol road, where a line of old London 'buses was waiting. They set off at 10.30 a.m. through St. Pol (which seemed surprisingly little damaged, although the shelling continued intermittently) and on via Frevent and Doullens, until they halted about nine miles from Arras; then a short march brought us to Bailleulmont about 3.45 p.m. Very heavy firing could be heard "up the line", and rumours filled the air-the most persistent being that the enemy had advanced from two to five miles on a ninety-mile front. (Actually the front attacked stretched for forty-three miles from Croisilles on the River Sensee to the River Oise.) But Bailleulmont seemed a comfortable billet, and when "the Army" with its usual inconsequence, ordained a pay-day immediately we arrived, even the most "windy" buried his fears and hoped that "the 10th" was going to keep out of the trouble after all.

However, matters soon began to look more serious; after tea orders came "to be prepared to move at twenty minutes' notice"; worse still, a percentage of each Company was detailed to return to the Quartermaster's Stores as reinforcements – the inevitable prelude to a battle.

The Battalion fell in at 8.30 p.m., but stood shivering and inactive near the village church till midnight, while a hellish strafe went on up the line, and an enemy 'plane dropped its bombs near the village.

That march, when at long last a move forward was made, is well-nigh indescribable. Certainly it was moonlight, but that only served to show up the severity of the bombardment which the villages along the road had suffered. Progress was hindered by houses which had collapsed across the road, while recent shell-holes had to be skirted, and to men unutterably weary after standing fully laden for three and a half hours, and only half able to guide their feet through lack of sleep, the march developed into a sheer test of will-power to "stick it", as hour after hour they blundered on. The men soon marched in a half-conscious state and had to be rudely shaken to awaken them after the regulation halts. To add to the horror, some building miles ahead was burning fiercely. This, in time, proved to be an Expeditionary Force Canteen, and that it was being burned to prevent it falling into the enemy's hands showed the seriousness of the situation.

At 6 a.m., as daylight broke, we reached our destination – a sunken road beyond Hamelincourt on the Army Line which ran to the east of Boisleux-au-Mont – and though it was now perishingly cold, we lay down and slept on the roadside, until awakened by the din of a bombardment from the

Bullecourt direction. With the sunshine, spirits rose again, particularly when we learned that those units of the 31st Division which had been rushed "up the line" by 'bus during the night had not "gone over"; it was doubtful whether the Germans had even captured our third line in these parts.

Actually, Sir Douglas Haig's despatch reports that "on the 23rd the 31st Division (Major-General R. J. Bridgford, C.B., C.M.G., D.S.O.) drove off the attacks of two enemy divisions about St. Leger, with heavy loss, although Croisilles had been evacuated by the 34th Division during the night".

Then, after a good breakfast, it was learned, as usual, that ours was "the reserve Battalion of the Brigade which was in Divisional Reserve". Despite this heartening news we spent the morning in improving a line of trenches which we now occupied, and in moving boxes of bombs and ammunition, to the accompaniment of heavy artillery fire.

About 2 p.m. the Battalion moved slightly south along the road into trenches near Ervillers (seven and a half miles south of Arras), the 92nd Brigade having taken over about 2,500 yards of line running north-west from the centre of the village. The 11th East Yorkshires were on the right of this front with the 11th East Lancashires on the left, whilst we were in reserve just west of Ervillers.

These trenches would appear to have been the rear line of the "battle zone" defences, but they were in a very half-finished state – scarcely waist deep and quite without dugouts or barbed wire. We started to dig at once, but the enemy soon spotted us and the position was heavily strafed for half an hour about 5 p.m.

Sunday, March 24th, was spent in still further improving the line and in waiting for something to happen. (Sir Douglas Haig reports that though the enemy had taken Mory early that morning, after continuous fighting, "our troops substantially maintained their positions – the Guards, 3rd and 31st Divisions, beating off a series of heavy attacks".)[31]

On the left of the 92nd Brigade was the 93rd Brigade, on the right the Guards Brigade, but south of Ervillers the line was uncertain and two Companies of the 10th East Yorkshires had been ordered up, early on the 24th, to form a defensive flank. During the afternoon it was evident that there was fierce fighting to the east and south of the village. (Actually, in the early afternoon the enemy had forced a gap between the Third and Fifth Armies, south of Le Transloy and captured Combles: his continued advance threatened to sever the two armies, so the IV and V Corps on the

---

31 The battalion lost 13 men killed in action.

right of the 92nd Brigade were ordered to withdraw to a line running from Bazentin, through Le Sars and Grevillers to Ervillers. This withdrawal was completed under great difficulty, but communication between the IV and V Corps was never properly established.)

About 8.30 p.m. the troops, who had been holding the line began to drift through Ervillers with the enemy in close pursuit and soon the 11th East Yorkshires were engaging him in the village streets. "A" and "B" Companies of the 10th Battalion moved up to help them, while "C" and "D" Companies also went forward. Our men did excellent work on the right flank, by dealing with the strong German patrols, who were causing much trouble; they captured an officer and ten men and one light machine gun.

March 25th was an anxious day as the enemy maintained great pressure from Ervillers towards the south. (Indeed the 10th Battalion Manchester Regiment (42nd Division) who reinforced the 11th East Yorkshires, claimed that they had repulsed eight attacks on Ervillers during the day.) From 7 a.m. to 10 a.m. the Germans attacked the village continuously, and again at 1 p.m. About 4 p.m. the position began to look very ugly, for the Trench Mortar Battery and the Machine Gun Company retired to defensive positions near Battalion headquarters. Soon afterwards the troops on the left began to evacuate hurriedly, and to make matters worse our Heavy Artillery started to fire "short" all round Battalion headquarters just after the 92nd Brigade headquarters had retired, and cut off telephonic communication, so that it was some time before a runner could correct the range for the gunners. At last, about 7 p.m., the Germans got a footing in the village – but they could not capture it.[32]

So Ervillers held out until orders came to withdraw at 9.30 p.m.; unfortunately, these orders never reached No. 5 Platoon, which, under Sergeant R. Emslie's command, held on until next morning when most of them were surrounded and captured soon after dawn. (The retirement was necessary because the IV and V Corps to the south had failed to establish communication, so that the right flank of the former had been pressed back until the Germans had captured Grévillers, while, further south still, hostile patrols had reached the right bank of the River Ancre, north of Miraumont and were pushing on towards Puisieux and Serre, nearly ten miles south-west of Ervillers. Hence, during the night, the IV Corps fell back to the line Bucquoy-Ablainzevelle.)

Ervillers was evacuated in good order, and our headquarters established in some disused gun-pits west of Gomiecourt. "B" and "C" Companies,

---

32 Battalion losses were 11 men killed or died of wounds.

together with the 11th East Lancashires, began to "dig in" along the railway embankment about 10 p.m. on a line at which the 12th K.O.Y.L.I.s, our "pioneer" battalion, had been working, while the 11th East Yorkshires took up a reserve position west of the railway. At this time the position was so uncertain that Gomiecourt was being shelled from both sides; actually there were no troops in the village. Early in the morning of the 26th, 92nd Brigade headquarters received orders from Division to withdraw to the Ablainzevelle-Moyenneville line, and to occupy a section comprising 500 yards just north of Ablainzevelle. It would seem that these orders were late in reaching the Battalion, for it was whilst breakfasting in the positions taken up overnight that bullets began to whistle overhead and it was found that strong German fighting patrols had found a way through gaps in the line, so that both the 31st and the 42nd Divisions were retiring precipitately. A scouting patrol under Second-Lieutenant Pretty, of "C" Company, went out, but failed to return, and so, acting under the above-mentioned order, the Battalion withdrew at 7.30 a.m. through Courcelles-le-Comte, where a Staff-Captain stood at the cross-roads coolly, as if on point-duty, directing each scattered party as it came along.

Amongst all the abandoned material, shovels were most eagerly sought, for now that we were back beyond the organised trench system, they became equally as valuable as rifles.

A continuous rattle of musketry could be heard just over the ridge we had crossed, as the Battalion reassembled in a deserted aerodrome half-way along the by-road linking Courcelles with Ayette and just astride the low-lying Ablainzcvelle-Moyenneville road. The men were split up into sections, each of which was ordered to dig a short isolated trench here and there over the old aerodrome landing-ground. Every man worked with such energy that both sides of the shallow valley soon resembled a series of gigantic molehills. Before long the Germans attempted to advance over the ridge of the skyline, but the Machine Gun Corps drove them back several times about noon. About this time our Field Artillery, who were now out in the open behind Douchy and were over perfectly strange country, began to drop their shells very "short" into the Battalion position, but the afternoon passed without further sight of the enemy.

A mysterious rumour that the Germans intended to use tanks in this sector, which led to the erection of a curious barrier of well-assorted scrap iron across the Ayette road may have been accounted for by the enemy's break through between Puisieux and Beaumont-Hamel, leading to the capture of Colincamps, which he held for a time with machine guns. Lewis gunners of the 8th Tank Bn., however, hastily rushed up by lorry from Acheux, captured the patrol after a skirmish in the street. In the afternoon the New Zealanders took over the village, while an Australian Brigade filled the gap between Hébuterne and Bucquoy.

On March 27th the Germans made their supreme effort on our immediate front. During the night they had crossed the River Ancre and captured Albert, about twelve miles to the south and some distance in the rear of our position, and about noon they launched a series of attacks all along the front from Hamelincourt to Bucquoy, almost midway between which lay our aerodrome.[33]

The morning broke bitterly cold, but we were to have little time to notice that. The German "sausage" balloons had crept up very close and scarcely seemed to rise clear of the forward ridge which was masking the enemy's movements. First his artillery became very active on our sector, then at 11.30 a.m. "C" Company sent up the "S.O.S". and things began to hum. Twice the enemy advanced over the ridge but twice he was driven back and a number of prisoners taken. Then, after his renewed attack, our men were forced back half-way down the slope, only to thrust him back a third and yet a fourth time by desperate bomb and bayonet work. The constant cry was for reinforcements, but there were none to send. (Later R.A.S.C. and R.O.D. drivers told us that as they came up from the Base all the training camps and billets were empty – the 10th East Yorkshires were indeed the last thin line of defence on this part of the front.) German 'planes buzzed everywhere, unmolested. Then the M.G.C. supporting our men received orders to withdraw their guns, as their position in rear of Battalion headquarters had been located and shelled, so that, forsaken by artillery, aircraft and machine-gunners, our plight seemed desperate.

About 3 p.m. the 42nd Division on our right was seen to be falling back, for Ablainzevelle had been captured, and as Moyenneville had been occupied by the enemy overnight, the position of our Brigade along the road joining these villages became untenable. Hence, a withdrawal to the partly-dug "Purple Line" between Ayette and Adinfer was ordered, though our front remained intact. This move, under the eyes of the enemy observation balloons was extremely hazardous; there was no alternative to dashing "over the top" to the sunken Ayette road, which itself was well marked by the enemy guns. Major D. D. Wilson, who was in temporary command of the Battalion (Major Hewson having taken over the 11th East Yorkshires, while Lieut.-Colonel Gurney was in temporary command of the 92nd Brigade) left behind a small rear-guard comprising Second-Lieutenant Rutherford – a very cool and gallant American officer who was killed later – a corporal and five men of Headquarters Company (Privates

---

33 Eight men were killed in action or died of wounds.

Bourne, Haines, Hobbs, Naylor and Porter); they stayed for an hour in a short trench near Battalion headquarters, and covered the retreat of the Battalion (and, since the 10th Battalion had been ordered to provide the rear-guard for the whole Brigade, of the 92nd Brigade, too) by blazing away blindly every time a German head showed above the skyline about 800 yards away. Thus they kept the ridge clear, and by the noise they made kept up the illusion that a strong force still held the Battalion position. None of the party expected to come out alive from this forlorn hope, but at the end of the hour they took their chances, slipped into the sunken road and retired slowly, halting to fire periodically to maintain the illusion. Presently they fell in with two "A" Company Lewis gunners and eventually all re-joined the Battalion in the "Purple Line" trenches to the east of Adinfer Wood. Here again all were digging frantically, momentarily expecting a renewal of the attacks, but the night passed surprisingly quietly, as the 4th Guards Brigade now held Ayette in front of us.

In the early hours of March 28th[34] the Brigade Composite Battalion (comprising the reinforcements left behind at their respective Quartermaster's Stores when the battalions marched up to the line) came up under Lieut.-Colonel T. A. Headlam's command and passed through our lines to take up an advanced position in closer touch with the Germans. This party was detailed after an appeal by a R.F.A. officer supporting us, to bring 18-pounder ammunition back from some evacuated gun positions by the roadside which were now within the German lines. This was successfully carried out during the night and materially aided the artillery in giving us that support which was so vitally necessary the next day. During this day the Germans made desperate efforts to capture Arras, attacking from Vimy all along the front as far south as Bucquoy; the 4th Guards Brigade were heavily engaged at Ayette, but the enemy made no headway whatever anywhere along the front. He had clearly out-run his communications, and got too far ahead of his big guns, so that his attacks were losing momentum, while the heavy rains of that day must have still further dislocated his programme. But though the continuous shelling of Adinfer Wood, just to our rear, on March 29th, proved that the German guns were slowly coming up, the danger of a big breakthrough was now over.[35] Next morning the Guards Division on our right was twice attacked, but the line held. Then, at 9.30 p.m. on March 31st, the 15th Highland Light Infantry of the 32nd Division relieved us. We had a meal at the field kitchens in Monchy, then marched back, "B", "D" and Headquarters to

---

34 Four men were killed during the day.
35 Five men were killed or died of wounds.

Gaudiempre, "A" and "C" to Pommier, where we turned in from 3.30 a.m. until noon, when we moved off again to Sus St. Leger, and here most of us enjoyed our first shave for eleven days. The following day, April 2nd, we returned to our old billets at Monchy Breton by 'bus.

Later we were gratified to learn that the 10th East Yorkshires was one of the battalions mentioned by Sir Douglas Haig for "exceptional gallantry on March 27th". Our losses from March 24th to 27th were four officers and 207 men,[36] but we felt that we had had a worthy share in the foiling of the German plans; using sixty-four divisions against our thirty-two he had thrust back our line thirty miles in places – but only five miles on the Battalion front – causing us enormous losses in men and material; never-the-less the Germans had very heavy losses, they had failed to capture Amiens, and, most important of all, the Allied front remained unbroken.[37]

---

36 The battalion losses for that period were 34 men killed or died of wounds and one officer died of wounds.
37 The German attacks on the Arras Front, code-named Alberich.

The "Tonics".

St Venant, 1916–17.

Merville, 1918.

Chapter 13

The Battle of the River Lys, April 1918

WE spent eight comparatively delightful spring days at Monchy Breton – days when Battalion Orders could be concerned, as on April 4th, with anything so important as "the instant removal of all East Yorkshire regimental buttons from tunics". That day also we were very glad to receive a reinforcement of seventy other ranks from the Base, followed next day by 256 from the XII Corps M. and R. Camp.[38]

On April 6th the G.O.C. 31st Division inspected the whole 92nd Brigade in the fields outside Monchy Breton.

On April 10th we should have sent a big 500 working party to Acq, though this was cancelled at the last moment and replaced by a Battalion route march towards Diéval. Soon after dinner, Battalion runners brought orders to prepare to move in battle order, so after a hurried tea we "fell in" at 3.45 p.m., marched, as on March 22nd, to join the buses on the St. Pol road, and set off in them about 6 p.m., through Diéval, Bethune and Merville to Vieux Berquin, a distance of a little under twenty-five miles as the crow flies, in a north-easterly direction.

The reasons for all this excitement were somewhat as follows. When the Germans were brought to a standstill after eighteen days' fighting on the Somme, Ludendorff decided to compel the French to use up their reserves, by attacking the British where they were notoriously weak; then when the Allies' last reinforcements were destroyed he would strike hard at Amiens, and so sever the communication between the English and French Armies.

The battle-ground he chose lay just north of the La Bassée Canal. Sir Douglas Haig had already withdrawn ten divisions from this area for the Somme fighting; most of its present defenders had suffered heavily in the last battle; it was far enough from Amiens to strain the Allied resources; important junctions like Bethune and Hazebrouck lay close behind the British front, whilst any advance there would be a direct threat to the Channel Ports.

---

38 Musketry and Reinforcement camp.

Ludendorff originally intended to use only nine divisions and had no intention of being drawn into a major action. He intended to push between La Bassée and Armentières, utilising the La Bassée Canal as a defensive left flank. Having captured Bethune he would turn north-west, aiming at Hazebrouck and the ridge north of Bailleul. He thus hoped to compel Haig to order a general retreat to a line west of Dunkirk; then in the midst of the general confusion he would strike at Amiens.

After thirty-six hours of intense bombardment along the British front from Armentières to Lens, the attack broke upon the front held by the 9th, 19th, 25th, 34th, 40th, 2nd Portuguese, and 55th Divisions between Messines and La Bassée, about 7 a.m. on April 9th. The Portuguese (who would have been relieved next day) broke first at Richebourg l'Avouée, causing the fronts of the 40th and 55th Divisions to collapse and that night a huge bite had been taken out of our line beginning at Bois Grenier in the north and passing through Croix du Bac, Sailly, Vieille Chapelle, Lacouture, Le Touret and Festubert to Givenchy in the south. But Bethune still held out and until it was taken the enemy left flank was not safe, and he could not open out the front of his attack.

Next day, April 10th, Armentières, Estaires, Steenwerck and Ploegsteert, further north, all fell. This meant, first a total advance of four miles, and also that the Germans were seeking the elbow room to the north, which the stubborn defence of Bethune by the 55th Division denied them in the south; and this was how matters stood when the 31st Division entered the battle.

We had arrived "somewhere beyond Vieux Berquin", where we left the 'buses at 1.30 a.m. on April 11th. As we lined up on the road the C.O. explained to the leading sections that the Germans had again broken through – this time on the Portuguese front at Richebourg l'Avouée and Neuve Chapelle – the front which we knew so well in the late summer of 1916. All that was certain was that the enemy was in Estaires, and so the 10th East Yorkshires were to push ahead and get into touch with them.

After marching some considerable distance, Battalion headquarters was established in a ruined farm, which lay on the west side of the Meteren Becque, adjoining Haute Maison, and which was temporarily occupied by a family of refugees from Steenwerck, whose Flemish patois we found very difficult to understand. After a few hours' much-needed sleep we woke to find that our horse-drawn transport had not yet arrived, so breakfast on April 11th was somewhat sketchy.

About 11 a.m. we moved forward to support the 50th Division (including the 4th East Yorkshires from Hull) which together with the 51st Division had been thrown in to support the 40th Division.

We took up a position 1,000 yards west of the hamlet of Doulieu, which lay about five miles north-east of Merville, where we "dug in". "D" Company was on the left, with its left flank on the Le Verrier road between Petite Ferme du Bois and Pont Wemeau, "C" was in the centre, due west of Doulieu, "B" Company (with one platoon of "A") on the right to the west of La Brielle Farm with the Meteren Becque on the right flank, while the remainder of "A" Company was in close support behind "C". Battalion headquarters was at Petite Ferme du Bois, about three-quarters of a mile west of Le Verrier. We were told that when the men in front of us could hold on no longer they were to withdraw through our line, leaving us to hold up the enemy. But when our patrols went out they soon found that there were no British troops ahead of us, though there were Germans in plenty.

Yet about 11 p.m., although Battalion headquarters had now moved back 500 yards from its morning position, we succeeded in advancing the Battalion left front to the crossroads at Pont Wemeau, almost due north of Doulieu. This move was made in conjunction with the 18th Durham Light Infantry, who captured La Becque and La Rose Farms, and the 13th York and Lancasters away on our left (but owing to the intervening troops being held up a gap was formed which was to be a source of much trouble next day). Nevertheless, this action brought us some credit as it was almost the only advance recorded that day along the whole British battle front.

Also it was the appropriate response to the stirring "order of the day" which we, along with all other units engaged had received from Sir Douglas Haig that day:

> "There is no other course open to us but to fight it out. Every position must be held to the last man; there must be no retirement. With our backs to the wall, believing in the justice of our cause, each one of us must fight on to the end. The safety of our homes and the freedom of mankind depend alike upon the conduct of each one of us at this critical moment".

But Messines had been lost that day, and Nieppe relinquished, so our line that night ran from Givenchy to Locon, then west of Merville and Neuf Berquin, north of Steenwerck and Nieppe, east of Wulverghem, west of Messines and along the ridge covering Wytschaete. It will be noticed that on our front the enemy was pushing hard in a north-west direction towards Hazebrouck.

So far he had not used more than sixteen divisions, but on the morning of April 12th, elated by his unexpected success, he decided to turn the attack into a major operation by throwing in his reserves, in the hope of reaching Calais and Boulogne.

About 8 a.m. he attacked heavily from the Estaires-Hazebrouck road as far as Steenwerck, in a supreme effort to grasp the important road and rail junction of Hazebrouck.

The 40th Division's remnants had withdrawn through the 31st Division by 7 a.m., and half an hour later enemy machine gun bullets and shells from east of Doulieu, warned us that it would not be long before we were attacked. By 8 a.m. Runners brought in news that the companies had been engaged with the enemy for some time. A German observation balloon crept unpleasantly near, and the air was alive with hostile aeroplanes, which swept low over our lines; one sinister black fellow almost razed the chimneypots at Battalion headquarters. Then along the road running south from Doulieu, and also in front of "D" company, crowds of Germans could be seen advancing. At 9 a.m. hostile fire on the right was intense. The houses on the eastern outskirts of Doulieu were full of Germans, and somewhere along the road just mentioned a field gun was driving back "B" Company's outposts on the right.

All the officers but one in this company and many N.C.O.s and men had fallen, killed or wounded; touch with the 2nd Royal Fusiliers on the right had been lost, and news came that the 93rd Brigade, on the left of the 92nd, was retiring. So about 10 a.m. we were ordered to withdraw in a north-westerly direction, and to occupy the east bank of the Meteren Becque between Haute Maison on the south and the point where the railway, running east and west, crossed the Becque just south of Outtersteene.

Orders concerning the positions to which we were to withdraw and the routes we were to follow had been issued overnight, but the enemy's advance was so rapid, our left flank was open, and the whole Division on our right was retiring at the same time along the very roads we should have used, so that it was exceedingly difficult to keep to the right roads.

This retreat – 2 miles as the crow flies – was terribly difficult. Deep dykes and hedges ran everywhere, facilitating the enemy advance, but badly handicapping our withdrawal, and these waterways were responsible for several parties becoming separated from the Battalion, which they did not rejoin until much later.

How the Battalion got away, for both flanks were exposed, and artillery, machine gun and rifle fire swept the position, is a marvel. Later, an extension of our line to the road junction south-east of Haute Maison was ordered by the Brigadier, so that we might link up with the 11th East Lancashires on the right, while we were told that we now had the 11th East Yorkshires on the left.

Having reached the Becque we made a stand, the companies fighting almost hand-to-hand with the Germans, until they found themselves driven in to within twenty yards of Battalion headquarters. But the 11th East Yorkshires did not appear so that our left flank was "in the air" and the enemy began to work round it. Then orders were given to cross the Meteren Becque, which those present describe as "like Queen's Road drain in Hull"; it was a little less than waist deep and no bridges were near. So the men just plunged in "at two paces interval" as though on manoeuvres, and, safely across, lined a short north and south railway embankment which carried a branch from the main line almost due south of Merris, 500 yards west of the Becque.

Here the C.O. (Lieut.-Colonel T. A. Headlam) realising that he had heard nothing from the 11th East Yorkshires for over an hour, sent out a small patrol which pushed into the eastern outskirts of Merris without finding them. (Actually, when we withdrew from before Doulieu, contact with them had been lost, and they, suspecting that both their flanks were "in the air" had withdrawn to the Outtersteene-Vieux Berquin road, so that they now lay to our right rear.)

We now know that the German attack this day drove in the British line from Doulieu as far north as La Becque Farm, which the Durhams had captured, thus creating an ugly gap through which the enemy, who later seized Outtersteene and Merris, was pushing straight for Hazebrouck. This was indeed one of the critical moments of the whole engagement.

Apparently owing to this gap on our left flank we had some difficulty in reaching the railway bank, but three gunners of the 29th Divisional M.G.C. lent us invaluable assistance in holding off the enemy by supporting their machine gun barrels against the tree trunks and firing from the shoulder in standing positions.

Next we received orders to extend our line along the main railway eastwards, in order to close the gap and to link up with Lieut.-Colonel Gurney's Brigade Composite Battalion. But instead of finding them along the railway we met the advancing Germans, so the movement came to an abrupt end.

Soon the overwhelming tide of German troops, powerfully supported by artillery and machine guns, compelled us to fall back still further. Acting under orders we withdrew gradually to hold the main railway line, about 1,000 yards south-west of Merris, and immediately south of Mont de Merris, at which point we linked up with the East Lancashires on our right and so established a line which ran in a south-westerly direction just clear of the northern limits of Vieux Berquin. Later on, contact was made with the Composite Battalion on the left and a line running from just west of Merris through the western outskirts of Vieux Berquin was eventually constructed (and later consolidated) from the pits and holes which each man originally scratched for his own protection.

On April 13th the German attacks on the weakly-held line in front of Bailleul – the next step towards the capture of Hazebrouck – were continued. Here the 29th and our own 31st Division, both very weak, held a front of 10,000 yards, behind which the 1st Australian Division was gathering, and it was imperative that this front should be maintained until the latter could get into the line.

In the early-morning fog the Germans launched their main attack, and with field guns firing at point blank range, they succeeded in taking Vieux Berquin, away on our right; the East Lancashires on our right were heavily attacked and our right company assisted them with machine guns and rifle fire. During the afternoon our right company was itself attacked by a force of 200 Germans, which they quickly drove back. On our front there was much shell fire, while towards evening machine guns and snipers became very active, but we had no large-scale infantry attack to meet that day, as we had anticipated.

The 1st Australian Division, whose detraining at Hazebrouck we had been covering since April 10th, was now entrenched close behind us. A message ordering us to withdraw through their line under cover of darkness should have reached us by 1.30 a.m. on April 14th. However, the country lying between Battalion and Brigade headquarters was shelled so heavily that it was impossible to maintain continuous telephone communication, though the Signallers worked heroically at line repairs. Eventually the message arrived at 4 a.m., when it was already beginning to grow light. So orders were rushed out to the companies to evacuate immediately and to get away before they could be seen by the Germans. It was quite light before the last men were ready to move, but a heaven-sent morning mist obscured all movement and the withdrawal was completed unobserved by the enemy. When the Germans attacked later in the day, they were met by the fresh Australian troops and completely repulsed. The road to Hazebrouck had been closed.[39]

"No more brilliant exploit", wrote Sir Douglas Haig, "has taken place since the opening of the enemy's offensive, though gallant actions have been without number . . ". and in this praise we felt that we had won some small share, though this action cost us thirteen killed, 141 wounded and 214 missing, the great majority of these latter being subsequently reported killed.

In the entry in the Battalion War Diary, which covers these operations, Lieut.-Colonel T. A. Headlam proudly concludes, "Close touch was kept practically the whole time with the 11th Battalion East Lancashire Regiment on our right, and no withdrawal was made except to conform to orders received".

---

39 During the period 12 to 14 April the battalion had 55 men killed or died of wounds and one officer killed.

Chapter 14

The Turn of the Tide

ON being relieved by the 1st Australian Division in the line near Merris, we marched back to billets on the railway siding to the north of Borre on April 14th; two days later we moved to the Chinese camp at La Kreule, and from here a composite battalion, drawn from the 10th and 11th East Yorkshires moved into the Hazebrouck defence system at Borre, with headquarters at L'Hoffand. On the 18th we relieved the 6th Australian Battalion in the support lines around Grand Sec Bois and Swartenbrouck; the 4th Guards Brigade were on the right, and the 11th East Yorkshires on the left. On April 26th we took over from the 11th East Lancashires in the front line at Seclin; we had the 4th Grenadier Guards on our right and the 11th East Yorkshires on the left.

At 3.30 next morning a party consisting of four officers and 120 other ranks, under Captain E. M. Pearce, raided the enemy trenches round La Becque Farm, held by the 221 R.I.R. of the German 48th Reserve Division. The raid was a great success, as twenty-four Germans and a machine gun were brought back, while the raiders reported that they had killed "about sixty of the enemy". We had two men killed and seven missing.[40] Both the Corps and Second Army Commanders sent congratulations to all concerned in this very successful operation.

We were relieved about midnight by the 2nd Leinsters (29th Division) and marched back to Haute Loge, west of Hazebrouck, from where we moved on May 2nd to the Chinese Camp at La Kreule. Until May 8th the days were spent between trench digging in the Hazebrouck defences and Company and specialist training.

During this period Major Carver proceeded to Linghem to take over his new duties as O.C. 31st Divisional Wing.

On May 3rd the following reference by Sir Douglas Haig to the 31st Division appeared in the Daily Mail:

---

40 Six men killed and one dying of wounds.

"The magnificent performance in holding up the enemy advance at a critical stage of the Lys Battle has already been publicly acknowledged. I wish to add my personal tribute to the fine fighting qualities displayed by this Division".

At this time there were persistent rumours that the 31st Division was to be disbanded; we even heard that the 92nd Brigade was to join the 61st Division; the 93rd Brigade to go to the 9th Division; and the 4th Guards Brigade to return to the Guards Division. Fortunately these were only rumours.

About this time Major-General John Campbell took over the command of the 31st Division from Major-General Bridgford.

On May 9th we moved via the La Brearde cross-roads to relieve the 3rd Australian Infantry Battalion in reserve in the Fletre area, with the 3rd Australian Brigade on our right and the 168th French Division on our left.

At this time Lieut.-Colonel E. H. Rigg (K.O.Y.L.I.) assumed command of the Battalion in place of Major D. D. Anderson.

The 92nd Brigade took over the front from the 93rd on May 15th, when we relieved the 18th Durham Light Infantry in the support lines – the 11th East Yorkshires taking the left front, the 11th East Lancashires the right, while the Durhams remained attached to our Brigade in reserve.

There was much enemy aerial activity each night and our anti-aircraft searchlights were kept very busy; also the enemy artillery was extraordinarily active over our back areas. On May 17th between 2,000 and 3,000 shells fell round Caestre Mill at about ten rounds per minute, while next morning Battalion headquarters was heavily shelled for an hour from 7.15, with 4.2, 5.9 and 9-inch shells.

A readjustment of the front line positions was made on May 19th, and we squeezed into the centre position in the Brigade front line, taking over a two-company frontage, which was occupied by "A" and "D" Companies, with "B" in support as counterattack company, while "C" were in reserve, with an officer and thirty-five men as a permanent garrison for La Besace Keep. Our right flank rested on the Fletre-Meteren road, our left on the Meteren Les Quatre Fils Aymon road. Then on May 21st the Brigade was relieved in the line by the 93rd, and we moved back to billets at Thieushouk, so picturesquely set at the foot of Mont des Cats, with its amazing Trappist monastery. This day Captain Le Blancq assumed command of "D" Company.

On May 24th we moved by 'bus to Lumbres (six miles south-west of St. Omer), arriving at 1.30 a.m. on the 25th at the camp at Val de Lumbres.

Until June 8th we put in a good deal of time in specialist training, range practice and ceremonial parades, these last in preparation for the inspection by the new G.O.C. 31st Division, who presented medal ribbons, after which the Battalion marched past the saluting base. Leave was readily granted to visit St. Omer, while our officers defeated those of our 11th Battalion at soccer, in addition to which there were Battalion and Brigade rifle meetings and a Brigade boxing competition. The Battalion also won the Divisional knock-out rugby competition.

But on June 8th we turned our faces once more towards the line, marching by Wizernes and Blendecques to Racquinghem, where we continued our training (including schemes of defence and retirement). Then on June 15th the Battalion moved via Belle Croix to improvised bivouacs (constructed of waterproof groundsheets) in a field near Wallon Cappel; orders were issued that no one might move more than 100 yards from his bivouac, as the Battalion must be prepared to move at an hour's notice. The next day R.S.M. Graham took a party of N.C.O.s to reconnoitre a position near Morbecque which we were to occupy "if the Germans attacked" on this front. On the 17th a move was made via Lynde to billets near Pont Asquin in the Blaringhem area; "A" and "D" Companies were billeted in Lynde, "B" on the road to Blaringhem and headquarters at Renescure; and on the 20th we marched via Sercus to the Transport Lines near Morbecque; late that night Captain G. A. Wright led a reconnoitring party to the headquarters of the 1st Battalion K.O.S.B.s on the bank of the La Motte Canal; they were then holding the line north-east of the Nieppe Forest. The remainder of our Battalion followed twenty-four hours later and took over from the Scottish Borderers with Battalion headquarters along the canal bank-west of La Motte-au-Bois Château. On June 23rd two officers and five men of the 177th Regiment, 78th Division U.S.A. Army joined us for instruction; after our experience of Canadians and Anzacs we found them – even their sergeants – remarkably docile – quite tame in fact. We were relieved on June 25th after a very quiet period (forever notable if only for the fishing expeditions with Mills bombs, organised by headquarters' details, in the canal – the Signallers' ninety-four roach with the first bomb being the best catch recorded – immediately after which the "professional" bombers drew a complete blank despite several casts).

Before we were relieved the C.O. and Company Commanders, in camouflage suits, had patrolled and reconnoitred our assembly positions in preparation for an attack on the enemy line from La Becque Farm to Le Cornet Perdu, which was intended to give us a new line along the Plate Becq, thus driving the enemy further back from the Forest of Nieppe, which he was constantly drenching with gas shells.

The 93rd Brigade were to be on the left with La Becque Farm as their left-flank objective; our 92nd Brigade on the right had a farm, Le Cornet Perdu, as our right-flank objective, while the 5th Division would carry on the attack further south. On our Brigade front the 11th East Yorkshires were to take the left, the 11th East Lancashires the centre, while we were on the right flank of the attack.

We were relieved by the 12th Norfolks on June 25th and marched back to the bivouac camp, west of Morbecque. June 26th was spent in practising the attack, but both the Battalion scheme in the morning and the Brigade scheme in the afternoon were interrupted by enemy shelling near the "final objective". On the 27th the scheme of attack was explained to all ranks by means of maps and aerial photographs, and then the Battalion paraded at 7.30 p.m. to march to the assembly positions on the north-eastern edge of Nieppe Forest, east of La Motte, and near the hamlet of Caudescure on the Merville road.

The assembly position was safely reached about 1.15 a.m. on June 28th, though Lieutenant J. St. C. Richardson was wounded on the way up. During the night Lieut.-Colonel Rigg and Captain Dugdale arranged the gaps in our wire and all was ready before dawn. Our barrage came down at 6 a.m. and the Battalion at once set off in four "waves" through the tall standing corn and passed through the "lanes" in the wire without difficulty. Before the barrage

The barracks, St Omer, 1918.

Château de la Motte, Hazebrouck, April 1918.

lifted we were close up to it and some casualties were caused through the impetuosity of the men. Major Traill (O.C. "C" Company) – a very well-loved officer, who had joined us at Hornsea in 1914 – who was killed at the beginning of the action, probably died from the shock of one of our shells which, falling short, burst close to him, as no wound could be found on his body.

The Germans belonging to the 208th Regiment having "stood down" when daylight came, were completely taken by surprise – as was proved by the boots and sets of equipment (including numerous automatic pistols) which were found in every deserted bivouac – and so put up very little resistance; the enemy machine guns were slow in coming into action and did comparatively little damage; it was not until 6.14 a.m. that their counter-barrage opened and then it was on our old front line and the edge of the forest where, although heavy, it was too late to cause many casualties; our barrage, on the contrary, was very effective.

Some resistance was later encountered by "C" Company (on the left front) at Gars Brugghe, but "D" Company on the right pushed forward so as to outflank this farm, while the Stokes Gunners brought their mortar into action, when the enemy garrison bolted, No. 5555, Private E. Thynne[41] being the first man to enter the farm. All our objectives were taken by 7.20 a.m.

41 Awarded the D.C.M. for brilliant gallantry on more than one occasion during the day.

Members of the Original Battalion at Armistice – St Omer.

All the officers of "C" Company having become casualties, Lieutenant W. H. Hall took command of our whole line, until Captain G. A. Wright (Battalion Intelligence Officer) was sent forward from Battalion headquarters to take charge of "C".

The newly-taken line was quickly consolidated behind a protective screen of Lewis gun posts, though long-range German machine guns hindered this work – but eventually a comprehensive line of unconnected posts was established.

During the afternoon parties of the enemy were observed, moving in the fields near La Becque Farm, evidently massing for a counterattack. The "S.O.S". went up and our barrage effectively scattered them. At the same time the new line near Gars Brugghe was heavily shelled, whilst a torrential downpour made conditions temporarily very difficult, and all day the support companies and the carrying parties, using the mule track through the cornfields prepared by the R.E.s, suffered from the enemy artillery. During the night the R.E.s succeeded in wiring the whole Battalion front, the necessary material being carried by the Battalion transport on pack mules.

Throughout the operation effective liaison was maintained with the 11th East Lancashires on the left and the 12th Gloucesters on the right, and eventually our front-line posts were linked up with theirs west of the La Becque stream.

The next day, June 29th, passed quietly enough, despite two "S.O.S.s" which proved to be false alarms.

"A" Company had now taken over the left front, while "B" had relieved "D" and that night a patrol under Lieutenant Sever searched "No Man's Land", but found no trace of the enemy west of La Becque Farm.

Then, after another comparatively quiet day, the 12th Royal Scots Fusiliers relieved us after tea on June 30th, and we marched back, very pleased with ourselves, to Morbecque Camp.

The attack had resulted in an advance of 1,500 yards on a front of between three and four miles, while 300 prisoners and twenty-two machine guns had been taken along the whole front. The prisoners were Saxons of the 32nd Division and Prussians of the 44th Division, and from both came confirmation of the rumour that influenza was rife in the German Army and that it had recently helped to hold up their advance.

Our casualties for the whole operation were: officers, one killed (Major C. B. Traill) and five wounded (including Captain C. E. Lloyd James, Second-Lieutenant C. Brooks, Second-Lieutenant K. M. Gordon, Second-

Lieutenant P. Owens); other ranks, twenty-four killed,[42] 126 wounded, two missing, one wounded believed killed, nine wounded at duty.

The operations were completely successful and were undoubtedly among the best things we accomplished; "the dashing courage of all the officers and men taking part was beyond all praise", says Colonel Rigg in the War Diary; but above all, the attack proved that we had left the bad days of March and April behind and that the initiative was once more in our hands.

About this time, the 4th Guards Brigade, those dour fighters whom we had been glad to have alongside us during the severe and harassing days of March and April, left the 31st Division and were replaced by the 12th Norfolks, 12th Royal Scots Fusiliers, and the 24th Royal Welsh Fusiliers. The first two were dismounted yeomanry and all three had come from Palestine. They formed the new 94th Brigade and from now on were to share with us the tours in the line, the offensives and whatever else the fates had in store for us.

---

42 Thirty-one men were killed or died of wounds.

Chapter 15

The Final Offensive

JULY 1st to 4th was spent in reorganising the companies and in musketry and box-respirator training, and Captain G. A. ("Jerry") Wright was appointed to command "C" Company.

During the night of July 4th-5th we relieved the 18th Durham Light Infantry in the line with Battalion headquarters at Swartenbrouck Farm. "C" and "D" Companies took the front line, with "A" and "B" in support. This was a remarkably quiet tour of duty, though the sector was difficult to work as it was impossible to approach the front line in daylight owing to the flatness of the country east of Nieppe Forest and the impossibility of entrenching in such a low-lying area. But the abandoned fields of new potatoes and green peas lying between the front and support companies made a welcome addition to Army rations, and headquarters several times carried out a supply large enough to feed them until they were again "in the line".

During this period Lieutenant W. S. Butter and Second-Lieutenants W. Buttery, R. Hey, W. Lindley, G. Lockwood, J. W. Marshall, and W. C. Taylor joined the Battalion from the Base.

It was raining heavily when the 11th East Lancashires relieved us just before midnight on July 8th, and we marched back into Brigade Reserve billets near Le Tir Anglais, though "A" and "B" Companies stayed in the reserve lines near Swartenbrouck. Continual thunderstorms and big working parties in these reserve lines made this an uncomfortable rest period, but rumours that the 11th Battalion had brought in many prisoners, and that the German morale was failing because they had "the wind up" about the Americans, showed that we were "tails up" once more.

On July 12th we relieved the 11th East Yorkshires in the line near Grand Sec Bois – "A" and "B" in front, "C" in close support, and "D" in reserve – and our first job was to consolidate the new line won by the 11th the previous day. (They had attacked and captured Tern Farm at forty-five minutes' notice, without a barrage, and advanced their line by 300 yards on a 500 yards front, while capturing sixty prisoners and five machine guns.)

On July 14th a "B" Company patrol located an enemy machine gun post just west of the Vieux Berquin road. As our men approached, the

German gunners fired a short burst, but, as our men held on their course, they then ran away. Our patrol thereupon took possession of the gun which they brought safely back to our lines.

During this spell one of our old "originals", Second-Lieutenant "Tommy" Shelton, our first Lewis gun Sergeant, returned to England to join the R.A.F., while Captain J. C. Dunn joined us as Medical Officer.

We were relieved by the 24th Royal Welsh Fusiliers early on July 16th, and returned to our camp north-west of Morbecque, where baths in the badly-flooded reserve trenches were very popular during the warm thundery weather.

On July 22nd we relieved the 13th York and Lancasters in reserve positions in Nieppe Forest, with headquarters at the junction of the rivers to the east of La Motte Château. "A" and "B" Companies were in line along the River Bourre, while "C" and "D" were in bivouacs along "A" Ride in the Bois d'Aval. The companies provided R.E. working parties until the 26th, when we relieved the 11th East Yorkshires on the right sector. "C" Company with its headquarters at Gars Brugghe, and "D" Company at Le Cornet Perdu (where they boasted a piano that would play) were in the front line, while Battalion headquarters were in "elephant" huts on "B" Ride in the Forest. This was almost exactly the ground which we had won on June 28th and consisted of sown corn fields – so flat that once again no movement was possible by day in the forward areas.

On July 28th an officer and twenty-nine other ranks of the 11th East Yorkshires came up to make a raid from our "D" Company headquarters on an enemy post which had been located between Cornet Perdu and the Plate Becque. They left our lines at 11.30 p.m., preceded by a creeping barrage. But as no enemy were holding the post, "D" Company provided a strong patrol to reconnoitre another slightly to the north, and due east of Cornet Perdu, which proved to be strongly held. At the same time, "C" Company found no signs of enemy occupation in the posts on their sector. Our patrols were active the next night, one from "D" finding the bridge across the Plate Becque partially destroyed.

On August 3rd at 12.15 a.m. – a very wet, dark night – a fighting patrol under Lieutenant Krog and Second-Lieutenant Hatfield with twenty other ranks, raided German shell-hole posts east of Gars Brugghe, under cover of a barrage. They brought back two prisoners of the 187th R.I.R., while the party had one man wounded. The 13th York and Lancasters relieved us that night and we marched back via Fettle Farm, Papote and Le Grand Hasard to our old Morbecque camp.

During this period out of the line the Battalion "soccer" team drew with the East Lancashires, 1-1, while the "rugger" game arranged with the

11th East Yorkshires had to be postponed because the officers needed the ground for a Polo practice, which the "ponies" seemed to enjoy more than most of the players.

This same day, August 8th, the 92nd Brigade in general, and the 11th East Yorkshires more particularly, suffered a severe loss through the death of Captain Oake, O.C. 92nd Brigade Trench Mortar Battery, as a result of an accident at a trench mortar demonstration. His appearances with "The Tonics" concert party as a singer of "Dixie" ragtime songs (like "Then they sent an Angel from the sky, and they called it Dixie Land ") had been very popular since 1916, and the news of his death caused very genuine sorrow in our camp.

Next day we relieved the 13th York and Lancasters in reserve in Nieppe Forest, with headquarters at Forest Camp, east of La Motte. "A" and "B" Companies were at Volley Farm and Cobley Cottage, with "C" and "D" in rear along the Bourre Becque.

On the 13th we were unexpectedly relieved by the 15th K.O.Y.L.I. so that we could move to the left to replace some B.1. men of the 8th Royal Irish Regiment (40th Division) at Swartenbrouck Farm. They had only done four days trench duty altogether, while their Signallers had had but six weeks training, and the whole battalion seemed amazed to find themselves actually in the fighting area.

They had been advancing by "infiltration", pushing forward their line at those points which seemed to be more thinly held; hence the situation of the forward posts when we took over was very indefinite. The line we eventually established ran about 250 yards west of the Vieux Berquin road, from abreast of that village, in a southerly direction.

At 7.30 next morning our fighting patrols pushed forward and occupied a series of posts which ran from a point south-east of Vieux Berquin (and east of the Vieux Berquin-Neuf Berquin road) in a south-westerly direction). This line had to be abandoned during the day as the troops on our left, the Royal Scots Fusiliers, had not gained their objectives; later, when these were secure, we again occupied the above line, which meant that we had captured the whole of Vieux Berquin. This line, which now faced south-east, about 400 yards south of Vieux Berquin village, was consolidated during the night; our patrols not only kept in touch with the enemy, but located his machine gun posts along the main road.[43]

At 4 a.m. on August 15th, "C" and "D" Companies "went over" to advance and strengthen our line.[44] All our objectives and one prisoner were taken.

---

43 Nine men were killed or died of wounds.
44 One man killed.

We were unexpectedly relieved by the East Lancashires at midnight, and moved back into Brigade Reserve, the Companies being billeted over a wide area with Battalion headquarters at the large farm À la Promenade, north-east of the estaminet Le Tir Anglais. Here the men rested ideally and bathed in the canal running from Hazebrouck past Le Motte Château during August 16th and 17th; at night on the second day we relieved the 11th East Yorkshires. "D" Company were in the front line with Company headquarters at La Becque Farm, "C" in close support in our old front line near Lug Farm, "A" in support in the Volley Farm-Cobley Cottage switch, while "B" were in the front line around Le Cornet Perdu and attached to the Camerons for the time. Battalion headquarters was to the left of "X" track on "B" Ride in Nieppe Forest. Our line of posts ran from the main road at the south extremity of Vieux Berquin, first south-west then south, then slightly south-east, so as to encircle the La Couronne cross-roads. At first, when daylight patrols pushed forward, they were held up by the enemy posts along the La Couronne-Caudescure road, but next day, August 19th, with help from the 11th East Yorkshires on the left, fighting patrols crossed the Vieux Berquin road and eventually organised new posts east of it.

The following day Battalion headquarters moved to Grenade Farm (on the Vieux Berquin road, which formed the northern boundary of the Forest) with a forward headquarters at La Becque Farm. That night the 10th K.O.S.B.s relieved us and we returned to the Le Tir Anglais area, but within twenty-four hours we made a hurried move to Cinq Rues (east of Wallon Cappel) on the Hazebrouck-Ebblinghem road, moving on again on August 24th to the Caestre area between Le Brearde and Le Peuplier in Divisional Reserve. Here our Battalion Transport Section won the second prize at the Divisional Horse Show. August 30th saw the heats of the Battalion Sports run off after tea in readiness for the finals next day, but by 10.30 next morning we were on the move again – via Caestre and Fletre for Phincboom Farm behind Meteren. The next day was spent by all ranks in salvage work around the old front line, and the morning of September 2nd in practising an attack on a two-company front, on the high ground around Meteren. Then, at 6 p.m., the Battalion paraded for a move forward "to an area east of Bailleul", but the parade was unexpectedly dismissed; it was rumoured we had been intended to assist in the capture of Hill 63.

Next day orders were received to relieve the 1st K.O.S.B.s in the line that night. Mounted orderlies were hurriedly sent to recall the companies from their morning exercises, and at 3.30 p.m. the Battalion set off through Meteren and Bailleul, both terribly battered, en route for the Nieppe area on the western bank of the River Lys, opposite Armentières. Tea was provided at La Crèche, and Battalion headquarters later established at

Ophir House, about one and a half miles north-east of Steenwerck; almost immediately headquarters was advanced another 2,000 yards north-east to Pont d'Achelles on the Bailleul-Nieppe Road. The relief was marred by one unfortunate incident. A platoon under Lieutenant Earle was led by a K.O.S.B. guide through Nieppe village, which had been heavily shelled during the day, and should have been skirted. A direct hit was made by the Germans on this platoon; its commander and ten other ranks were killed, six other ranks were wounded, and the relief was delayed until 4 a.m.[45]

Meanwhile orders had been received for a general advance by patrols on a frontage of 2,000 yards to a depth of 1,500 yards on the right and of 2,000 yards on the left – the Battalion occupying the line between Les Trois Pipes and Nieppe itself, with advanced headquarters at Prompt Farm.

At 5.30 a.m. on September 4th, Lieut.-Colonel Rigg and Major Hewson visited the front line and found our patrols well concealed in the Nieppe trenches and waiting the signal to advance. Then at 8 a.m. the 29th Division on our left advanced under a barrage to occupy Hill 63, and it was noticed that the enemy put down an immediate barrage on our positions.

"Zero" for us was 8.35 a.m.; we had no barrage and our men found the Germans both very strong and very alert. The ground over which we attacked was exceedingly flat and quite devoid of cover, so that most of our casualties were caused by machine gun fire. By 11 a.m. "C" Company had advanced about 1,000 yards, "D" Company 500 yards, while "B" had been compelled to withdraw to its original line. Later, orders came to "push ahead" if this were possible without heavy loss. This attempt was made at 3 p.m., but was not persisted in owing to the strength of the opposition encountered.

Second-Lieutenant Cheesbrough was killed, Captain Wallace, Lieutenant Oakden and Second-Lieutenant Rayner were wounded, and there were sixty-nine casualties in the ranks.[46]

During the night we were relieved by the 11th East Lancashires and marched back to bivouacs between La Crèche, and Bailleul. It is on record that the Signal Section laid out 7,000 yards of telephone wire (much of which they had salvaged in Steenwerck by working the whole night) in the course of this day's operation around Prompt Farm.

On September 6th the C.O. was hurriedly summoned to Brigade headquarters while the Battalion moved to a field near Steenwerck Station. The Colonel learned that the Battalion was to deliver another attack with an artillery barrage "with the River Lys as the final objective". He rode back to

---

45 On 3 September one officer and thirteen men were killed.
46 One officer and ten men were killed.

Steenwerck, collected his Company commanders and returned with them to the 92nd Brigade, where the details of the barrage were arranged, while the Brigade Intelligence Officer prepared the maps showing the objectives. These were distributed at 6 p.m. and found to be invaluable later. None of the Battalion's officers had had time or opportunity to reconnoitre the assembly positions by day, so the task of selecting these was entrusted to the Intelligence Officer of the 11th East Yorkshires – Second-Lieutenant Hall, who did his work really well – and at dawn on September 7th the Battalion was in position, well concealed and with headquarters once more at Prompt Farm. The Germans were evidently nervous and their artillery was very active along a line 500 yards east of our position.

The attack was launched at 10 a.m. Smoke was to have been mixed freely with our barrage, but for the first two minutes it failed to blanket our men; also the barrage started, as arranged, 500 yards ahead of the assembly position, which distance was found to be too great, as it left the German machine-gunners untouched, and they let our men reach their uncut wire before opening out. Nevertheless, by 11 a.m. our line had been advanced to the light railway near Harrisburg junction, though it was still about 1,200 yards north-west of the Armentières loop of the River Lys; we had lost Lieutenant Krog and Second-Lieutenant Bradbury, killed, Second-Lieutenant K. M. Gordon and Second-Lieutenant Myhall, wounded, and there were fifty casualties in the ranks.[47] The Germans shelled the whole of our area heavily all the afternoon, and the position was still very uncertain when the 11th East Lancashires relieved us at midnight. We marched out through the rain and mud to some German bivouacs a mile north of Steenwerck; it rained heavily all the next day, but by 5.30 p.m., after much less than twenty-four hours out of the line we relieved the East Lancashires again, and took up a line running from the old trenches east of Nieppe to a point south-east of Harrisburg Junction; "A" and "D" Companies were in the front line with "B" and "C" in support; the wet weather made the ground very difficult.

During the morning of September 9th a patrol from the right company found that Pontceau Farm was unoccupied. Therefore the two front companies swung round to the south-east and took up a line from the south of Harrisburg Junction on the north to the west outskirts of the village of Pont de Nieppe on the south. This was successfully accomplished in the afternoon as a result of careful patrol work, though only slight opposition was encountered. During the night "B" relieved "A" Company in the front line. Next day, September 10th, Lieutenant Hutchinson, the Brigade Intelligence Officer, was sniped and killed from Soyer Farm whilst out reconnoitring.

---

47 Two men died of wounds and 28 were killed.

That night we again changed over with the 11th East Lancashires and marched back to the Steenwerck area. September 11th was spent in cleaning and reorganising, and during the day came the welcome news of a move back – first to Hazebrouck, then further back to Staple for a rest.

So next day we marched to Bailleul, where we entrained and crossed the "No Man's Land" of our April retreat, passing close to Vieux Berquin and through Strazeele to Hazebrouck, where there were now English nurses in the hospitals. We detrained here and marched via Wallon Cappel to Staple, of which the general first impression was that it looked the most prosperous and pleasant village in which we had been billeted since Robecq days. Colonel Rigg, in the Battalion Diary, says:

> "This was the first opportunity the Battalion had had for some months of living for a short time in a comparatively civilised area, and the change was very welcome".

Here the Sergeants established a very comfortable Battalion Mess at the Estaminet de la Couronne; Headquarters beat "A" Company by 5 goals to nil; the Battalion XI lost to a team of giants from the M.T. (A.S.C.) attached to the R.E. Pontoon Park, while the Rugger XV played two very close games with the 11th Battalion, losing 9-0 at Staple, and 14-9 on their ground at Hondeghem; we visited the quaint old hill-top town of Cassel; French classes were started as part of our Educational Scheme; the "Nissen Nuts" gave several open-air shows in the village for our entertainment; most of us went over to Hondeghem to see "The Tonics" in their new black and white costumes, while our holiday ended with a Brigade Church Parade service at Hondeghem.

During this ten days' rest, Lieutenant L. J. Yorke and Second-Lieutenants B. W. Pickering, F. Frayne, F. Copley, E. Banham, F. Pygott, F. R. Dobson, and F. Heath, joined us from the Base, and on September 20th the companies reconnoitred support trenches in the Borre area in case the Battalion was called in to take up a defensive position whilst in Divisional Reserve.

At last, on September 23rd, the Battalion started to move back to the battle area by marching to Hazebrouck, where we were billeted in a boys' school. Most of us saw the 40th Division's "Gamecocks" at night – a fine variety show; it was almost full moon and the German 'planes were soon overhead on a bombing raid. Next day we reached Bailleul about noon by train, and marched to the new Transport Lines on the Bailleul-Armentières road, from where we set off after tea to relieve the 12th Royal Scots Fusiliers of the 94th Brigade. "C", "B", and "A" Companies were in almost exactly the same front line we had left on September 10th (running from just north of Pont de Nieppe in a north-easterly direction to Soyer Farm) with "D" in support. Battalion headquarters was in the De Seine Lines, about 1,000 yards east of Prompt Farm; there was nothing to report until the 119th Brigade relieved us on the night of September 25th, and we moved back to a hut camp near the badly-damaged Neuve Eglise.

After thirty-six hours' rest we were off again at 9.30 p.m. on September 27th to relieve the 11th East Lancashires behind Ploegsteert Wood in readiness for the morrow's big battle. "A", "B" and "C" Companies took up their assembly positions, while "D" and headquarters were in a most marvellous and intricate system of tunnels which the Germans had excavated in the chalk hillside near Hyde Park Corner.

The morning of September 28th was marked by storms of rain so heavy that the attack was postponed from breakfast time to 1.30 p.m. Then the Battalion advanced under cover of a creeping barrage with the intention of working along the north-eastern edge of Ploegsteert Wood, thus protecting the right flank of the 11th East Lancashires, who were fighting on our left. We were to turn right and work south through the wood and finally take up a position outside its south-eastern edge. But owing to the very effective barrage which the enemy put up as soon as ours opened, and also to the very heavy machine gun fire from the wood, the two right companies were unable to advance beyond the road which ran north-east from Hyde Park Corner. The left company ("B" Company) however, was able to push ahead, keeping in touch with the East Lancashires and covering their flank.

In the first few minutes of the attack, "A", "B" and "C" Company Commanders became casualties and the Battalion lost heavily during the afternoon. Early in the evening, "D" Company, under Captain Le Blanc, was ordered up to reinforce and reorganise the Battalion front, and a line was satisfactorily established linking up with the East Lancashires at Prowse Point, immediately west of St. Yves post office, 400 yards north of the wood and with the 18th Durham Light Infantry on the right, 200 yards south of Hyde Park Corner. During the evening the enemy attempted a counter-attack against "B" company, but was driven off with loss.[48]

We found next morning that, owing to the weight of the allied attacks, which extended northwards to the North Sea, the enemy was steadily retiring on our front. Patrols were therefore pushed forward along the Battalion front and meeting with no opposition they went right through the wood. The Battalion followed (headquarters being established in a German pill-box in the wood) and reached a line running along Border Avenue, where

---

48 Eight men were killed in action.

they met considerable fire from snipers and machine gunners. It was found that most of the enemy machine gun posts and concrete pillboxes were quite untouched by our artillery fire, which accounted for the difficulty experienced by the Battalion in assembling on the slopes at Hyde Park Corner and for the cross-fire from which our men suffered as soon as they started to attack.[49]

Early on the morning of September 30th "B" Company on our left flank was relieved by a company of Durham Light Infantry and moved over to the right flank, thereby displacing another Durham Light Infantry company.

At 6.15 a.m. orders came to occupy the line of the River Warnave, in collaboration with the Durhams on the left and the 40th Division on the right. Little opposition was encountered and this move was satisfactorily carried out.

On October 1st we noticed that enemy machine gun and rifle fire was very light when compared with that of the day before. Consequently, at noon a general advance was ordered with the line of the road running parallel with and on the south side of the River Warnave, but half a mile beyond it, as the immediate object. The two right companies reached this without difficulty, but our left flank and the Durham Light Infantry had to meet heavy artillery and machine gun fire. "D" Company actually went forward, but the Durhams being held up compelled them to come back to Desperrier Farm. That night our Battalion front, with advanced headquarters at the ruined convent (or rather in the cellar which was all that remained), well clear of the wood, was taken over by the 11th East Lancashires, and we returned to Neuve Eglise camp just before dawn.

The Battalion went into the battle with twenty-five officers and 520 men; we came out on the night of October 1st with twelve officers and 394 men.

The following were the officers who went into the line on September 27th: Lieut.-Colonel E. H. Rigg, Major Riall, Captains Braithwaite (C.F.), Dugdale, Dunn (R.A.M.C.), Le Blanc, Naylor, Pearce, and Wright, Lieutenants Eycott, and Yorke, and Second-Lieutenants Banham, Chaplin, C. W. Clark, Copley, Dobson, Frayne, F. Hall, Heath, Oliver, Pickering, Pygott, Rendle, and Young.

Our officer casualties were Captain Dugdale (a very popular "original" member of the Battalion, who with his violin introduced many of us to Dvorak's "Humoresque"), and Second-Lieutenants Dobson, Pygott, and Rendle, killed; Captains Le Blanc, Dunn, Pearce and Wright, Lieutenants

---

49 Thirty men killed and three died of wounds.

German field kitchen captured at Harlebeke, October 1918.

Loading transport for home, 1919.

Eycott and Yorke and Second-Lieutenants Copley and Heath, wounded; Second-Lieutenant Banham, missing.

We stayed at Neuve Eglise until October 6th, when we moved via Steenwerck to a camp under canvas between La Crèche, and Bailleul, which we took over from the 12th Norfolks, but moved again on the 8th to camp amid the ruins of the Asylum at Bailleul. Here training was carried on until October 12th, when we entrained at the Duke of York siding and travelled back to Hyde Park Corner, from where we marched via Bakery Post to take over the front line from the 24th Royal Welsh Fusiliers of the 94th Brigade. "C", "B" and "D" Companies occupied posts along the River Lys, from left to right, well clear of Ploegsteert Wood, with "A" Company in support near Battalion headquarters.

Next day our front was extended on the right to Pont Rouge, and "B" Company withdrawn into support. "C" Company's front now stretched to the Sugar Refinery, while "D" lay between that point and Pont Rouge, due east of the convent, and south of Deulemont.

About midnight on October 14th a patrol of "A" Company crossed the River Lys on a raft, meeting little opposition but capturing two prisoners, one of whom was of French origin living in Alsace-Lorraine and he volunteered much valuable information, explaining to us that he had been forced to serve in the German army. At 3 o'clock in the early morning the same Company sent a platoon across by the raft, which established posts on the east bank, opposite the Sugar Refinery, though the enemy still held the trenches along the Deulemont-Warneton road. Twelve hours later the remainder of the Company crossed the river and advanced under a barrage to this road, where they established their posts. At 5.30 p.m."B" Company followed across the river and were able to organise posts east of Deulemont. Soon afterwards the 11th East Yorkshires passed through our lines to carry on the "nibbling" process, so our posts were withdrawn to our original position west of the river.

On October 16th we moved by route march to Le Blanc Coulon, about two miles east of Deulemont and a mile south of Comines. All companies were billeted along 2,000 yards of the railway line immediately behind Ste. Marguerite, the Battalion being in support to the 11th East Yorkshires. Next morning we passed through their positions along the La Vigne-Wervicq road, and advanced in company columns, preceded by cyclist screens (where had we carried out this manoeuvre the last time – at Hornsea or Ripon?) and finally taking up a line along the Roncq-Bondues Road (this was really the main Lille-Menin road) with headquarters east of Comines and south-west of Wervicq. Next morning the 11th East Lancashires passed through us and advanced towards Tourcoing, so our companies were withdrawn at 9 a.m. to billets near Croix Blanche, though we moved again at 3 p.m. to Wattrelos, an eastern suburb of Roubaix, where we stayed for a very exciting and enjoyable week until October 25th.

The frenzied throngs of people in the be-flagged streets almost exactly fulfilled our 1914 dreams of how King Edward Street would look when we came home again. Ordered marching was impossible, women pressed flags and flowers upon us and when we were free to fraternise we found every house open to us. Food and drink of every kind were pressed upon men who, even when they realised what sacrifices were involved, found it very difficult to recompense their delighted hosts; and to crown all, we slept in their best feather beds!

Indeed they could not do enough for us to show their delight and gratitude at their deliverance from the Germans, who had occupied Wattrelos since the beginning of the War. The Band came into its own again here and gave nightly performances, much to the enjoyment of the inhabitants.

But on October 25th we marched northwards via Mouscron, Sterhoek, Aelbeke, Marcke and Courtrai to Cuerne, and next day travelled by lorry to Belgiek, whence we marched to Ooteghem to relieve the 12th Camerons and 18th Seaforths in the line. "B" and "C" were in front on the right and left respectively, with "A" and "D" in support behind them.

The following day there was a very heavy bombardment of the whole area by the enemy, who put down a counter-preparation barrage near the Ooteghem-Kleinronsse road, while we suffered several casualties from gas, which was largely used.

On the 28th[50] our line was pushed forward slightly to Biest Farm in conjunction with the 35th Division and the 11th East Lancashires. The next night we again advanced, under cover of darkness, establishing posts east of Ooteghem and south of Ingoyghem, between the Beck Te Biest stream and the road, before we were relieved by the 24th Royal Welsh Fusiliers and moved back six or seven miles north-west to billets between Harlebeke and Deerlyck, north-east of Courtrai. Battalion headquarters were at Harlebeke, where the cooks were particularly proud of their captured German field kitchen, with its gleaming copper boiler (which was eventually brought back to Hull when the "Cadre" came home). Here also was an abandoned German field gun in good condition, just outside the headquarters farm. One of the day's diversions was to fire this gun using mangold wurzels as ammunition! At this time Lieut.-Colonel Rigg, D.S.O., left the Battalion for six months duty in England; Major Hewson assumed command of the Battalion, whilst Lieutenant Hadrill became Captain and Adjutant.

---

50 Two men were killed in action.

On October 31st the Battalion "stood to" from 11 a.m. as our Brigade was in support to the 94th Brigade, who were attacking. We moved at 2.30 p.m. by Belgiek, Vichte, and Ingoyghem to Ooteghem, in reserve to the 24th Royal Welsh Fusiliers, who were attacking in conjunction with the 34th Division and the French; we were not called on as we heard later that they gained their objective, and that eighteen field guns and 586 prisoners were captured in the whole operation. It should be pointed out here that the line in these parts ran slightly east-north-east, as the Germans were now retiring to the line of the River l'Escaut (Scheldt) in the direction of Avelghem.

On November 1st we learned that an Armistice was to be granted to Austria, Hungary and Turkey at noon that day. This really began to look like the end of the War. Appropriately enough we spent the morning in clearing up this part of the war area, by salvaging the plentiful war material which the Germans had abandoned in their hurried retreat. Incidentally, at Ooteghem there was a great slaughter of fat Belgian hares which had been left behind when their owners fled before the approach of the tide of battle; it was long since most of us had tasted such rabbit pies as followed. But we moved back to our old billets at Harlebeke about noon at fifteen minutes' notice, as we were not needed.

On November 3rd we marched via Courtrai, Marcke, Lauwe and Reckhem to Halluin, a suburb of Menin, where the whole Battalion was billeted in a large factory to the south-west of the town. Four days later we marched back to Lauwe and on to Marcke. Immediately we arrived a fatigue party of ten men was ordered to proceed to the River Lys just north of the town to prepare the "boats" for a practice river crossing, in preparation for the approaching attempt to cross the River L'Escaut by the 31st Division (who were now attached to the XIX Corps).

Two collapsible boats had been allotted to the Battalion, each capable of holding eight men, and "B", "A" and "D" Companies in turn crossed the River Lys; owing to the failing light there was not time for "C" Company's trip. So they stayed behind to dismantle the "boats" which they carried back to the Quartermaster's stores. Later in the evening, Colonel Hewson lectured the officers and N.C.O.s on the coming crossing of the River L'Escaut and the attack which was to follow.

Next day we marched via Courtrai and Sweveghem to farm billets near Ooteghem. About 2 p.m. a French civilian who had swum the river, brought news that the enemy was falling back, and the 11th East Lancashires crossed the L'Escaut without opposition. There was now to be a general move forward along the Corps front, with the 11th East Yorkshires passing through the East Lancashires to form the new front line. Consequently, our "A" and "B" Companies with headquarters Company, including the Band

and the Transport, marched through Avelghem and Rugge, where we had tea. Then about 5 p.m. we crossed the river by an improvised R.E. pontoon bridge, and marched through Amougies to Reussignies. We were cheered and greeted all along the road by the civilians who were overjoyed at their liberation, and were billeted for the night in a fine large house attached to a brewery or flour mill, which was in working order, and where "C" and "D" Companies joined us. That Saturday night, Captain Braithwaite, the Padre, astounded us all by telling us that he thought the War was over; at first we refused to take him seriously.

We were off again next morning, November 10th, and marched through Renaix, quite an important looking little town, where all the public notices were printed in German. One overjoyed civilian marched backwards the whole way through the town at the head of the Battalion, playing the National Anthem on a violin. There was much traffic on the road, all pushing eastward as rapidly as possible, so that progress was necessarily slow; occasional stray shells and the rattle of musketry reminded us that we were very close on the heels of our 11th Battalion, who formed part of the front line of that day's advance. It was 5.30 p.m. when we reached the Haisette area, which we were to occupy that night – one Company being at Houppe, with Battalion headquarters at Ellezelles, a very squalid, poverty-stricken village.

But it was here that news reached the orderly room at 2 a.m. on November 11th[51] that an Armistice had been signed and that hostilities would cease at 11 a.m. Battalion Runners carried the news to the Companies at 6 a.m., when such a heavy bombardment was in progress so very near at hand that most of our men turned over, for that last hour in bed, well-nigh incredulous! Later, when the men began to stir and to discuss the momentous news there was a surprising lack of enthusiasm. The war had continued so long that we had come to know army life pretty well- civilian life would mean taking a fresh plunge, besides breaking up what seemed lifelong friendships.

We continued to hear stray shells during the morning and learned later that our 11th Battalion had actually had a man killed on that Armistice morning; then as 11 a.m. approached, little groups gathered in that very drab village street, under a grey sky, standing almost breathless, watches in hand, until it was all over, and we had come through!

We fell in at 11.30 a.m. and marched forward through Puvinage to Everbecq, and took up the line which the Germans had evacuated that

---

51 One soldier died of wounds and one died in hospital, probably of flu/pneumonia.

morning, which was infinitely more desirable than passing through the 11th Battalion, in leap-frog fashion, and going into action that day as we should have done had the war continued. There were flags at cottage windows, gaunt cottagers who cheered as we marched past, church bells ringing across the fields, but it was a very grey November day and the rain had steadily increased as we marched.

It was a strange experience to take over billets which had been occupied by Germans in the morning, and even to see the villagers removing the fixed seats round the estaminet walls to get out the bicycles which had been hidden there since the Germans had commandeered all rubber, brass and copper. There were some French troops in Everbecq whose dancing in the estaminets to the music of the automatic pianos added to the gaiety of Armistice night, though our road had been so hilly and so badly in need of repair that we were all exceedingly weary.

Everbecq, the nearest point to Berlin we were destined to reach, was two and a half miles from the River Dendre, and twenty-four miles from Brussels.

Chapter 16

After the Armistice

On November 12th came a Brigade order, "There will be no move to-day", but we learned to our great disgust, that although the Second Army, to which we had been "loaned", was to form part of the Army of Occupation, yet the 31st Division was to be transferred to the new Fifth Army and to return to France. We therefore turned our steps westwards – and homewards – on November 13th,[52] and were billeted that night at Rigaudrye, which was really the other end of the village of Ellezelles, where we had spent the eve of the Armistice. Next day we retraced our steps through Renaix, Reussignies and Amougies to Orroir; on November 15th[53] we re-crossed the Schelde and passed through Avelghem and Heestert to Sweveghem and on the 16th to Marcke, where we had eight days' rest in a big school-quite a good billet, though it had been hit by a bomb. Here, on November 21st, we learned that the Censorship restrictions on letters home were released, so that men might mention and describe their situation and surroundings; also Captain Naylor was promoted to be Major, while on the 23rd, the G.O.C. 31st Division (Major-General J. Campbell) inspected the Brigade at the aerodrome and presented medal ribbons to about fifty men of the 92nd Brigade.

On November 25th we started to march still further back, spending that night in Menin; next day we followed the ghostly Menin road through Gheluwe and Gheluvelt, passing the many derelict "tanks" and Hell-Fire Corner into Ypres, past the ruined Cloth Hall, to a camp west of Vlamertinghe; then through Poperinghe and Steenvoorde to Terdeghem; next day through mediaeval Cassel, with its little electric trams running down the hill, to Le Nieppe and Ebblinghem, and finally, on November 29th, through Renescure and Arcques to St. Omer, our immediate destination, where we were billeted in the huge fortress-like cavalry barracks-the Caserne de la Barre.

---

52 One soldier died of wounds
53 Private Bilbe died of pneumonia.

Cadre on parade at Paragon Station, Hull, 26 May 1919.

Here, on December 6th, elementary education classes were organised in order to fit men for a return to civil life; on December 9th the pivotal men whose services were most needed in industry at home, began to cross over to England for demobilisation, the coal miners being the first group released.

On December 17th, "A", "B" and "D" Companies and headquarters moved out to billets at St. Martin-au- Laert (a roadside village two kilometres out of the town on the Boulogne road), while "C" Company moved to another barracks in the Rue Carnot, as French troops were taking over the Caserne de la Barre. At St. Martin an old dance hall was adapted for use as a school, fitted up with electric light by the Signallers and partitioned off with sacking walls by the Pioneers, and, except when large working parties were demanded for the filling in of trenches and similar work, education classes occupied most of our mornings, the afternoons being given over to football matches and cross-country runs. On December 24th, at a Brigade ceremonial parade in the Grand Place at St. Omer, Brig.-General Williams presented the Croix de Guerre to some members of the Battalion.

By those of us who remained with the Battalion to the end, our Christmas dinner, held in the gymnasium, will for ever be remembered. Turkeys, and plenty of them, with vegetables; also Christmas pudding flavoured with rum sauce, which was the genuine article. The canteen funds provided four barrels of beer, all of which was served to the men by the W.O.s and Sergeants on real plates and in good mugs, the nearest approach to home life for three years.

Early in the New Year men going home on leave in the usual way were automatically demobilised, whilst more and more "groups" were constantly being sent home. But the system was not working quickly enough to suit some men and on January 29th, at 1.30 a.m., orders came for the Battalion to move at once to Calais in consequence of serious disturbances there. We entrained at St. Omer station at 7 a.m., and at Calais found the whole of the 31st and 35th Divisions assembled, because the R.A.O.C. and R.O.D. were causing trouble. We marched to Beau Marais Camp, where we were accommodated in tents, though there was snow on the ground and the weather was bitter. That day the 105th Brigade picketed Calais to prevent the disorder spreading beyond the docks and storehouses which the R.A.O.C. had seized.

Next day, at 11 a.m., we paraded in fighting order and moved off to take up a position in support to the 35th Division, but General Sir W. R. Birdwood, G.C.M.G., met the men's representatives, and by 1 p.m. we were back in camp.

On January 31st both the R.A.O.C. and the R.O.D. were back at work and the G.O.C. 31st Division, knowing how inhospitable were our quarters, induced the Governor of Calais to send us back immediately to St. Omer, where we arrived at 9 p.m. and returned to the billets we had recently left.

We learned later that Armourer-Sergeant Good, late of the Battalion headquarters Signal Section and of "D" Company, lost his life in these Calais riots.

On February 4th the Corps Commander visited the Battalion to inspect billets and the Education Classes, while next day the King's Colour was consecrated.

Demobilisation proceeded steadily and on February 14th the four depleted companies were amalgamated, while on the 17th the 92nd Brigade took charge of the Education Classes – a Brigade Central School being opened. But on March 26th even this Brigade School closed down through lack of students.

On March 3rd we had sent a draft of two officers and forty-two men to the 9th Northumberland Fusiliers, while by April 1st the Battalion was reduced to "cadre" strength, and this skeleton Battalion eventually returned to England on May 22nd and disembarked at Southampton. They travelled by train to Sheffield, reaching the Hillsborough Barracks at 10 p.m. on May 23rd, and remaining there for demobilisation until 8 a.m. on Monday, May 26th. When all was completed the "cadre" made an official journey to Hull with the Battalion colours, arriving at Paragon Station at 10.33 the same morning.

The party consisted of Lieut.-Colonel Hewson ("a youthful-looking officer" according to the Hull Daily Mail), Captain W. H. Hall, Second-Lieutenant W. S. Leech, Lieutenant and Quartermaster Moore and thirty-seven men. Second-Lieutenant Leech carried the colour with Sergeant "Bob" Lee and Sergeant Simpson as escort, and the men had with them the captured German cooker which had rendered headquarters good service since the previous October.

The Lord Mayor of Hull (Councillor Peter Gaskell) was on the platform to meet the party. With him, amongst many others, were Lord Nunburnholme (Lord Lieutenant of the East Riding), Major-General Sir Stanley von Donop (Humber Garrison), Brig.-General O. de Lisle Williams, C.M.G. (92nd Brigade), Colonel Sir George Duncombe (Hon. Colonel 3rd East Yorkshires), Lieut.-Colonel W. H. Blackburn (5th East Yorkshires), Colonel H. R. Pease (12th East Yorkshires), Lieut.-Colonel K. W. Savory (13th East Yorkshires), Major Ridsdill Smith and Captain Clifford Sherburn.

Almost immediately afterwards, the "cadres" of the 11th East Yorkshires (three officers and thirty-five men) and the 146th Heavy Battery – formerly the 3rd Hull Heavy Battery (one officer and seventy-two men) – arrived from Catterick.

When all had detrained, the "cadres" marched out into the square on the south side of the station, where a large number of discharged and demobilised men of the four Hull Battalions of the East Yorkshire Regiment were drawn up under Major W. H. Carver's command, together with representatives of the "Discharged and Demobilised Soldiers and Sailors Federation" and the "Comrades of the Great War".

Lord Nunburnholme inspected the men, after which he welcomed and thanked them, besides reviewing briefly their achievements during the War and mentioning the services of Colonels Richardson, D.S.O., Burges, V.C., Pearson, Stapledon, Headlam, Rigg, D.S.O., Hewson, M.C. (of the 10th East Yorkshires) and of Colonels St. Clair Ford, Pease, Ferrand, Gurney, Wellesley, Dewar, and Savory (of the other Hull Battalions), while Major-General von Donop, as Officer Commanding the Humber Garrison, added a few words of welcome, addressed in particular to the Artillerymen.

Then to the strains of "Home, Sweet Home" and "The Yorkshire Lass" the whole parade marched along the Anlaby Road and Alfred Gelder Street to the Guildhall, where the Lord Mayor, after taking the salute, addressed the parade in Lowgate from the Guildhall balcony.

He then invited them to refreshments in the Banqueting Chamber, and later entertained the officers to luncheon, while to celebrate the occasion the shipyard workers and the school children enjoyed a holiday in the afternoon.

And so, after a period of almost exactly four years and nine months, ends the story of the 10th (Service) Battalion East Yorkshire Regiment.

Any stranger who had last seen the Battalion when it left England would only with difficulty have recognised it as the same body of men at the Armistice. The photograph taken in the Park at St. Omer in January, 1919, shows that five officers and about 120 men of the original Battalion still remained with the unit.[54]

Of these, only the Officer Commanding, Lieut.-Colonel R. C. Hewson, M.C., had joined us at Wenlock Barracks as a subaltern; the others had all served in our ranks, whilst it may not be out of place here to record Major

---

54 The total is impressive compared with many similar battalions, especially as they had all been offered the choice of becoming an officer.

Carver's oft-repeated statement that "more than one-half of the original Battalion received commissions."[55]

Further, War Office statistics show that in all actions we had 574 men killed (though many of these belonged to later drafts) and that we were entitled to the following battle honours: Somme (1916); Albert (1916); Ancre (1916); Scarpe (1917); Arras (1917-18); Oppy (1917); Bapaume (1918); Lys, Estaires, Hazebrouck, Scherpenberg (1918); Ypres (1918).

The Battalion colours were eventually placed in Holy Trinity Church, where they still rest, and the final chapter in this record of the "Hull Commercials" may well close with the words of the Lord Mayor when he addressed the "cadres" in Lowgate on May 26th, 1919: "You have fought a fight, you have gained a victory, you have won a peace".

---

55 The total number commissioned during active overseas service was 163 out of 1454, far short of half but still a considerable number from such a battalion. The total does not take into account the number of men who are untraceable: whilst many of them only served for a short period, some may well have been commissioned and their records lost or are untraceable.

Appendix I

Roll of Honour

Officers, N.C.O.s and men who were killed or died of wounds serving with the Battalion.

MAJOR

Traill, C. B., M.C.

CAPTAINS

Addy, J. C., M.C.
Carlisle, R.
Clark, W. S., M.C.
Dugdale, D.
Leech, N. B.
Rice, B. N.

LIEUTENANTS

Flintoff, R. A.
Hutchinson, L. G.
Jackson, H. W.
Krog, E. J., M.C.
Palmer, D. W. O.
Pierson, L. D.
Robinson, W. L.[56]

SECOND LIEUTENANTS

Bradbury, W. R.
Buttery, W.
Cheesbrough, H.

---

56 Not listed as a death by the CWGC

Davis, O. M.
Dobson, F. R.
Earle, C.
Fricker, A. C.
Houghton, A. W.
Johnston, A.
Jones, A. G.
McDermott, E., M.C.
Marshall, A. F. W.
Piggott, F.
Rayner, H.
Rendle, G.
Rutherford, W. M.
Sanger, H. K.
Southern, M.
Stringer, D.
Spink, C. C.
Webster, A. C.

Sergeants and Lance-Sergeants

No.[57]	Rank and Name.
12/574	Sergt. Arnell, G.
10/693	L/Sergt. Bone, W.
17067	Sergt.Cain, T.
10/1072	L/Sergt. Chalmers, F.
10/723	Sergt. Clubley, B. A.
10/92	A/L/Sergt. Dawson, E. W.
220642	Sergt. Drasdo, A. W.
16595	Sergt. Graham, J. C., M.M.
10/430	Sergt. Harrison, W. E.
10/1029	A/Sergt. Hermann, E., M.M.
10/717	Sergt. Huntington, T.

---

57 Other ranks were given a regimental number which varied for some of the
battalions. Numbers prefixed by 10/, 11/, 12/, 13/ and 14/ were original Hull
Pals who had enlisted originally in the 10th, 11th, 12th, 13th or 14th Battalions
respectively. Volunteers to other East Yorkshire Regiment battalions numbered
between 10600 and 26000 approximately. Conscripts received numbers greater
than around 26000. A number prefixed by 3/ was a Special Reserve soldier and
six figure numbers were originally soldiers from the Territorial Force. Soldiers
with numbers less than 10600 were pre-war regulars.

10/622	Sergt. Johnson, J. A.
10/621	Sergt. Jones, R. P.
13/1134	Sergt. Mennell, F.
10/493	A/Sergt. Miller, R.
10/932	Sergt. Nash, A. H.
10/78	Sergt. Newbert, F. E.
36605	L/Sergt. Piggott, W. J.
36626	Sergt. Pollon, F.
225198	Sergt. Roo, J. W., M.M.
10/205	Sergt. Stather, J. N., M.M.
10/45	L/Sergt. Tindale, A.
9609	Sergt. Walker, E. J.
41442	Sergt. Ward, W., M.M.
12/61	Sergt. Whiteley, C.
10/1038	L/Sergt. Wilkinson, J. H., M.M.
36562	L/Sergt. Woolfenden, J. B.

Corporals and Lance-Corporals

No.	Rank and Name.
220017	L/Corpl. Arksey, A.
10/286	Corpl. Bailey, W.
25942	A/Corpl. Balmforth, M.
36356	Corpl. Blackshaw, S.
7883	Corpl. Blanchard, H.
10/1207	L/Corpl. Bowen, G. E.
10/528	Corpl. Browne. R. E.
10/806	Corpl. Buck, T.
30136	L/Corpl. Clarke, J. A.
220431	L/Corpl. Clough, B.
24218	L/Corpl. Cobby, W. H.
41447	L/Corpl. Coulson, D. C.
26168	A/Corpl. Cryer, R. E.
28362	Corpl. Cullum, W.
28179	L/Corpl. Daniels, H. A.
10/1356	Corpl. Dixon, W.
36661	L/Corpl. Duffield, E. S.
10/990	Corpl. Dunn, E. C.
36403	Corpl. Escott, G. H.
30149	Corpl. Grace, J.
41449	Corpl. Greenwood, F. L.

28058	Corpl. Hall, A. W.
10/431	Corpl. Hall, C. G.
41072	L/Corpl. Hewitt, A. W.
10/681	L/Corpl. Hicks, H.
10/627	L/Corpl. Jackson, F.
225176	L/Corpl. Jackson, J.
12/1366	Corpl. Jackson, W.
10/797	L/Corpl. Jeynes, L.
27244	L/Corpl. Johnson, J.
41450	L/Corpl. Jones, G. W.
12/934	L/Corpl. Jordan, J.
25371	L/Corpl. Keenan, B.
10/1223	L/Corpl. Langthorpe, G. F.
30104	L/Corpl. Lawton, P.
29297	L/Corpl. Ling, B.
30170	L/Corpl. Lord, H. I.
10/287	L/Corpl. MacPherson, W. A.
23963	L/Corpl. Mallory, A.
39448	L/Corpl. Martin, N.
10/318	L/Corpl. Mayer, J. R. H.
220003	Corpl. McNally, J.
14324	L/Corpl. McNally, R.
10/702	L/Corpl. Metcalfe, J.
51120	L/Corpl. Morton, G. T.
8775	Corpl. Murphy, E.
36313	Corpl. Oxford, W.
10/1155	L/Corpl. Peek, L. E.
10/841	L/Corpl. Perkins, E. R.
10/939	Corpl. Potts, A.
41445	Corpl. Price, C.
16632	Corpl. Redpath, J., M.M. and Bar
10/14	Corpl. Saunderson, T. E., D.C.M.
9461	L/Corpl. Smith, A.
10/1231	L/Corpl. Smith, R. H.
10/836	L/Corpl. Spring, G. L.
10/1106	Corpl. Stevens, E. B.
10/17	L/Corpl. Taylor, A. W.
10/1268	Corpl. Thomas, W.
10/950	Corpl. Turner, A.
51167	Corpl. Vasey, R. N.
25965	Corpl. Williams, C.

Privates

No.	Rank and Name.
10/483	Pte. Abba, H.
30317	Pte. Abel, F.
7723	Pte. Adams, J. H.
3031	Pte. Adams, R. F.
37886	Pte. Adams, R. N.
10/1040	Pte. Adams, T.
10/525	Pte. Adamson, W. E.
41034	Pte. Akers, A.
10/478	Pte. Allen, J. W.
30322	Pte. Allen, R. C.
226045	Pte. Allcock, C. E.
202954	Pte. Allcock, E. R.
37260	Pte. Allston, H.
19592	Pte. Andrew, P. C.
33354	Pte. Annis. R. E.
36306	Pte. Arbon, W.
10/1392	Pte, Archer, G.
14147	Pte Armes, S.
30109	Pte. Armstrong, J. F.
10/277	Pte. Ascough, W. B.
36640	Pte Ashworth, H. E.
30327	Pte. Askem, W. R.
10/1230	Pte. Atkinson, J. B.
30332	Pte. Bailey, W. E.
28038	Pte. Baker, E. W.
42187	Pte. Baldwin, G. L.
25352	Pte. Ballard, S.
35013	Pte. Balmforth, C.
23939	Pte. Bancroft, D.
10/100	Pte. Barker, A.
14260	Pte. Barrass, H.
25597	Pte. Barrett, F.
37049	Pte Barrs, G. T.
21257	Pte. Bachelor, J. A.
33105	Pte. Bateman, H
220035	Pte. Baxter, J.
28034	Pte. Bell, A. E.
3/6868	Pte. Bellamy, J. W.

30337	Pte. Beven, F. G.
51117	Pte. Biggs, F.
10/923	Pte. Bilbe, C.
23878	Pte. Blacker, R.
51215	Pte. Blagg, S.
10/527	Pte. Blakemore, A.
10/73	Pte. Blenkin, G.
30245	Pte. Boardman, J.
21812	Pte. Booty, G. W.
39345	Pte. Botham, W. R.
30121	Pte. Boulton, A. G.
201350	Pte. Bower, J.
30344	Pte. Boxall, G. T. Y.
10/655	Pte. Boyd, P.
30345	Pte. Bradbrook, A. A
19003	Pte. Bradley, J.
51207	Pte. Bramley, W.
40933	Pte. Bramwell, J.
10/855	Pte. Bray, G. W.
27921	Pte. Brealey, W. G.
10/218	Pte. Briggs, W. H.
27871	Pte. Britton, J.
10/653	Pte. Brocklehurst, J.
36336	Pte. Brook, W.
3/6493	Pte. Brotherton, F.
12/578	Pte. Brown, A.
23959	Pte. Brown, H.
33445	Pte. Brown, H. W.
21587	Pte. Brown, L. H.
51197	Pte. Brown, N. P.
10/734	Pte. Brown, P.
28037	Pte. Brumby, T. S.
10/466	Pte. Brunyee, J.
10/1297	Pte. Buck, G. W.
12/236	Pte. Burdon, J. W.
10/1131	Pte. Caley, S.
29944	Pte. Canham, F.
14/126	Pte. Canty, C.
28765	Pte. Carrick, P.
21563	Pte. Cawkwell, F.
28047	Pte. Chambers, G. H.

33213	Pte. Chapman, A.
10/1221	Pte. Cheney, J.
28504	Pte. Chrispen, V.
225889	Pte. Cordon, J. G.
51724	Pte. Clapton, T. E.
23964	Pte. Clark, E. W.
19733	Pte. Clark, J.
31048	Pte. Clark, J. B.
10/1286	Pte. Clark, J. W.
28044	Pte. Claxton, R.
37890	Pte. Clayford, D.
26316	Pte. Clayton, C. M.
10/958	Pte. Cleary, W. J.
35028	Pte. Coates, E. J.
10/1355	Pte. Cobby, J. H.
28042	Pte. Cockerline, G. F.
10/338	Pte. Collingwood, J. W.
10/31	Pte. Comins, J.
10/787	Pte. Conyers, S.
12/350	Pte. Cook, J. A.
28046	Pte. Cook, J. T.
10/561	Pte. Coop, S.
39561	Pte. Cooper, G. H.
36408	Pte. Cooper, J.
36371	Pte. Cooper, J.
10/459	Pte. Corden, H. S.
15748	Pte. Cosgrave, J.
30101	Pte. Cowley, J. T.
25391	Pte. Cox, G.
37914	Pte. Cox, H. W.
18994	Pte. Cresswell, W. J.
202878	Pte. Crockford, A.
33051	Pte. Crombie, J. B.
30238	Pte. Crump, H. B.
10/341	Pte. Dalton, W. H.
30142	Pte. Dawson, C.
29042	Pte. Dawson, G. W.
26364	Pte. Deighton, E.
10/1247	Pte. Deighton, G. K.
10/1123	Pte. Dempsey, H.
10/641	Pte. Dennison, W.

37045	Pte. Dickinson, C.
36976	Pte. Dinsdale, J.
10/1059	Pte. Dixon, A. H
21098	Pte. Dixon, E.
37093	Pte. Dixon, R. I.
10/507	Pte. Dobbs, J. A., M.M.
3/6754	Pte. Dodsworth, J. W.
25379	Pte. Doherty, J.
10/959	Pte. Dougherty, H.
22367	Pte. Douglas, D.
41119	Pte. Dowten, P.
37902	Pte. Dunn, J. H.
36319	Pte. Eastwood, H.
36350	Pte. Eden, G.
36397	Pte. Edmunds, A.
12/1389	Pte. Edwards, C. S.
29950	Pte. Elliott, T.
10/639	Pte. Emery, A. V.
41249	Pte. Ettridge, J. H.
10/875	Pte. Everingham, W.
38897	Pte. Everitt, A.
10/813	Pte. Farnill, J. R.
30145	Pte. Flavell, J.
26092	Pte. Flinton, W.
18906	Pte. Fletcher, Z.
22126	Pte. Fisher, G. F.
210258	Pte. Fisher, R.
10/894	Pte. Fitton, R.
10044	Pte. Ford, E.
34257	Pte. Ford, H. R.
16843	Pte. Foster, H.
10/1291	Pte. Fowler, W. E.
220038	Pte. Fox, D. P.
12/587	Pte. Franks, R. P.
3/6594	Pte. Frith, S. D.
33129	Pte. Fussey, H.
10/25	Pte. Gale, H.
19007	Pte. Gallear, N.
10/180	Pte. Galt, J.
51171	Pte. Garnham, A. J.
10/505	Pte. Garton, H

51773	Pte. Gasgoyne,
29769	Pte. Gash, E. J
10/764	Pte. Gill, G. W.
38921	Pte. Gill, E.
41223	Pte. Gilliver, H. H.
26066	Pte. Gilyead, G.
36642	Pte. Gladwell, E.
203211	Pte. Goldsmith, J.
28054	Pte. Goldspink, H. D.
51193	Pte. Goodey, E. A.
39675	Pte. Gosling, E.
51141	Pte. Graham, H.
11561	Pte. Grayburn, W.
33451	Pte. Grindell, F.
12033	Pte. Guest, E.
37898	Pte. Gutherless, F.
39681	Pte. Hagestadt, J.
35084	Pte. Haigh, E. S.
12/42	Pte. Hall, H.
21684	Pte. Hall, J. W.
10/886	Pte. Hall, P. C.
30156	Pte. Hallywell, G.
41749	Pte. Hamenway, A. H.
10/1248	Pte. Harding, F. E.
19725	Pte. Hargreaves, J. H.
51118	Pte. Harris, J.
28057	Pte. Harris, J. A.
20019	Pte. Harrison, A.
37899	Pte. Harrison, G.
22122	Pte. Harsley, S. H.
25365	Pte. Hawkins, B. W.
39204	Pte. Hawksworth, A.
31065	Pte. Haxby, E.
36333	Pte. Hayter, E.
33228	Pte. Hayton, B.
32958	Pte. Hayton, W. W.
9767	Pte. Heaven, E. G.
33095	Pte. Heeson, W. E
5129	Pte. Henderson, J. A.
13/814	Pte. Hester, J. W.
37206	Pte. Hewitt, J. S.

37923	Pte. Hicks, F. T.
27888	Pte. Hill, A.
23939	Pte. Hill, F.
30288	Pte. Hill, F.
37901	Pte. Hillyard, H.
28227	Pte. Hinchsliff, F.
51179	Pte. Hindmarsh, F.
29192	Pte. Hoad, S.
14/208	Pte. Hodds, H.
30332	Pte. Holmes, A.
52800	Pte. Holmes, E. E.
10/305	Pte. Holmes, F.
37094	Pte. Holroyd, R. H.
10/968	Pte. Homan, W. R.
10/20	Pte. Horsfall, W.
10/716	Pte. Horsfield, S.
21671	Pte. Hotson, R.
36711	Pte. Howarth, H.
38151	Pte. Hoyle, H. L.
12/05	Pte. Hunt, A. E.
29467	Pte. Hunt, J.
28220	Pte. Hunt. R.
30261	Pte. Hutchinson, D.
31904	Pte. Hutchinson, J. F.
22603	Pte. Hutton, R. G.
29950	Pte. Hutton. S.
10/1028	Pte. Hyde, E.
10/261	Pte. Ireland, B.
9844	Pte. Jackman, J. W.
51103	Pte. Jackson, F.
27339	Pte. Jackson, R.
10/626	Pte. Jackson, W. J.
18926	Pte. Jagger, F.
18965	Pte. James, J.
10/422	Pte. Jeffrey, L. F.
10/708	Pte. Jessup, G. H.
10/1210	Pte. Johnson, F.
10/519	Pte. Johnson, F. H.
10/845	Pte. Johnson, G. H.
10/532	Pte. Johnson, H.
51725	Pte. Johnson, N. J. P.

36705	Pte. Johnson, P. V.
51770	Pte. Joiner, A. E.
21970	Pte. Pte. Jones, P. G.
10/819	Pte. Joys, C. S.
220041	Pte. Jubb, R.
31445	Pte. Kay, B.
10/676	Pte. Keal, R.
10/160	Pte. Keene, E.
30168	Pte. Kelly, C. N.
10/232	Pte. Kidd, R. L.
10/998	Pte. Kingdon, C. H.
33115	Pte. Kirkby, F. W.
33030	Pte. Kirkby, J. W.
10/118	Pte. Kirkman, H.
18919	Pte. Knight C
11402	Pte. Lake, J .W.
10/1133	Pte. Langdale, W. S.
10/295	Pte. Latus, S.
51150	Pte. Laws, I.
10/170	Pte. Lazenby, W.
37047	Pte. Ledger, J. H.
22121	Pte. Lee, W.
27980	Pte. Leeson, G.
10/128	Pte. Leighton, O. R.
22418	Pte. Lilley, G. E.
10898	Pte. Linford, J.
10/65	Pte. Linsley, R.
51175	Pte. Little, J. H.
220490	Pte. Little, T.
10/136	Pte. Lockey, P.
21921	Pte. Loftus, H.
11/1407	Pte. Long, W.
51112	Pte. Longstatf, J.
29957	Pte. Luxnsdon, J. J.
30176	Pte. Madden, W.
11/1395	Pte. Maddra, J.
30174	Pte. Maher, J.
31077	Pte. Maitland, J.
22598	Pte. Mann, J. F.
51777	Pte. Manners, C.
10/79	Pte. Marr, S.

220635	Pte. Marriott, F. L.
220043	Pte. Marritt, E.
12136	Pte. Marshall, A.
24897	Pte. Marshall, T. C.
10/672	Pte. Martindale, P.
36338	Pte. Masters, C. E.
10/609	Pte. Matthews, G.
17737	Pte. May, S. C.
10/931	Pte. McBride, J.
40937	Pte. McCabe, J.
210869	Pte. McGuire, W.
30308	Pte. McIlvride, N. J.
27046	Pte. Mercer, T. J.
10/1233	Pte. Messenger, A. E.
30351	Pte. Middleton, A. E.
10/381	Pte Millard, T. P.
26583	Pte. Miller, E.
51213	Pte. Miller, R. H.
30292	Pte. Miller, T.
10/557	Pte. Miller, W. V.
18890	Pte. Milton, G.
37018	Pte. Mitchell, A.
29972	Pte. Moment, F.
10/207	Pte. Monday, J. H.
39139	Pte. Moore, W.
10/225	Pte. Morack, M. W.
10/1380	Pte. Morley, J. H.
25394	Pte. Morrell, T. C.
10/266	Pte. Moss, A.
12/971	Pte. Motherby, F.
19000	Pte. Munday, J.
11941	Pte. Murphy, B.
28210	Pte. Mutter, E.
10/572	Pte. Nasby, T. A.
41103	Pte. Nash, F.
11/464	Pte. Naylor, A. B.
10/867	Pte. Neill, R. C.
10/1249	Pte. Newton, J. E.
36314	Pte. Nicholas, B. C.
28205	Pte. Nichols, C.
27990	Pte. Nichols, W.

17629	Pte. Nicholson, M.
33021	Pte. Nicholson, W.
10/1285	Pte. North, A. B.
10/366	Pte. North, A. H.
18745	Pte. Oldfield, F.
10/604	Pte. Page, F. K.
29959	Pte. Parker, J.
3/5568	Pte. Parker, W.
26096	Pte. Parkinson, W.
10/543	Pte. Pattern, E.
10/1413	Pte. Pawson, H. H.
21796	Pte. Pearce, F . W.
36611	Pte. Pears, J.
51312	Pte. Pickersgill, H.
18902	Pte. Pickles, J.
30295	Pte. Pickup, T.
51686	Pte. Pink, T.
39492	Pte. Place, T. V.
51148	Pte. Pollard, J.
39073	Pte. Potter, W.
10/574	Pte. Powell, T. A.
30105	Pte. Powell, W.
23656	Pte. Pregden, A. W.
39055	Pte. Prescott, T.
203649	Pte. Price, W.
30313	Pte. Prior, A. E.
39426	Pte. Procter, W. H.
36981	Pte. Proudfoot, W. B.
51133	Pte. Rainbow, G. W.
10/560	Pte. Raney, W. R.
27399	Pte. Rawson, S.
30204	Pte. Reid, W.
10/1045	Pte. Reuben, I.
36733	Pte. Rhodes, H.
39190	Pte. Richards, J.
30268	Pte. Richards, W. H
12/433	Pte. Richardson, C.
33086	Pte. Richardson, N.
10/520	Pte. Riley, C. W.
10/751	Pte. Roberts, D. A.
31141	Pte. Robson, F. S.

30202	Pte. Robinson, H.
10/1101	Pte. Robinson, W.
30234	Pte. Rudkin, H.
28234	Pte. Runkee, C.
10/67	Pte. Russell, P.
13/469	Pte. Rusling, A.
18919	Pte. Schofield, F.
26099	Pte. Scrubbs, A.
39429	Pte. Seagrave, A.
220435	Pte. Seaman, G.
25353	Pte. Seckerson, L.
10/1054	Pte. Sellers, E. W.
39413	Pte. Shackler, E.
27347	Pte. Shaw, A.
30214	Pte. Shaw, J. R.
51682	Pte. Shearing, L. C.
30216	Pte. Shenton, H.
39407	Pte. Shouler, E.
225120	Pte. Sill, H.
14133	Pte. Simmons, J. L.
21806	Pte. Simon, H. S.
30293	Pte. Simpson, A.
31099	Pte. Simpson, J. T.
23011	Pte. Singleton, A. E.
225291	Pte. Sissons. A. E.
6148	Pte. Sizer, U.
21718	Pte. Skelton, VV. R.
23961	Pte. Sleight. G.
36321	Pte. Smart, E. VV.
3/6334	Pte. Smethurst, E.
12/1445	Pte. Smith, C.
21162	Pte. Smith, F.
10/1251	Pte. Smith, H.
10/838	Pte. Smith, J.
37068	Pte. Smith, N.
225794	Pte. Smith, R. J. T. C. R.
29963	Pte. Smurthwaite, T. L.
30273	Pte. Sorby, W.
26084	Pte. Southcott, S. C.
35073	Pte. Spencer, G.
51201	Pte. Spivey, T. F.

10/1172	Pte. Stead, R. B.
22914	Pte. Stewart, W.
10/1140	Pte. Stone, F.
10/890	Pte. Storr, H.
10/677	Pte. Summers, H.
30213	Pte. Sutton, C. E.
10/396	Pte. Sykes, A.
51326	Pte. Telford, H,
12/1035	Pte. Taylor, E. W.
30219	Pte. Taylor, J.
10/1008	Pte. Taylor, S.
10/313	Pte. Tennison, C. F.
10/314	Pte. Tether, B.
10/951	Pte. Tether, G. W.
51734	Pte. Tindell, J. W.
41867	Pte. Thomas, J.
10716	Pte. Thompson, E. M.
41344	Pte. Thompson, J. J. W.
3/6758	Pte. Thurloe, F.
10/859	Pte. Todd, H.
25412	Pte. Travis, F. E.
36799	Pte. Tucker, G. S.
36344	Pte. Tumblety, J.
27783	Pte. Turner, G.
220189	Pte. Tweddle, G.
30300	Pte. Verity, C.
30241	Pte. Vickers, C. E., M.M.
55019	Pte. Waddingham, G.
39412	Pte. Waddingham, J. H.
29966	Pte. Wade, T.
17867	Pte. Walker, A. J.
36420	Pte. Wallace, V.
51194	Pte. Wallington, A. H.
18978	Pte. Walters, C. H.
200854	Pte. Walton, A.
10/103	Pte. Walton, F.
39655	Pte. Ward, C. E.
21720	Pte. Ward, G. A.
10/401	Pte. Warn, E. H.
30233	Pte. Warne, C. F.
31473	Pte. Warren, F. C.

19285	Pte. Watson, J. W.
10/39	Pte. Watson, J. S.
37065	Pte. Watson, W.
51742	Pte. Watts, H.
10/774	Pte. Webb, W.
10/407	Pte. Webster, A.
10/346	Pte. Webster, L.
10/738	Pte. Wells, G. A.
10/1144	Pte. West, A. E.
10/148	Pte. West, G. W.
39389	Pte. Westmoreland, I.
30315	Pte. White, A. T.
30226	Pte. White, E.
30229	Pte. Whittingham, J.
18998	Pte. Wilkes, R. E.
30303	Pte. Wilkinson, J.
30234	Pte. Williams, C.
30235	Pte Williams, W. L.
14/172	Pte. Williamson, G. F.
51330	Pte. Williamson, L.
28236	Pte. Wilmot, A. E.
10/793	Pte. Wilson, M.
36797	Pte. Wilson, R.
28679	Pte. Wilson, W.
30280	Pte. Wilstrop, L.
51753	Pte. Winder, J.
10/1186	Pte. Winter, G. W.
30483	Pte. Womar, A.
52811	Pte. Wood, J. W.
33463	Pte. Wood, R.
10/744	Pte. Woodcock, F. K.
33117	Pte. Woodifield, F. W.
21053	Pte. Woffinden, R.
39188	Pte. Wright, A.
10/856	Pte. Wright, A. H.
13022	Pte. Wright, E.
38586	Pte. Wright, J. E.
10/350	Pte. Young, L.

Total, N.C.O.s and Men – 573.

List of Awards

British

1. Won by Officers serving with the Battalion. (The ranks shown are those held at the time of the award.)

2nd BAR to D.S.O.

Lt.-Col. Rigg, E. H., D.S.O. (K.O.Y.L.I.)

Military Cross

Capt. Addy, J. C.
2/Lieut. Anderton, W. H.
Lieut. Clark, G. W.
2/Lieut. Clark, W. S.
Capt. Deacon, J. N. (R.A.M.C.)
2/Lieut. Gcraghty, T.
2/Lieut. Hadrill, C. I.
Lieut. Hall, W. H.
Capt. Hewson, R. C.
Lieut. Krog, E. J.
Capt. Lambert, G. F.
2/Lieut. McDermott, E.
Capt. Naylor, W. E.
Capt. Pearce, E. M.
2/Lieut. Piper, C. H.
2/Lieut. Shaw, J. S.
2/Lieut. Stewart, R.
Lieut. Shaw, D.

2/Lieut. Hutton, W. S.
Capt. Traill, C.
2/Lieut. Wallace, C. C., M.M.
Capt. Wright, G. A.

BAR to M.C.

2/Lieut. McDermott, E., M.C.

2. Won by Other Ranks serving with the Battalion

D.C.M.

No.	Rank and Name.
7127	C.S.M. Graham, J.
10/47	C.S.M. Street. C.
10/317	Sergt. Sendall, H. E.
10/765	Sergt. Willis, F.
10/251	Corpl. Collinson, C.
10/721	Corpl. Edlington, S.
10/14	Corpl. Saunderson, T. E.
21924	Pte. Green. T.
10/868	Pte. Nowell, L.
10/1134	Pte. Singleton, W., M. M.
3/5555	Pte. Thynne, E.
10/742	Pte. Vollans, C. H.

Military Medal

No.	Rank and Name.
10/697	Sergt. Abba, A. C.
10/656	Sergt. Baldwin, A.
10/986	Sergt. Best, E.
10/735	Sergt. Boag, W. R.
10/913	Sergt. Bold, F.
10/736	Sergt. Brown, J. W.
10/1201	Sergt. Charlesworth, A.
10/243	Sergt. Ellis, J.
10/445	Sergt. Fisher, H.

10/847	Sergt. Hall, W.
10/1029	Sergt. Hermann, F. E.
10/1000	Sergt. Lee, R.
225198	Sergt. Roo, J. W.
10/342	Sergt. Thompson, W. A.
10/1262	Sergt. Winter, W. H. V.
10/589	Sergt. Youngson, H.
10/102	Corpl. Baker, F.
10/188	Corpl. Clarke, C.
10/992	Corpl. Crooks, J. H.
10/296	Corpl. Davie, F.
10/246	Corpl. Dixon, J.
10/437	Corpl. Goodman, J.
10/439	Corpl. Hermann, C.
10/115	Corpl. Nunns, E. A.
10/603	Corpl Page, F. G.
10/768	Corpl. Pippett, J. G.
10/205	Corpl. Stather, J. N.
10/135	Corpl Terry, R.
10/691	L/Corpl. Brumby, B.
10/464	L/Corpl. Clipson, F.
10/1191	L/Corpl. Jarvis, L.
10/1185	L/Corpl. Mowforth. E.
10/1099	L/Corpl. Petty, J. D.
10/1361	L/Corpl. Rawling, H.
10/586	L/Corpl. Robinson, W.
10/664	L/Corpl. Schottlander, S.
10/663	L/Corpl. Smith, G. A.
13/267	L/Corpl. Verity, C.
10/1335	L/Corpl. Ward, J.
31498	Pte. Bell, B.
10/1014	Pte. Dawson, W.
10/507	Pte. DobbS. J. A.
10/2110	Pte. Dover, H.
10/633	Pte. Graystone, H.
10/102	Pte. Ledraw, G. E.
10/1306	Pte. Lewis, J.
10/4195	Pte. Marsden, E.
10/668	Pte. Reynolds, C. C.

10/1371	Pte. Shapero, L.
10/583	Pte. Simpkins, C.
10/361	Pte. Simpson, J. E.
10/1134	Pte.Singleton, W., D.C.M.
10/138	Pte. Stringer. T.
10/1308	Pte. Walsh, A.
10/1038	Pte. Wilkinson, J. H.

1st BAR to M.M.

10/603	Sergt. Page, F. G., M.M.
11/493	Corpl. Noble, W. H., M.M.
10/1101	Pte. Jarvis, L., M.M.

M.S.M.

10/603	C.Q.M.S. Grindelle, A. H.
10/637	Sergt. Fenwick, J. M.
10/660	Sergt. Swift, H.
10/143	Sergt. Wrigglesworth, L. M.
10/553	Corpl. Pudsey, D. A.

3. Officers and Other Ranks Mentioned in Despatches

Rank and Name.

Lt.-Col. Headlam, T. A.
Major Hewson, R. C.
Capt. Le Blancq, S. E.
Lieut. Pierson, L. D.
2/Lieut. Petty, J. D.

No.	Rank and Name.
10/607	R.Q.M.S. Milns, J. P.
10/419	C.S.M. Pinchon, R.
10/1086	C.Q.M.S. Cressy, S.
10/927	Sergt. Moses. S. H.
10/143	Sergt. Wrigglesworth, L.M.

10/992	Corpl. Crooks, J. H.
10/159	Corpl. Mooton, E.
10/539	L/Corpl. Gibson, G. E.
10/437	L/Corpl. Goodman, J.
10/1402	L/Corpl. Tindale, H.
10/830	Pte. Andrews. W. G.
10/236	Pte. Bailey, W.
10/294	Pte. Clark, H.
10/1430	Pte. Middleton, W.
10/140	Pte. Reveler, H.
10/379	Pte. Rodham, J. T.
10/915	Pte. Wilson, F. C.

Foreign Decorations

Belgian Croix de Guerre

Rank and Name.

Capt. Penn, C. L.
Lieut. Sever, J.

No.	Rank and Name.
10/847	R.S.M. Hall, W., M.M.
10/1306	Sergt. Lewis, J., M.M.
10/1262	Sergt. Winter, W. H. V., M.M
10/761	L/Sergt. Jackson, A.
10/478	Pte. Allen, J. W.

French Medaille Militaire

No.	Rank and Name.
10/1308	Sergt. Walsh, A.

French Medaille d'Honneur avec Glaives (en argent)

No.	Rank and Name.
10/88	C.Q.M.S. Davison, T.

French Croix de Guerre

Rank and Name.

Lt.-Col. Hewson, R. C., M.C.

No.	Rank and Name.
10/586	Corpl. Robinson, W., H.M.
10/1134	Corpl. Singleton, W., D.C.M.

Italian Bronze Medal for Military Valour

No.	Rank and Name.
10/996	Pte. Fisher, J. W.

Appendix III

Chronological Diary of Movements

(Distances in brackets – Miles in England, Kilometres overseas.)

1914.

Sept.   1 Battalion formed at Wenlock Barracks, Hull.
Nov.   17 Rolston Camp, Hornsea.

1915.

June   21 Beverley (14).
        22 Pocklington (18).
        23 York (14).
        24 Boroughbridge (18).
        25 Ripon (7).
Nov.   6/7 Hurdcott Camp.
        16 Larkhill Camp.
Dec.   2 Hurdcott.
        7 Left Hurdcott.
        8 Devonport. Embarked SS *Minnewaska*.
        9 Sailed.
        12 Gibraltar.
        16/17 Malta.
        20 Alexandria.
        21 Port Said.
        27 "B" Co. to Salt Works.

1916.

Jan.   10 "B" Co. re-joined.

19 Left Port Said.

    "A"   Company to El Kab.

    "B"   Company to Ballah.

    "C"   Company to El Aish.

    "D"   Company to Kantara and 50.8 Post.

Bn. H.Q. to Ballah.

21 Bn. HQ. to Swing Bridge.

Feb.   28 Transport personnel left Port Said in H.M.T. *Northlands.*

29 Battalion left Port Said in H.M.T. *Tunisian.*

March 7 Arrived Marseilles.

9 Arrived Pont Remy (11-45 p.m.).

10 Longpré-les-Corps-Saints (Somme).

22 Advance Party to trenches for instruction.

25 Flesselles.

26 Beauquesne.

27 Engelbelmer.

28 Trenches: Auchonvillers.

April   3 Engelbelmer.

4 Bertrancourt.

12 Courcelles.

16 Trenches: Colincamps.

21 Bus-les-Artois.

May   6 Colincamps.

10 Trenches: Colincamps.

14 Bus-les-Artois.

15 Warnimont Wood.

24 Bus-les-Artois.

28 Trenches: Colincamps.

June   4 Bus-les-Artois.

12 Trenches: Colincamps.

14 Bus-les-Artois.

23 Trenches: Colincamps.

July   2 Bus-les-Artois.

5 Beauval.

6 Bernaville.

8 Entrained, Auxi-le-Château. Detrained, Thiennes.

9 Robecq.

15 Riez Bailleul.

20 Trenches: Fauquissart (Lonely Post)

23 Pont du hem.

24 Richebourg St. Vaast.

30 Trenches: Richebourg l'Avouée.

Aug. 5 Richebourg St. Vaast.

11 Trenches: Richebourg l'Avouée.

20 Kings Road (Lacouture).

23 Trenches: Richebourg l'Avouée.

31 Kings Road (Lacouture).

Sept. 4 Trenches: Richebourg l'Avouée.

10 Seneschal Farm (Lacouture).

16 Trenches: Richebourg l'Avouée.

22 Seneschal Farm and Kings Road.

28 Trenches: Richebourg l'Avouée.

Oct. 4 Seneschal Farm.

5 Merville.

8 Entrained Merville. Detrained Candas (Vauchelles).

16 Sailly Dell (Bivouacs).

17 Rossignol Farm, Coigneux.

18 Sailly-au-Bois.

20 Trenches: Hébuterne.

21 Coigneux and St. Leger (Huts).

30 Warnimont Wood.

Nov. 10 Bayencourt.

12 Trenches: Vercingetorix (Reserve to 12th and 13th Bns.).

13 Battle of the Ancre. Bn. less carrying parties and two Lewis gun Teams, remained in Vercingetorix.

14 Bayencourt. Warnimont Wood.

21 Trenches: Hébuterne.

27 Coigneux (Huts).

Dec: 3 Trenches: Hébuterne.

9 Authie (H.Q., "C", "D" Companies), Famechon ("A", "B" Companies).

21 Sailly (H.Q., "B", "C" Companies), Hébuterne Keep ("A", "D" Companies).

28 Trenches: Hébuterne.

1916

Jan. 2 Authie, St. Leger.

10 Amplier (Camp).

22 Gezaincourt (Billets).

31 Berneuil (Billets).

Feb. 18 Terramesnil.

19 Bayencourt (Nissen Huts).

20 Sailly Dell.

25 Trenches: Papin, Hébuterne, Vercingetorix, Pasteur.

26 Crossed "No Man's Land" to Nameless Trench.

27 Couin.

March 3 Trenches: Bn. H.Q., K.18.a.05 (German Lane).

5 Hébuterne: Dugouts in Vercingetorix.

9 Trenches: Bn. H.Q. in Berg Graben, nr. Rossignol Wood.

12/13 Couin.

19 Terramesnil (13 ½).

20 Bonnnieres (22).

21 Wignacourt and Croisette (13 ½).

22 Pernes (18 ½).

24 Estrée Blanche (16).

25 Robecq (27).

April 8 Marles-les-Mines.

11 Bruay (4).

14 Diéval (9).

25 Mingoval and Villers Chatel (13 ½).

28 Maroeuil (13 ½).

29 Ecurie (5).

30 H.1.c.

May 1 Old trenches on top of Vimy Ridge.

2 Trenches and shell holes, Oppy.

3 Attack on Oppy Wood.

4 Camp at G.4.a. (Roclincourt).

6 Trenches: Oppy.

8 St. Catherine. Camp.

13 H.1.c.

16 Camp at G.9.c. (Roclincourt).

18 H.1.c.

19 Camp at G.9.c.

20 Camp at G.6 (Old British Line).

June 3 Mont St. Eloi.

10 St. Catherine.

19 Trenches: Gavrelle.

26 Railway Cutting (behind Bailleul).

27 Camp at Roclincourt.

28 Red Line: In reserve to 94th Brigade.

29 Railway Cutting.

30 Camp at A.28.c.

July　1 Railway Cutting.

2 Trenches: Gavrelle.

4 Mont St. Eloi.

13 Trenches: Bn. H.Q. T.22.a.83 (Mont Forêt Quarries).

21 Bivouacs, Vimy and La Folie Wood.

31 Frazer Camp, Mont St. Eloi.

Aug.　6 Trenches: Bn. H.Q., Mont Forêt Quarries.

15 Bivouacs, Vimy and La Folie Wood.

25 Frazer Camp, Mont St. Eloi.

Sept.　2 Bray.

6 Roclincourt, Wellington Camp.

7 Trenches: Arleux.

13 Red Line and Vimy.

19 Camp at Ecurie (Bn. H.Q., "A", "D" Companies). Longwood ("B", "C" Companies).

25 "A" and "D", "B" and "C" changed over.

Oct.　1 Trenches Arleux.

7 Support in Red Line.

13 Ecoivres.

25 Trenches: Arleux Loop.

31 Support in Red Line.

Nov.　9 Bray.

18 Roclincourt, Aubrey Camp.

19 Trenches: Gavrelle.

25 Support: H.1.c.

Dec.　1 Trenches: Gavrelle.

7 Wakefield Camp (Arras-Lens Road).

22 Bray.

1918.

Jan　3 Ecurie Camp.

9 Trenches: Arleux.

15 Mont St. Eloi; Lancaster Camp.

27 Support in Red Line. Trenches: Arleux.

Feb.　4 Mont St. Eloi.

10 Trenches: Arleux.

16 Ecurie.

22 Support in Red Line.

27 Trenches: Acheville.

March　3 Mont St. Eloi.

        4 Monchy Breton.

        22 Bailleulemont and Army Line (E. of Boisleux-au-Mont).

        22/23 W. of Ervillers and Ervillers.

        25 Evacuated Ervillers, took up line E. of Courcelles-le-Comte, nr. Gomiecourt.

        26 Retired to W. of Moyenville-Ablainzevelle Road (Aerodrome).

        27 Retired to E. of Adinfer Wood (Battalion provided rear-guard).

        31/Apl. 1 Pommier and Gaudiempré.

April   1 Sus-St. Leger.

        2 Monchy Breton.

        10 Embussed for Lys Area.

        11/13 Vieux Berquin and Haute Maison and Battle of the Lys.

        14 Borre.

        18 Grand Sec Bois and Swartenbrouck.

        26 Trenches: Seclin.

        28 Haute Loge.

May   9 Fletre.

        15 Support Position (Bn. H.Q.X.2.d85.25).

        19 Trenches.

        21 Thieushouk.

        24 Lumbres.

June   8 Racquinghem.

        15 U.17. Central.

        17 Renescure and Lynde.

        20 C.16.b.5.5.

        21 Trenches: Nieppe Forest. H.Q. Canal Bank, nr. La Motte.

        25 Camp (W. of Morbecque).

        27 Trenches: H.Q. near "A" Ride - Nieppe Forest.

        28 Attack on Gars Brugghe.

July   1 Camp at D.19.a.8.8 (W. of Morbecque).

        4 Trenches: H.Q., Swartenbrouck Farm.

        8 D.6.d. and D.12.

        12 Trenches: H.Q., Grand Sec Bois.

        16 Camp (W. of Morbecque).

        20 Nieppe Forest ("A" Ride), H.Q. D.25.d.46. Reserve-Beyond Sawmill, La Motte.

        26 Trenches: H.Q. "B" Ride, Nieppe Forest.

Aug.   4 Morbecque.

        9 Reserve: Forest Camp, Nieppe Forest.

        12 Trenches: Swartenbrouck Farm.

        16 Reserve: H.Q. D.12.a.31 (À la Promenade).

17 Trenches: H.Q. near "X" Track, "B" Ride.

20/21 Le Tir Anglais. H.Q. at À la Promenade.

21 Cinq Rues Hazebrouck, Ebblinghem.

24 V.I2.b.99: Camp between Le Brearde and Le Peuplier.

31 Phincboom Farm.

Sept. 3 Trenches: H.Q., Ophir House, Steenwerck.

4 Advanced H.Q., Prompt Farm, nr. Nieppe.

4/5 Bivouacs, nr. Bailleul.

5 Bivouacs, nr. La Crèche.

6 Trenches.

7 Camp at A.11.b.63 (W. of Steenwerck).

8 Trenches: Prompt Farm.

10 Camp at A.11.b.94, Steenwerck

12 Staple.

23 Hazebrouck.

24 Trenches: H.Q., B.10.b.44 (De Seine Lines).

26 Camp at Aldershot Lines-Neuve Eglise.

27 Trenches: Charing Cross Corner-Ploegsteert Wood.

28 Attack on "Plug Street" Wood.

29 H.Q. in Pill Box-Ploegsteert Wood.

Oct. 1 Camp at Aldershot Lines, Nieppe.

6 Camp A9: Central (in Steenwerck and Bailleul).

12 Trenches.

16 Billets in V.17.a and V.28.b.

17 Advanced through the 11th Bn. to Roncq-Bondues Road.

18 Croix Blanche (A.14.d).

25 Cuerne.

26 Trenches: Ooteghem.

29 Billets: I.15.d.99 (Harlebecke).

31 Billets: P.1 and P.2 (Ooteghem).

Nov. 1 Harlebecke.

3 Halluin.

7 Marcke.

8 Ooteghem.

9 Russeignies.

10 Ellezelles.

11 Everbecq.

13 Rigaudrye.

14 Orroir.

15 Sweveghem,

16 Marcke.

25 Menin.
26 Vlamertinghe.
27 Terdeghem.
28 Ebblinghem.
29 St. Omer.
Dec.   17 St. Martin-au-Laert.

1919.

Jan.   29 Calais.
          31 St. Martin-au-Laert.
April   1 Reduced to Cadre.
May   22 Cadre returned to England (Southampton).
          23 Hillsborough Barracks, Sheffield.
          26 Cadre officially received at Hull.

Appendix IV

Nominal List of Original Battalion

1	Sgt. Joseph Tholander
3	Pte. George Quest
4	Pte. William Wells
5	Pte. Harold Whittle
6	Pte. Robert Edward Gordon Lucas
7	Pte. G E Ledraw MM
9	Pte. George Lilley
11	Pte. Cyril Fletcher Waterhouse
13	Pte. Robert Tall
14	Cpl. Thomas Ernest Saunderson DCM
15	Pte. Harry Stout
16	Pte. James W Sisson
17	L/Cpl. Albert W Taylor
18	Pte. Ernest Russell
19	Pte. Albert Johnson
20	Pte. W Horsfall
21	Pte. Albert Edwin Holding
22	Pte. Harold Espin
23	Pte. William James Hall
24	Pte. Claud G Graves
25	Pte. Herbert Gale
26	Pte. Maurice Freeborough
27	Sgt. Walter Samuel Leech
28	Pte. William Dawe
29	Pte. Arthur Crane
31	Pte. Jonathan Comins
33	Pte. Edmund Power
34	Pte. Rowland Bryant*
35	Pte. Percy Bourner
36	Pte. Frederick Barraclough
37	Sgt. Seymour Custon Watson
38	Pte. Henry Morris Wacholder

39	Pte. James S Watson
40	Pte. T Adams
41	Pte. Frederick William Wardill*
42	Pte. John Charles Bennett
43	Sgt W E Harrison
44	Pte. Charles Walter Tune*
45	Sgt. Arthur J Tindale
47	CSM Clifford Street DCM
48	Pte. Harold Sneetson Richardson
49	Pte. Lawrence Read
51	Pte. Sydney James Pybus
52	Sgt. George Pickering
53	Pte. Claude Leslie Penn*
54	Pte. Cecil Wright Mason
55	Sgt William Benjamin Hoyle
56	Pte. W R Raney
58	Pte. John Good*
59	Pte. Richard Cowl*
60	Pte. Samuel G Cawley
63	Pte. Horace Stanley Johnson
64	Pte. Alfred Armistead Kennedy*
65	Pte. Robert Linsley
66	Pte. Frederick Cecil Watson Niven
67	Pte. Percy Russell
68	Pte. Walter Sheppard
69	Pte. Harold R Gibbons
70	Pte. Harry Watson*
71	Pte. Ernest William Young
73	Pte. G Blenkin
74	Pte. John Bailey
75	Pte. George W Butler
76	Pte. Charles Reginald Finding
77	Sgt. Newton Farrar
78	Sgt. Frederick E Newbert
79	Pte. Stanley Marr
80	Pte. James Smith
81	Pte. James Arthur Fairhurst
82	Pte. Ernest Earnshaw Jackson
84	Pte. A E Wilson
85	Pte. George Edward Bell
86	Pte. Alexander Gemmell

87	CSM Samuel Cash
88	CQMS Thomas Davison (Medaille d'Honneur)
89	Pte. John Arnott Elliott
90	Pte. Albert Horden
91	Pte. Edmund John Britnell
92	Sgt. Ernest W Dawson
93	Pte. Lawrence Dalgleish
94	Pte. Robert Dewson
95	Pte. Harold Draper
96	Pte. Ernest E Crane
97	Sgt. David Boddy
98	Pte. Sidney Birkbeck
99	Cpl. E C Dunn
100	Pte. A Barker
101	Pte. Alfred Boland
102	Cpl. Frank Baker MM
103	Pte. Frederick Walton
104	Pte. Robert Wright
105	Pte. Stanley Wright
106	L/Cpl. George Sanders
107	Pte. Thomas Norwood Prince
108	Pte. Herbert Riches
109	Pte. Arthur Sugden
110	Cpl. Ernest Smith
111	Pte. William Percy Skevington*
113	Pte. Donald McLachlan
114	Pte. F Stone
115	Sgt. Edwin Arthur Nunns MM
116	Pte. Harold Owen
118	Pte. Horace Kirman
119	Pte. Frank Douglas Lacey
120	Pte. George Lacey
121	Pte. Harold Reed Lidgley
122	Pte. Arthur Moore
123	Pte. J B Atkinson
124	Pte. John Nelson
125	Pte. Walter Gillingwater
127	Pte. George Thomas Lotherington*
128	Pte. Oscar Rounding Leighton
130	A/C.Sgt. Harry Lamb
131	Pte. Llewelyn Owen Owens

132	Pte. George Leslie Naylor*
134	Pte. G Sanders
135	Cpl. Ralph Terry MM
136	Pte. Percy Lockey
137	Pte. Charles Randolph Stevenson
138	Pte. Terence Stringer MM
139	Pte. Harry Smith
140	Pte. Harry Reveler MID
141	Pte. Harry Smith*
142	Pte. John William Shaw*
143	Sgt. Leonard Martin Wrigglesworth MID
144	Pte. Allen Boughton Wells
145	Pte. Maurice Watson
146	Pte. Frederick C Wilson*
147	Pte. Charles Woodcock
148	Pte. George William West
150	Pte. George W Taylor
151	Pte. William Taylor*
152	CSM Dudley Stringer*
153	Pte. Ernest Sleight
154	Pte. James Louis Stephenson
155	Pte. Frederick John Smith
156	Pte. Alfred Smith*
157	Pte. George Frederick Stephenson*
159	Cpl. Edgar Mooton MID
160	Pte. Edmund Keene
161	Pte. Philip Sydney Kendall
162	Pte. Clarence George Kay
165	Pte. George Augustus Hughes*
166	Pte. John Hodgson
167	Sgt. Charles Searby Henson
168	Pte. Charles Henry Horberry
169	Pte. Ellis Hobson
170	Pte. Wilson Holmes
171	Pte. George Albert Haines
174	Pte. Benjamin Green
175	Pte. Arthur Godfrey
176	Pte. Harry Godfrey
177	Pte. Ernest Belton Gooch
178	Pte. Horace Seymour Gibson
179	C/Sgt. Herbert Edwin Gibson*

180	Pte. J Galt
181	Pte. William Harold Footit
182	Pte. Frederick Finding*
183	Pte. Jesse Fenton
184	Sgt. Richard Emslie
185	Pte. Harold Dixey
186	Sgt. John Douglas Cowl*
187	Pte. A Chippendale
188	Cpl. Charles Augustus Clarke MM*
189	Pte. William Arthur Cheeseman
190	Pte. Carl Edgar Chatterton*
191	Pte. John Buchanan
192	Pte. F Burn
193	Pte. Harry Burn
194	Pte. George F Brittain
195	Pte. Lawrence Gardham Baynes
197	Pte. Frank Atkinson
198	Pte. William Norman Langley Barr
200	Pte. Frederick Charles Robins
204	Pte. Alfred S Robins
205	Sgt. J N Stather MM
206	Pte. Kenneth Bertram Spink*
208	Pte. Kenneth George Shackles*
209	Sgt Edgar Thrale*
210	Pte. George Walter Waddington^^*
211	A/Cpl Alfred P Wells *
212	Pte. Wilfred Williamson
214	Pte. Alfred Carr Warne*
216	L/Cpl Frederick J Walsh
218	Pte. Norman Walker
220	Pte. Arthur Samuel Pratt
221	Pte. Alfred James Pratt
222	Pte. Harry Oughton
224	Pte. Percy Naylor Murray
225	Pte. Maurice W Morack
226	Pte. Vincent West Maw
228	Sgt. Rhys Lloyd*
229	Pte. Richard Loynes
230	Pte. Arthur Allison Lamb
231	Pte. Maurice Kitching
232	Pte. Roger Leslie Kidd

233	Pte. Austin Hutchinson*
234	Pte. Mennell Horncastle*
235	Pte. Leonard Maxwell Holmes*
236	Pte. James Herbert Holmes
237	Sgt. William S Coates
238	Pte. Cyril Kenneth Hindson*
239	Pte. Harold Kennington Havercroft
240	Pte. Lewis William Gregory*
241	Pte. Harold Elvin
242	Pte. Oscar James Elphick
243	Sgt John Ellis MM
245	Pte. David Dudding
246	Cpl. John Dixon MM*
247	Pte. Harry Dixon*
248	Pte. Harry Day
249	Pte. Harry Cowperthwaite MSM
251	Cpl. C Collinson DCM
253	Pte. Frederick David Brown*
254	Pte. Frederick Bennett
255	Pte. Francis Henry Bell*
256	L/Cpl. Charles William Backwell*
257	Pte. J R Ansdell
259	Pte. Frank Hope
260	Pte. Harry Hodgson
261	Pte. Benjamin Ireland
262	Pte. Victor Ingamells
263	Pte. Leslie William Green*
264	Pte. Sydney Gray
266	Pte. Alfred Moss
267	Pte. John H Monday
268	Sgt. G W May
269	Pte. Frederick McManus
270	Pte. George Wells
271	Pte. Leonard E Wilson
272	Pte. Harold Frederick West
273	Pte. G Watt
274	Pte. Eric Samuel Willis*
275	Pte. A Wilson
276	Pte. A Yates
277	Pte. W B Ascough
278	Pte. William Martin Anderson*

279	Pte. S Arnott
281	Cpl. George Herbert Burton*
282	Pte. Frank Bernard Bradley
283	Pte. Albert Batty
284	Pte. Frank Butler
285	Cpl. Harry Brown*
286	Cpl. W Bailey MID
287	Sgt. Frank Leslie Corlett
288	Pte. Walter Harry Corlett
289	L/Cpl. George Wilson Clark*
290	Pte. Herbert Dover MM
292	Pte. William Catron Carter
294	Pte. Harold Clark MID
295	Pte. Sydney Latus
296	Cpl. Frank Davie MM*
297	Pte. Harold Leslie Cooper*
298	Pte. Clifford Carter*
299	Pte. John Dale
300	Pte. C T England
301	Pte. Harold Robert Barr Fullerton
302	Pte. Leonard Fox
303	Pte. Basil Fallowfield
304	Pte. George Hodge*
305	Pte. Frank James Holmes
306	Pte. Francis William Harrison
307	Cpl. Harold Holdsworth
308	Pte. Albert James Hancock
309	Pte. Henry Thomas Frederick Hall
310	Pte. Harry Gyngell
311	Pte. Horace Gill*
313	Pte. C F Tennison
314	Pte. B Tether
315	Pte. L Surfleet*
316	Pte. P Saunders
317	Sgt. Harold Edward Sendall DCM
318	L/Cpl. Joseph R Mayor
319	Pte. Frank R Mallison
320	Pte. Robert Ormston
321	Pte. Edward Kingsley Parrish*
322	Pte. Fred Portergill
323	Pte. Walter Ramsay

324	Pte. Frank Riley
325	Pte. Arthur Riley
326	Pte. John Henry Hall
328	Pte. John William Everett
329	Pte. Frederick James Everett
330	Pte. Reginald Charles Freeman
331	Pte. John Henry Forward
332	Pte. Stephen Harvey Hall*
333	Pte. Wilfred Brown
334	Cpl. Richard Bertram Bulmer
335	Pte. Frank Bird
336	Pte. Ernest Booth
337	Pte. Harry Coupland
338	Pte. Joseph W Collingwood
339	Pte. Edward Dalby
340	Pte. William Irvine Cattley
341	Pte. William Henry Dalton
342	Sgt. William Archbutt Thompson MM
343	Pte. Victor Malon
344	Pte. James William Taylor
345	Pte. Thomas Wordsworth
346	Pte. Leonard Webster
347	Pte. Harold Woolhouse
348	Pte. Frederick Wilkinson*
349	Pte. Frank Young
350	Pte. L Young
351	Pte. John Armstrong
352	Pte. Harry Victor Anfield
353	L/Cpl. Charles William Bourne
354	Pte. Alan Porter
355	Pte. Charles Ernest Pattison
356	Pte. Eric Zacharia Charles*
357	Pte. Harold Godfrey Richardson
358	Pte. John Rishworth*
359	L/Cpl. M Spikings
360	Pte. Watson Smith
361	Pte. John E Simpson
362	Pte. John Alfred Skipsey
363	Pte. E Booth
364	Pte. Frederick Thomas Moss
365	Pte. Frederick McWilliam

366	Pte. A H North
367	Pte. William Henry Newton
369	Pte. Harold Robert Gibbons
371	Pte. Richard Ingamells
372	Pte. E T Jackson
374	Pte. Robert Taylor l'Anson
375	Pte. William Reginald Jones
376	Cpl. Llewellyn Hill Jones
377	Pte. Arthur Kirk*
378	Cpl. Lewis Koplick
379	CSM. Charles Kenneth Lonsdale*
380	Pte. Archie L Lamming
381	Pte. Eric Lear
382	Pte. James H Lown
383	Pte. Albert Henry Martin
384	Pte. Thomas Percival Millard
385	Pte. Ernest Mainprize
386	Pte. Jack Peck
387	Pte. Charles Turnbull
388	Pte. Arthur Leeming
389	Pte. Arthur Stanley Wright*
390	Pte. Charles William Searle
391	Pte. Herbert Smales
392	Pte. John C Stanton
393	Pte. Charles G Shackleton
394	Pte. William Mackay Scott
395	Pte. Rowland Scott
396	Pte. A Sykes
397	Pte. Fred Taylor
398	Pte. Frank Starling
399	Pte. John Percy Tuxworth
400	Pte. Harold Turner
401	Pte. William Henry Warn
403	Pte. Albert Edward Wheelband
405	Pte. Robert Wardell
406	Sgt. Walter Watson*
407	Pte. A Webster
408	Pte. Harold Reuben Watson
411	Pte. Walter Charles Waddington*
412	Pte. Samuel Arthur Wigby
413	Pte. John Wilson

415	Pte. Alfred Taylor*
416	Pte. Harry Parker
417	Pte. Sydney Clayton Pacey
418	Pte. Wilfred Poulson
419	CSM Roy Pinchon MID
420	Pte. William Kitching
421	Pte. Harold Kemp
422	Pte. Lawrence Frederick Jeffery
423	Pte. Allan Kenneth Ingram
424	Cpl. Reginald Peace Hudson*
426	Pte. Leonard Hobson
427	Pte. James Norris Houldsworth*
428	Pte. Henry Ernest Hodge
429	Pte. Carl Hermann* MM
430	Sgt. William Ernest Harrison*
431	Cpl. C G Hall
434	Pte. James Hastings*
435	Pte. Frank Hall *
436	Pte. Henry Edmund Harrison
437	Cpl. Joseph Goodman MM
438	Pte. Robert Gillingswater
439	Pte. Joseph Gibson
440	Pte. Basil Montague Gibbs
442	Pte. Thomas Geraghty*
443	Pte. George H Atkin
445	A/Sgt Horace Fisher
446	Pte. J Feldman
447	Pte. Ernest Fewster
448	Pte. Hugh Parker Freeborough*
449	Pte. Percy Fox
451	Pte. William Eastwood
452	Pte. Douglas Duncan
453	Pte. Robert Douglas Dunham
454	Pte. Edwin Stanley Duffield
455	Sgt. H Fisher MM
456	Pte. Philip Morris Davidson*
457	Pte. William Dalton
458	Pte. John Noton Cooper
459	Pte. H S Corden
460	Pte. Wilfred Toft Corlass
461	WO2 Herbert Cowling

462	Pte. William Jarvis Clark
463	Pte. Farnill Clayton
464	L/Cpl. Fred Clipson MM
465	Pte. Robert Thomas Buttimer
466	Pte. John Brunyee
467	Pte Arthur Brealey
468	Pte. Herbert Brown
469	Pte. George Edward Boyd
470	Pte. Bryan George Bowen*
472	Pte. Geoge Birks
473	Pte. Benjamin Brettell
474	Pte. George Bartlett
475	Pte. James R Atkinson
476	Pte. Andrew Ashford
477	L/Cpl. G Andrew
478	Pte. Joseph W Allen C-de-G (B)
479	Pte. William Henry Alexander
480	Pte. Charles Richard Aistrop
481	Cpl. Oscar Randall Waldemar Agerskow*
482	Pte. Thomas H Agerskow
483	Pte. Harold Abba
484	Pte. Cyril Wrigglesworth*
485	Pte. James Stennett Watson*
488	Pte. Thomas H Slater
489	Pte. John Spring
490	Sgt. James Regan
491	Sgt. Frederick Edwin Railton
492	Pte. Arthur Thomas Jackson*
493	Sgt. Richard Miller
495	Pte. Ernest Marsden
496	Pte. George Stanley Mansfield*
497	Pte. George Frederick Knowles
498	Pte. Paul Kershaw
500	Pte. James Frederick Holmes
501	Pte. S E Harwood
503	Pte. Wilfred Mark Harrison
505	Pte. H Garton
507	Pte. J A Dobbs MM
508	Pte. Thomas Hamblion Clarke*
509	Cpl. Gerald Duncan Butters
510	Sgt. Uriah Ellis Butters*

511	Cpl. Wilfred Lessey Brown*
514	Pte. Frederick Batty
515	Pte. James John Allen
516	Pte. George H Atkin
517	Pte. Edwin Akester
518	Cpl. Gordon Akester
519	Pte. Frank Herbert Johnson
520	Pte. Cyril W Riley
521	Pte. Rupert George Smedley
522	Pte. Robert Laurie Stevenson
523	Pte. Arnold Vernon Sylvester
524	L/Cpl. Cyril George Watts
525	Pte. William E Adamson
526	Pte. Hugh Frank Blakemore
527	Pte. A Blakemore
528	Cpl. Ralph E Browne
529	Pte. Alfred Hardern
530	CQMS Alfred Holmes Grindelle
531	Pte. Robert M Ireland
532	Pte. Harry Johnson
533	Pte. Harry Ramsay
534	Pte. Herbert Powell
535	Sgt. John C Stocks
536	Pte. John Cundall Stocks
537	Sgt. James Iveson
538	QM/Sgt. Herbert Victor Ireland*
539	Cpl. George Edgar Gibon
540	Pte. John Murdoch
541	Pte. William Murdock
542	Pte. Robert Knowles Oxley
543	Pte. E Pattern
544	L/Cpl. H Harold Redmore
545	Pte. Harry Woodmansey
546	Pte. Hubert Ellis
547	Pte. Charles Wilfred Elton
548	Pte. Joseph Benson Fay
549	Sgt. Albert Edward Frank
550	Pte. Lawrence Martin
551	Cpl. Thomas Hewitt
553	Cpl. David Alfred Pudsey MSM
554	Pte. Thomas Joseph Willis

555	Pte. Robert Henry Stutt
556	Pte. Wilfred Newlove
557	Pte. William Vincent Miller
558	L/Cpl. John William Fearnley*
559	Pte. Allan Hastings Dale
560	Pte. W R Raney
561	Pte. S Coop
563	Pte. Peter McRorie
564	Pte. Percy Atherton
565	Pte. William Brown
567	Pte. William Kay
568	Pte. William Claxton Smith
569	Pte. Percy James Todd
570	Sgt. Samuel Windle
571	Pte. Sidney Smith
572	Pte. Thomas A Nasby
573	Pte. Charles H Newton
574	Pte. Thomas Albert Powell
576	Pte. John Henry Deyes
579	Pte. R W Smith
582	Pte. T E Rust
583	Pte. Cecil Simpkins MM
584	Pte. Robert Frank Scaife
585	Pte. E S Leonard
586	L/Cpl. William Robinson MM C-de-G (F)
588	Pte. Solomon Shapero MM
589	Sgt. Harold Youngson MM
590	Pte. Frank Westerby
591	Pte. Harold Wray
593	Pte. Reginald Warren White
594	Pte. John Wollaston
595	Pte. Joseph Wood
596	Pte. James William Wilson
597	RSM Christian Wilkie Thirsk*
598	Pte. F Thompson
599	Pte. James William Pront
600	Pte. William Andrew Pickering
601	Pte. Harold Parrish
603	Sgt. Fred Graham Page MM & bar
604	Pte. F K Page
606	Pte. Ernest Henry Mills

607	RQMS John Percy Milns MID
608	Pte. James Richardson McAllister
609	Sgt. Joseph Alfred Johnson
611	Pte. Lawrence Martin
612	Pte. George Albert Mankel
613	Pte. Henry Lewsley
615	Pte. Thomas Headley Kirby
616	Pte. Richard Henry King
617	Pte. Edward Kilvington
618	Pte. E L Kidd*
620	Pte. Norman Loftus Kelsey
621	Sgt. R P Jones
622	Sgt. J A Johnson
623	Pte. William Johnson
624	Pte. Will Jenkins
625	Pte. Philip James ^^
626	Pte. William James Jackson
627	L/Cpl. F Jackson
628	Pte. Noel Westgarth Holmes
629	Pte. George Hodgson*
630	Pte. Robert Hayes
632	Sgt. James Guest
633	Pte. Herbert Graystone MM
634	Pte. James William Graystone
635	Pte. William Gray
636	Pte. John Edgar Garton
637	Sgt. John Matthews Fenwick MSM*
638	Pte. J A Elliott
639	Pte. AV Emery
640	Pte. Alfred Eastaugh
641	Pte. W Dennison
642	Pte. Walter Dick
643	Pte. William Henry Dickinson*
644	Pte. Wilfred Davis MSM
645	Pte. Thomas Curtis
646	Pte. David McGavin Cowell
647	Pte. Albert Edward Collett
648	C/Sgt. Harry Colquhoun
649	Pte. Harry Connaughton
650	Pte. David Frank Chapman
651	Pte. Wilfred Cartledge

652	Pte. Stanley Williams Brown
653	Pte. James F Brocklehurst
654	Pte. Henry Stracham Briggs
655	Pte. Percy Boyd
656	Sgt. Arthur Baldwin MM*
657	Pte. George Winter Anson
658	Pte. Harry Cressy Abercrombie
659	Sgt. Cecil Fritz Wikner
660	Sgt. Herbert Swift MSM
661	Pte. Horatio Swift
662	Pte. Frederick Charles Seller
663	Cpl. George Austin Smith MM
664	L/Cpl. Solomon Schottlander MM
665	Pte. Wallace Snowden
666	Pte. Ernest Stevens
667	Pte. H. Summers
668	Pte. Charles Cleveland Reynolds MM*
669	Pte. Herbert Sutton
670	Pte. Stanley Victor Oliver
671	Pte. Lawrence William Newlove
672	Pte. Percy Martindale
673	Pte. Harold Lancaster
674	Pte. Herbert Ansley Lambert*
675	Sgt. Sidney Keal
676	Pte. Robert Keal
677	Pte. Thomas Brinton Johnson
678	Cpl. Arthur Ernest Huzzard
679	Pte. J Williams
680	Pte. Francis Izon Hirst
681	L/Cpl. H Hicks
682	Pte. Alfred Lowther Harrison
683	Pte. William Sydney Gerbutt
684	Pte. Charles Edward Fox
685	Sgt. Frank Alfred Ellis*
686	Pte. Harry Eckles*
687	Pte. Edmond E Draper
688	Pte. Samuel John Cook
689	Pte. Hugh Collinson*
690	Pte. William Foster Brunton
691	L/Cpl. Bernard Brumby MM
692	Pte. Arthur Gordon Brown

693	Sgt. Wilfred Bone
694	Pte. James Biddlecombe
695	Pte. John Beeken
696	Pte. James Alfred Bailey
697	Sgt. Archibald Clifford Abba DCM, MM*
699	Sgt. Walter Barnett*
701	Pte. Sydney Meeton
702	L/Cpl. J Metcalfe
704	Pte. Walter Linsley*
705	Pte. George Moss
706	Pte. Douglas McAndrew
707	Pte. Frederick Maud
708	Pte. George Herbert Jessup
709	Pte. William Ellis Johnson*
710	Pte. Arthur Harris*
711	Pte. Harold Hunter
712	Pte. Cyril Hirst
713	Pte. Willaim Hunt
714	Pte. Harry Gamble
715	Pte. Clarence Graham
716	Pte. Stanley Horsfield
717	Sgt. Thomas Huntington
718	Pte. Thomas Hunter
719	Pte. Francis Edmund Furley*
720	Pte. Walter Fussey
721	Cpl. Sidney Edlington DCM*
722	Pte. Jospeh Holliday Ellis
723	Sgt. B A Clubley
724	Pte. Walter Victor Carey
725	Pte. Sydney John Cornwall
726	Pte. Percy Clark
727	Cpl. Robert Granville Bennett*
728	Pte. Frank Taylor Armitage
729	Sgt. Walter Barr
730	Pte. Thomas Joseph Boag
731	Sgt. Spencer Bailey
732	Pte. William Bird
733	Cpl. Harold E Burgoyne*
734	Pte. Percy Brown
735	Sgt. Walter Reinsford Boag MM
736	Sgt. John William Brown MM*

737	Pte. William Atkinson
738	Pte. George A Wells
739	Pte. Walter Herbert Wreghitt
740	Pte. Hugh Graham Wheeler*
741	Pte. David Wilkinson
742	Pte. Charles Henry Vollans DCM
743	Pte. George Edward Wade
744	Pte. F K Woodcock
745	Sgt. Charley Tennison*
746	Sgt. Thomas James Shelton*
747	Pte. Frederick James Simpson
748	Pte. John Smelt
749	Pte. Leonard Stubbs
750	Pte. Shirley Redfern
751	Pte. D A Roberts
752	Pte. Wilfred L Smith
753	Sgt. George Clifford Sugden*
755	Pte. Tom Sherburn
756	Pte. Norman Clark Smith
757	Pte. George Frederick Sleight
758	Pte. S Scott
759	Pte. George Herbert Nicholson
760	Pte. Harry H Gill
761	L/Sgt. Arthur Jackson C de G (B)*
762	Pte. Frederick Edward Purcell
763	Pte. Archibald B Shipley
764	Pte. G W Gill
765	Sgt. Frederick Willis DCM*
766	Pte. Robert Sewell
767	Pte. Frank Scoffin
768	Cpl. John Gilbert Pippett MM*
769	Pte. R M Leake
770	Pte. William Lazenby
771	Cpl. Reginald Sydney Newman
772	Sgt. Walter Arnold Wilby
773	Pte. Geoffrey Wilcockson
774	Pte. Wilson Webb
775	Pte. Arthur Stuffins*
776	Pte. Eric Linnell*
777	Pte. Edward Kell
778	Pte. Robert Henry Key

779	Pte. Cyril Johnson
780	CQMS Frank Illingworth*
782	Pte. Henry Burn Hewitt*
783	Pte. Arthur Reginald Hasnip
784	Pte. George Frederick Arnold Floyd
785	Pte. John William Duce
786	Pte. Cyril Arthur Credland
787	Pte. S Conyers
788	Cpl. William Alfred Cliffe*
789	Sgt. Arthur Thomas Barrett
791	Pte. Thomas Anderton
792	Pte. Wilfred Leslie
793	Pte. M Wilson
794	Pte. Frederick Wilde
795	Pte. John Spence
797	L/Cpl. Leonard Jeynes
798	Pte. Alfred Gill MM
801	Pte. Alan Pearson Adamson
802	Pte. Thomas Weldon Bailey
803	Pte. Edward Crompton
804	Pte. Christopher Pentith*
805	Pte. James Edwin Brown
806	Cpl. Thomas Buck
807	L/Cpl. W B Billany
809	Pte. William John Linaker Downes
810	Pte. George Thomas Chapman
811	Pte. Leonard Caley
812	Pte. Wilfred Arthur Fletcher
813	Pte. J R Farnill
814	Pte. John Ferry
815	Pte. Harold Farnley
816	Pte. Francis Geraghty*
817	Pte. William Adrian Goodwill
818	Sgt. Fred Johnson
819	Pte. C S Joys
820	Cpl. Herbert Johnson
822	Pte. Fred Kirby
823	Pte. Rupert Reese Lewis
824	CSM Bernard L Littlewood
825	Pte. Thomas Lidgard
826	Pte. Frederick Monkman

827	L/Cpl. W A MacPherson
828	Pte. Charles W Mason
829	Pte. Harold Arhur Walsh
830	Pte. Wlliam George Andrew MID
831	Pte. Charles Henry Selkirk
832	Pte. Wilfred Elsworth Sykes*
833	Pte. Alexander Smith
834	Pte. Reginald Noel S Sinderson
835	Pte. Bernard Ellis Smith
836	L/Cpl. George Lewis Spring
838	Pte. John Smith
839	Pte. Frederick Arthur Smith
840	Sgt. George Maurice Sheppard*
841	L/Cpl. Edward Randolph Perkins
842	Pte. Alfred Ernest Nicholson*
843	Pte. M Malon
844	Pte. Percy William Littlewood
845	Pte. George Henry Johnson
846	Pte. Frederick William Harrison
847	RSM Walter Hall MM C-de-G (B)
849	Pte. Douglas William Garrett
850	Pte. C J W Finch
851	Pte. Algernon Ellmer*
852	Pte. William Henry Drake
853	Pte. Gerald Blackmore
854	Pte. Harold Bentley
855	Pte. George W Bray
856	Pte. A H Wright
857	Pte. Ernest Wilkinson
858	Pte. Harold Wakeling
859	Pte. H R Todd
860	Pte. Reginald Edward Saunby
861	Pte. Herbert Spink
862	Pte. Walter Storr
863	Pte. Arthur Ernest Smith
864	Pte. Aaron Petersen*
865	Pte. Eric Pentith*
866	Pte. Arthur H Oliver*
867	Pte. Reynold C Neill
868	Pte. Lawrence Nowell DCM
869	Pte. George Ephraim Selby

870	Pte. Henry Seymour Ryley*
871	Pte. Fred Walker
872	Cpl. Cyril Travis
874	Pte. James Frederick Wiles
875	Pte. W S Everingham
876	Pte. Alfred Kersh
877	Pte. Harold Jackson
878	Pte. Ernest Jenkins
879	Pte. H Illingworth
880	Pte. H E Hyde
881	Sgt. Thomas Gregory*
882	Pte. Frederick C Cowell
883	L/Cpl. William Edward Chapman
884	Pte. Thomas Brayton Bell
886	Pte. Percy Cameron Hall
887	Pte. Frederick Thomas Sleight
888	Pte. Rupert Cameron Hall
889	Pte. Charles Wade
890	Pte. Harry Storr
891	Pte. Robert Broxham
892	L/Cpl. Kenneth Saxelbye Evers*
893	Pte. Herbert James Fell
894	Pte. H Fitton
895	Pte. F M Fell
896	Pte. John Forrester*
897	Pte. George Fearnley
898	Pte. George William Warriner
899	Cpl. Stanley Booth Wilson*
900	Pte. Reginald Verity
901	Pte. Hartman Smith
902	L/Cpl. F Stevenson
903	Pte. A J Candy
904	Pte. Herbert William Monkman
905	Pte. Dennis Faulkner Jordan
906	Pte. George Thomas Johnston*
907	Pte. Walter Henry Kirk
908	Pte. Bertie Chambers
909	Pte. William Alfred Collins
910	Pte. John William Dunn
911	Pte. William Girdlestone Bromby*
912	Pte. Albert H Brooks

913	Sgt. Frank Bold MM
914	Pte. William Robert Witty
915	Pte. Frederick Charles Wilson MID
916	Pte. Walter Watts
917	Pte. Wilfred Young
918	Pte. John Appleyard
919	Pte. F Ancient
920	Pte. W Allison
921	Pte. Walter Edward Aust
922	Pte. Ezra William Busby
923	Pte. Clarence Bilbe
924	Sgt. John Law Barton*
925	Pte. Harold Medforth
926	CQMS Norman T Metcalfe
927	Sgt. Sydney Henry Moses MID
929	Pte. Baron Barnett Moss
930	Sgt. Arthur Moody
931	Pte. J McBride
932	Sgt. Albert H Nash
933	Pte. Reginald W Veale
934	Pte. Dick Norton
935	Cpl. Henry Needham
936	Pte. John Churchill Oxtoby
937	Pte. William E Oxley
938	Pte. Alfred Henry Pitts
939	Cpl. Alfred Potts
940	Pte. Denis Richard Pack
941	Pte. Harold Patrick
942	Pte. William Albert Phillips
943	Pte. Harold Ernest Robinson
944	Pte. Reginald Ernest Savage
946	L/Cpl. Walter Silverwood*
947	Pte. John Edmond Sherwood
948	Cpl. Stanley Scarr*
949	Pte. Herbert Cecil Thompson
950	Cpl. Arthur Turner
951	Pte. George William Tether
952	Cpl. Wilfred Trowill
953	Pte. Herbert Tinn
954	Sgt. Gerald Ashley Wright*
955	Pte. Harry Winter

957	Pte. Ashling Cundy
958	Pte. W J Cleary
959	Pte. H Dougherty
960	Pte. William Relly
961	Pte. Charles Hewison
962	Pte. Ernest Hayes
963	Cpl. Oswald Anthony Haller*
964	Pte. Albert Hall
965	Pte. William Garton
966	Pte. Joseph Hilary Hobbs
967	Pte. William George Hughes
968	Pte. Walter R Homan
969	Pte. Ernest Hancock
970	RSM Fred Stanley Ives C-de-G (B)
971	Cpl. Reginald William Johnson
972	Pte. Frank Jackson*
973	Pte. Ernest Jobling
974	Pte. Hubert Kettle*
975	Pte. William Edward Lambert
976	Pte. Arthur Roxland Lea
978	RQMS Charles Frederick Taylor
980	Pte. Tom H Gunnee*
981	Pte. Amaziah Harrison
982	Pte. Charles King Palmer
984	L/Cpl. Joseph Wharf
985	Pte. Robert Yallop
986	Sgt. Ernest Best MM*
987	Sgt. Sidney James Clark
990	Cpl. Eric Claude Dunn
991	Pte. Branton Auistin Rider
992	Cpl. James Henry Crooks MM MID
993	Pte. Thomas Alan Goodwill
994	CSM John Melton Bateman*
995	Pte. Gilbert Popple
996	Pte. John William Fisher Bronze Medal For Bravery (I)
997	Pte. James Hamilton
998	Pte. C Kingdom
999	Pte. Thomas Elmer Stephenson
1000	Sgt. Robert Lee
1005	Pte. Leonard Dale
1006	Cpl. Francis William Green

1008	Pte. Sidney Taylor
1009	Sgt. Robert Sydney Lamming
1010	Pte. Edward Robinson
1012	Pte. John William Chapman
1013	Pte. William Taylor Coleman
1014	Cpl. William Dawson MM
1015	Pte. Arnold Reid
1016	Pte. James Hughes
1017	Pte. John Todd
1018	QMS. Henry Cooper
1019	Pte. Fred Fellowes
1020	Pte. Herbert Dearing
1021	Pte. Harry Gordon Wood
1022	Pte. Allan Hewitt
1023	Pte. Reginald William Everingham
1026	Cpl. Henry Allan Houldsworth
1027	Cpl. William Stanley Bartindale
1028	Pte. Edgar Heidrich
1029	Sgt. Edgar F Hermann MM
1031	Sgt. Arthur Francis Goldthorpe*
1032	Pte. Norman Larard
1033	Pte. Cyril H Shakesbury
1034	Pte. Charles Ronald Oxtoby*
1035	Sgt. John Peacock Day*
1038	Pte. J H Wilkinson MM
1039	Pte. G A B West
1040	Pte. Thomas Adams
1041	Pte. Hewson O'Connor
1042	Pte. Arthur Milton Woods
1043	Pte. Tom Dalby
1044	Pte. Harold Stainton
1045	Pte. Isaac Reuben
1046	Pte. Harry Harris
1047	Pte. Harry Cooper Crossland
1049	Pte. James Willey
1050	Pte. Eric Crowston
1051	Pte. Oscar Bolmeer
1052	C/Sgt. Harold Scruton
1054	Pte. Ernest W Sellers
1055	Pte. Stanley Sharp
1056	Pte. H R Rushton

1057	Sgt. Aythan Powell
1058	Pte. William Henry Chew
1059	Pte. Arthur H Dixon
1060	Pte. Charles Henry Shallcross*
1061	Pte. Harry Fanthorpe
1062	Pte. Eric Friis Smith*
1063	Cpl. Claude Marsh Hornstedt
1064	Pte. Arthur Charles Vaughan Smith*
1065	Cpl. Frank Pinder Aitken*
1067	Pte. James Watson Fowler
1068	Pte. Cyril P Townsend
1069	Pte. William Henry Atkin
1070	Pte. Ralph Snowdon*
1071	Pte. Leonard Heidrich
1072	Sgt. Frank Chalmers
1073	Pte. Harold Raymond Harper*
1074	Pte. John C Gibson
1075	Pte. Fred Russell*
1076	Pte. Harold V Dixon
1077	Pte. Fred Hall*
1078	Pte. Henry Bird
1079	Pte. Edward Bird
1080	Pte. Walter Maddison Barlow*
1083	Pte. Frank Hargreaves
1084	Pte. Harry Pickard
1085	Sgt. Wilfred Parker
1086	CQMS Sydney Cressey MID
1087	Pte. Cyril Sharp
1088	Pte. Thomas Langley Frazer
1089	Sgt. Arthur Bell
1090	Pte. Arthur Cleminshaw
1091	Pte. Fred Moore
1092	Pte. Leonard Donkin
1093	Pte. Harold Ernest Hatfield
1094	Pte. Albert Cunliffe*
1095	Pte. James F Edson
1096	Pte. Leonard Bolderson
1097	Sgt. Harold Farnaby Strachan
1099	L/Cpl. John Darneley Petty MM*
1101	Pte. W Robinson
1102	Pte. Harold Charles Needham

1103	Pte. Sydney Temple Heald
1104	Pte. Lawrence Joseph Chapman*
1105	Pte. Harry Booth
1106	Cpl. E B Stevens
1107	Pte. Christopher William Binning
1109	Sgt. Alfred Kemp
1111	L/Cpl. Richard B Ezard
1112	Pte. Horace Charles Marris
1113	Pte. William Park Beas
1114	Pte. Joseph Henry George Boyes
1115	Pte. Thomas Percival Bennett
1116	Pte. Frank Bernard Barnby
1118	Pte. Philip Moore
1119	Cpl. Douglas Harold Scott*
1120	Pte. Leon E Watt
1121	Pte. Allan Rawstorn
1123	Pte. Hubert Dempsey
1124	Pte. Tom Crayton
1125	Pte. Harold Flintoft
1126	Cpl. Samuel Downs
1127	L/Sgt. Walter Samuel Leech*
1128	QMS. John Henson
1129	Pte. Frank Allvin
1130	Pte. Frederick Kendrew
1131	Pte. Samuel Caley
1132	Pte. Cyril Martin
1133	Pte. William Sykes Langdale
1134	Pte. William Singleton DCM, MM, C-de-G (F)
1135	Pte. Edward Owen Rutherford*
1136	Pte. Herbert William Charity
1137	Sgt. Thomas Mitchell*
1138	Pte. John Laurie
1139	Pte. Harry Bland Cooper
1140	Pte. Francis Stone
1141	Pte. Percy Walker
1142	Pte. Charles William Philpott
1143	Cpl. Alfred Masters
1144	Pte. Arthur Ernest West
1145	Pte. Bertram Rider
1147	Pte. Thomas B Lowson
1148	Pte. Archie Stewart

1149	Pte. Albert Topham
1150	Pte. Alfred Clayton
1151	Sgt. Edward Ormonde Hutchinson
1152	Pte. George William B Dainton
1153	Pte. George Henry Derby
1154	Pte. Fred Downes
1155	L/Cpl. Lewis E Peek
1156	Pte. James Louis Page
1157	Pte. William Good
1158	Pte. Edgar Oswald Clegg*
1159	Pte. John Lumley
1160	Pte. Asia Predgen
1161	Pte. John Ernest Hailstone
1162	Pte. Roland Hyde
1163	Pte. Richard F Goodworth
1164	Pte. John Newborn
1165	Pte. Charles Edward Campbell
1166	Pte. Alfred Boddy
1168	Pte. James Leslie Abbott
1169	Pte. George Henry Hain (served as Henry Howard)
1170	Pte. Ernest Carter Bell
1171	Pte. George C Walker
1172	Pte. Robert B Stead
1173	Pte. Michael James Dakin
1174	Pte. G B Robson
1175	Pte. Alexander Hodgson Martin
1176	Pte. Albert Binns
1177	Pte. Thomas Marshall
1178	Pte. John Reginald Martin
1180	Pte. Reginald Hardey Pearson
1181	Pte. William Lindridge
1182	Pte. Percy Haynes
1183	Pte. James Edward Whitfield
1184	Pte. Fred Longhorn
1185	L/Cpl. Edward Mowforth MM
1186	Pte. George W Winter
1187	Pte. Alfred Ferraby
1188	Pte. Bernard Rowland Middlewood
1189	Pte. Hendry Hunter
1191	L/Cpl. Leonard Jarvis MM & bar
1192	Pte. Job Petch

1194	Pte. Cecil Ratcliffe
1195	Cpl. Morley Edward Hanby*
1196	Pte. William Robert Lancaster
1197	Pte. Alexander Matthews
1198	Pte. Allanson Hick
1199	Pte. Charles Percival Coleman
1201	Sgt. Alexander Charlesworth MM
1202	Pte. Sydney Henry Hastie
1203	Sgt. George William Darnell
1204	Pte. Edwin Percy Close
1207	L/Cpl. George Ernest Bowen
1208	Pte. Fred Little*
1209	Cpl. Mark Ethenbert Barr*
1210	Pte. Frank Johnson
1212	Pte. Joseph Alban Doran
1214	Pte. James Harold Markham
1215	Pte. William High
1216	Pte. Joseph Day
1217	Pte. Thomas Scott Larman
1218	Pte. William H Briggs
1219	Pte. Cecil Charles Burrows
1220	Cpl. Joseph E Wilson
1221	Pte. Joseph Cheney
1223	L/Cpl. George Frederick Langthorpe
1224	Pte. Thomas G Cook
1225	Pte. William Dawson
1226	Pte. Edwin Stephenson
1227	Pte. Harold Atherton*
1228	Pte. Allan McCurrach
1229	L/Cpl. F O'Dell
1230	Pte. J B Atkinson
1231	L/Cpl. R H Smith
1232	Pte. William Graham Hill*
1233	Pte. Alfred E Messenger
1234	Pte. John George Scruton
1235	L/Cpl. Robert H Barker
1236	Pte. Ronald Graudin Boulton
1237	Pte. C W Hackney
1238	Pte. George Marris
1239	Pte. Samuel K Elliott
1240	Pte. Hector Smith

1241	Pte. Alfred Ernest Knowland
1242	Pte. Robert Hurd
1243	Pte. Charles W Hackney
1244	Pte. John Rotherham Hayward
1245	Pte. F Cowey
1246	Pte. Stanley Joplin Bryan
1247	Pte. George Kilby Deighton
1248	Pte. Frank E Harding
1249	Pte. John E Newton
1250	Pte. James Clark
1251	Pte. Harold Smith
1252	Pte. William Fox
1253	Pte. Frank Cowey
1254	Pte. Harry Hope
1255	Pte. Francis D Boast
1256	Pte. John Fergusson
1257	Pte. Albert Edward Denton
1258	Pte. Thomas Danby
1259	Sgt. William F Williams
1260	Pte. William Bowes
1261	Cpl. Robert Ranson
1262	Sgt. W H V Winter MM C-de-G (B)
1263	Pte. Percy Brown
1264	Pte. Thomas Jackson
1265	Cpl. Robert John Edson
1266	Pte. Wilfred Hoggard
1267	Pte. G Goodill
1268	Cpl. Walter Thomas
1269	Pte. Charles William Popplewell
1270	Pte. Herbert Cross
1271	Pte. Sydney Carter
1272	Pte. Harold Smith
1273	Pte. L C Wilkinson
1274	Pte. Alfred W Clark
1275	Pte. Leonard Lynch
1276	Pte. Percy Allen Haines
1278	Pte. Horace Mabbott
1279	Pte. Frank Cecil Cocker
1281	Pte. James Cecil Tait
1282	Pte. George Ernest Bethel Robinson
1283	Pte. Albert Higgins

1284	Pte. A A Kennedy
1285	Pte. Alfred Barrett North
1286	Pte. John W Clark
1287	Pte. Victor W Corlyon
1288	A/Cpl. William D Dymock
1289	Pte. Cyril A Mainprize
1290	Pte. John H W Gleadow
1291	Pte. William E Fowler
1293	Pte. John R Kendrew
1297	Pte. George Walter Buck
1298	Pte. John E Robson
1299	Pte. John George Wardle
1300	Pte. Robert Edward Clappison
1301	Pte. Leonard Stork
1302	Pte. Arthur William Lucas
1304	Pte. Samuel Crossland
1305	Pte. John Edward William Smith
1306	Sgt. John Lewis MM C-de-G (B)
1307	Cpl. William Henry Mawer
1308	Sgt. Abraham Walsh MM, MM (F)
1309	Pte. Francis Lloyd
1310	Sgt. Benjamin Charles Nicholls*
1311	A/Sgt. James Grange
1312	Pte.Thomas Wright
1313	Pte. G W Gunnell
1314	Pte. Edward E Boynton
1315	Pte. William Herbert Anderton*
1316	Pte. George William Mitchell
1317	Pte. Arthur Douglas Gladwin*
1319	Pte. George Linford
1320	Pte. Harry Francis Wharf
1321	Pte. Walter Whitehead
1322	Sgt. Clarrie Alcock
1323	Pte. Anderson Needham
1324	Pte. Frank Tindale
1325	Pte. Charles Tomlinson
1326	Pte. Sidney George Turner
1327	Pte. Cyril Pope
1328	Pte. Frederick Linsley
1329	Sgt. George H Dimmock
1330	Pte. Albert Jordan

1331	Pte. Samuel Sugarman
1332	Pte. James William Branford*
1333	Pte. William James Smith
1334	Cpl. Sydney Frank Atkinson
1335	L/Cpl. John Ward MM
1336	Pte. W Beecroft Rockingham
1337	Pte. Percy R Dickels
1338	Pte. William Ward
1339	Sgt. Charles H Thompson
1340	Pte. William Oxley
1341	Cpl. Henry Johnson
1342	Pte. Claude Mattison
1343	Pte. Alfred Werner
1344	Pte. W J Whyte
1346	Pte. Robert Fish
1347	Pte. Harold Stonehouse
1348	Pte. Charles W Richardson
1349	Pte. G W Taylor
1350	Pte. George Henry Dewick
1351	Pte. Harry Jipson
1352	Pte. Harold Milner
1353	Pte. George Sterry Alexander
1354	Sgt. Samuel Lyons
1355	Pte. Joseph H Cobby
1356	Cpl. William Dixon
1357	Pte. Edward Newton Bland
1358	Pte. William S Hargreaves
1359	Cpl. Leslie Scarr
1360	Pte. N Coverdale
1361	L/Cpl. Harold Rawling MM
1363	Pte. Ernest Garbutt
1364	L/Cpl. John Masters
1365	Pte. Edwin Francis Field
1366	Pte. R E Clappison
1367	Sgt. Frederick George Palmer*
1368	Pte. Edward Hirst
1369	Pte. Edward Towse
1370	Pte. Samuel Esmond Wright
1371	Pte. Louis Shapero MM
1372	Pte. Joseph Bowran Slide
1373	Pte. James Edward Martin

1374	Pte. Nehemiah J Queskey
1375	Pte. Albert Campbell
1376	Pte. Harry MacDonald
1377	L/Cpl. Charles Guise
1378	Pte. Charles Harrison
1379	A/L/Cpl John Thomas Rodham MID
1380	Pte. Joseph Henry Morley
1381	Pte. William Storey
1383	Pte. John Whitehead
1384	Pte. J J Board
1385	Pte. Edgar Smith
1386	Pte. Harry Kneshow
1387	Pte. George C Thornham
1388	Pte. Arthur Hornby
1391	Pte. Sidney Henry Butler
1392	Pte. George Archer
1394	Pte. Richard A Gray
1395	Pte. William Holmes
1396	Pte. John Akester
1397	Pte. John H Bartram
1398	Pte. Alfred Stanley Sutton
1399	Pte. Thomas Edwin Croudson
1400	Pte. Ernest Ratcliffe
1402	L/Cpl. Harold Tindale MID
1403	Pte. M H Holmes
1404	Pte. M Harkstone
1405	L/Cpl. William George O'Dell
1406	Pte. Thomas W Marshall
1407	Pte. John Edgar Dunn
1408	Pte. Alfred Conman
1409	Pte. Harold Harry Roberts
1410	Pte. Fabian Charlton*
1412	Pte. Matthew Robinson
1413	Pte. Herbert Harold Pawson
1414	Pte. Fred Robinson
1415	Pte. Matthias Cobb
1416	Pte. Harry Warkup
1417	Pte. Wilfred Thompson
1418	Pte. William B Storey
1419	Pte. Jim Blenkin
1420	Pte. Harry Brabben

1424	Pte. Roland Percy Haselhurst
1425	Pte. Thomas Wiliam Burgess
1426	Pte. Stanley Tonkinson
1427	Pte. Edwin Huzzard
1428	Pte. Robert Revell
1429	Pte. William Bamford
1430	Pte. William Middleton MID
1432	Pte. Harold H Jordan
1433	Pte. Albert Bell
1434	Pte. Charles Frederick Thompson
1435	Pte. Walter Nicholson
1436	Pte. Albert Bricklebank
1437	Pte. George Mellor
1438	Pte. Edwin Noel Gray
1439	Pte. Alexander Gouldthorpe
1441	Pte. John H Archbutt
1442	Pte. Edward Robert Oliver
1443	Pte. Henry Bush
1444	Pte. Percy Wilson
1445	Pte. William Calvert
1446	Pte. F Ellis
1447	Pte. Arthur Cruddas
1448	L/Cpl. Martin Vivian Jude
1449	Cpl. Jess Heyhoe
1450	Pte. Charles Edward Homersham
1451	Pte. Arthur J Sutton
1452	Pte. Frederick Richard English
1453	Pte. Donald Grey
1454	Pte. George Storr

KEY

^^	Stayed in the army
*	Commissioned or accepted for commission before war ended
DCM	Distinguished Conduct Medal
MID	Mentioned in Dispatches
MM	Military Medal
C-de-G	Croix de Guerre
(B)	Belgium
(F)	France
(I)	Italy

Ranks given are from the 1915 Star Medal roll, from the 1914–19 War Medal roll, from Soldiers Died in the Great War, Find My Past or from the Honours section of the Regimental History.

Appendix V

Additional Photographs

Sergeant Tholander, the first Hull Commercial. He never served abroad with the battalion and was transferred to the Army Ordnance Corps and invalided out in 1918. (Hull Museums)

An early practice marching with guns. (Hull Museums)

Measuring a potential recruit's chest. (Hull Museums)

a/O.R.S Tholander   No. 1.

1st HULL BATTALION
The East Yorkshire Regiment.

STANDING ORDERS.
MISCELLANEOUS.

King's Regulations and Standing Orders.—All ranks are to make themselves acquainted with Extracts from King's Regulations issued October 1914. and with these Standing Orders. Company Commanders will have a copy of each issued to all Officers and others joining.

Venereal Disease.—All men becoming affected with venereal disease to report sick without delay.

Smoking.—Cigarettes are prohibited on all duties and fatigues and during the whole time men are out of barracks on marches or for training

Dogs and Animals.—Are prohibited unless a permit is previously obtained from the Adjutant.

Hawkers.—No edibles or drinkables are to be purchased from hawkers within half a mile of barracks, &c., or during marches, manoeuvres, training or work.

As a military unit, there were regulations to follow. This is the copy used by the first Orderly-room Sergeant, Sergeant Tholander. (Hull Museums)

464. La Grande Guerre 1914-15-16

Aspect de l'Eglise d'HÉBUTERNE bombardée et incendiée par les allemands

VISA PARIS. 464

A. R.

The condition of the church in Hébuterne when the Commercials arrived.

The newly constructed huts at Hornsea waiting the arrival of the battalion. (Hull Museums)

RSM Thirsk, one of the authors of the book.

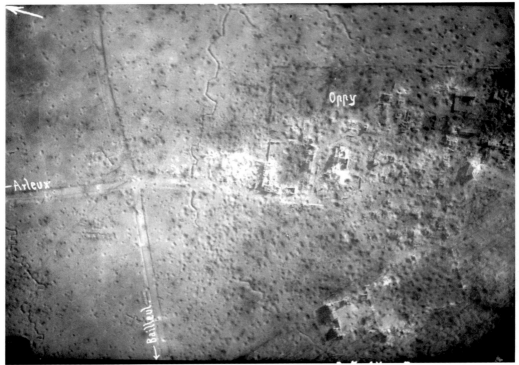

A German aerial photograph of the Oppy battlefield taken on 3 May 1917 while the battalion lay in No-Man's-Land waiting for darkness to allow them to withdraw.

2190 HAZEBROUCK bombardé   Rue de Lille - Maison Decool
                                              Lille street

Hazebrouck when the Commercials arrived in 1918.

On a tram like this Captain Glossop encouraged his company to run faster, earning them the soubriquet 'Glossop's greyhounds'.

Wenlock barracks where the commercials enlisted.

Index